A History of Canada's Peoples

The Canadian Odyssey

The Greek Experience in Canada

Peter D. Chimbos

Published by McClelland and Stewart Ltd. in association
with the Multiculturalism Directorate,
Department of the Secretary of State
and the Canadian Government Publishing Centre,
Supply and Services Canada.

Government Catalogue No. CI44-4/1980E

The Canadian Publishers
McClelland and Stewart Limited
25 Hollinger Road
Toronto, Ontario

CANADIAN CATALOGUING IN PUBLICATION DATA

Chimbos, Peter D.
  The Canadian odyssey

(Generations, a history of Canada's peoples)

Bibliography: p.
Includes index.

ISBN 0-7710-1964-5 bd.   ISBN 0-7710-1965-3 pa.

1. Greeks in Canada.   2. Greeks in Canada –
History.   3. Greek Canadians.*   4. Greek
Canadians – History.*   I. Title.   II. Series.

FC106.G7C55   971'.0048   C80-094164-0
F1035.G7C55

Picture researcher: Jill Patrick
Printed and bound in Canada

DEDICATION

To my children, Tina and Demetri

Contents

Editors' Introduction

Canadians, like many other people, have recently been changing their attitude towards the ethnic dimension in society. Instead of thinking of the many distinctive heritages and identities to be found among them as constituting a problem, though one that time would solve, they have begun to recognize the ethnic diversity of their country as a rich resource. They have begun to take pride in the fact that people have come and are coming here from all parts of the world, bringing with them varied outlooks, knowledge, skills and traditions, to the great benefit of all.

It is for this reason that Book IV of the *Report of the Royal Commission on Bilingualism and Biculturalism* dealt with the cultural contributions of the ethnic groups other than the British, the French and the Native Peoples to Canada, and that the federal government in its response to Book IV announced that the Citizenship Branch of the Department of the Secretary of State would commission "histories specifically directed to the background, contributions and problems of various cultural groups in Canada." This series presents the histories that have resulted from that mandate. Although commissioned by the Government, they are not intended as definitive or official, but rather as the efforts of scholars to bring together much of what is known about the ethnic groups studied, to indicate what remains to be learned, and thus to stimulate further research concerning the ethnic dimension in Canadian society. The histories are to be objective, analytical, and readable, and directed towards the general reading public, as well as students at the senior high school and the college and university levels, and teachers in the elementary schools.

Most Canadians belong to an ethnic group, since to do so is simply to have "a sense of identity rooted in a common origin . . . whether this common origin is real or imaginary."[1] The Native Peoples, the British and French (referred to as charter groups because they were the first Europeans to take possession of the land), the groups such as the Germans and Dutch who have been established in Canada for over a hundred years and those who began to arrive only yesterday all have traditions and values that they cherish and that now are part of the cultural riches that Canadians share. The groups vary widely in numbers, geographical location and distribution and degree of social and economic power. The stories of their struggles, failures and triumphs will be told in this series.

As the Royal Commission on Bilingualism and Biculturalism pointed out, this sense of ethnic origin or identity "is much keener in certain individuals than in others."[2] In contemporary Canadian society, with the increasing number of intermarriages across ethnic lines, and hence the growing diversity of peoples ancestors, many are coming to identify themselves as simple Canadian, without reference to their ancestral origins. In focusing on the ethnic dimension of Canadian society, past and present, the series does not assume that everyone should be categorized into one particular group, or that ethnicity is always the most important dimension of people's lives. It is, however, one dimension that needs examination if we are to understand fully the contours and nature of Canadian society and identity.

Professional Canadian historians have in the past emphasized political and economic history, and since the country's economic and political institutions have been controlled largely by people of British and French origin, the role of those of other origins in the development of Canada has been neglected. Also, Canadian historians in the past have been almost exclusively of British and French origin, and have lacked the interest and the linguistic skills necessary to explore the history of other ethnic groups. Indeed, there has rarely ever been an examination of the part played by specifically British – or, better, specifically English, Irish, Scottish and Welsh – traditions and values in Canadian development, because of the lack of recognition of pluralism in the society. The part played by French traditions and values, and particular varieties of French traditions and values, has for a number of reasons been more carefully scrutinized.

This series is an indication of growing interest in Canadian social history, which includes immigration and ethnic history. This may particularly be a reflection of an increasing number of scholars whose origins and ethnic identities are other than British or French. Because such trends are recent, many of the authors of the histories in this series have not had a large body of published writing to work from. It is true that some histories have already been written of particular groups other than the British and French; but these have often been characterized by filio pietism, a narrow perspective and a dearth of scholarly analysis.

Despite the scarcity of secondary sources, the authors have been asked to be as comprehensive as possible, and to give balanced coverage to a number of themes: historical background, settlement patterns, ethnic identity and assimilation, ethnic associations, population trends, religion, values, occupations and social class, the family, the ethnic press, language patterns, political behaviour, education, inter-ethnic relations, the arts and recreation. They have also been asked to give a sense of the way the group differs in various parts of the country. Finally, they have been asked to give, as much as possible, an insider's view of what the immigrant and ethnic experiences were like at different periods of time, but yet at the same time to be as objective as possible, and not simply to present the group as it sees itself, or as it would like to be seen.

The authors have thus been faced with a herculean task. To the extent that they have succeeded, they provide us with new glimpses into many aspects of Canadian society of the past and the present. To the extent that they have fallen short of their goal, they challenge other historians, sociologists and social anthropologists to continue the work begun here.

Jean Burnet
Howard Palmer

[1] *Report of the Royal Commission on Bilingualism and Biculturalism.*
[2] Ibid. Paragraph 8.

Acknowledgements

I am grateful to the Department of the Secretary of State for providing me with the opportunity to write the social history of Greek Canadians.

Grateful acknowledgement is made to Professors Jean Burnet (York University) and Howard Palmer (University of Calgary) and Dr. John A. Petrolias (Department of the Secretary of State) for reading the manuscript and offering useful comments and constructive criticism. I am also grateful to John Roberts and Randal Montgomery for editorial revisions to the monograph. The above-named persons are in no way responsible for the limitations of the book.

I wish to thank those Greek Canadians who co-operated in making this study possible, including the leaders of the Greek-Canadian communities and the official representatives of Greece in Canada. Thanks also to Professor Christos Jecchinis for preparing the chapter on the socio-economic aspects of the home society, and Bobis Giannokopoulos for his assistance in the chapter dealing with the political life of Greek Canadians. Peter D. Prattas of Montreal and Zaharias Jack C. Prattas of Toronto must also receive thanks for their efforts in collecting and translating useful materials.

Finally, my wife Eugenia deserves special thanks for sharing with me the tiring moments of my work. Her compassion and encouragement made my work more pleasant and rewarding.

Introduction

The Hellenes, or Greeks as they are known to North Americans, boast an historical legacy of 3,000 years. From their native land, consisting of a Mediterranean peninsula ringed by many mountainous islands, large numbers of Greeks have emigrated to all corners of the world. Wherever they have gone they have proudly called themselves "Hellenes." In Canada the Greeks have constituted only a small fraction of the population.[1] They are one of many ethnic groups participating in the multicultural fabric of Canadian society and contributing to its economic and cultural enrichment.

During the last few decades, a number of studies have been made of the Canadian ethnic mosaic. Such research has provided us with useful information about new Canadians: their historical background, their social institutions, and their problems in adjusting to their new society. However, research on Greek Canadians,[2] especially their history, migration and institutions, is limited. The available studies[3] are confined to particular cities and deal with single aspects of Greek life, such as social mobility or integration, and thus lack an overall historical and sociological perspective. It is hoped that the present study will fill a gap by presenting a comprehensive examination of many aspects of Greek life in Canada, both past and present.

The author and his associates had many questions about Greek Canadians. What were their socio-economic conditions when they left Greece? What problems did they have on arriving in Canada? Did they come alone or with their families? Did they move into Greek communities and seek jobs with Greeks, or did they try to strike out on their own? What successes or failures did they encounter, and what changes did they go through? Where are the Greek communities located and how are they structured? Do the people live in harmony or are there frustrations and conflicts? Have Greek Canadians risen up the socio-economic ladder over the years, or have they remained in menial jobs or been unemployed? How many have given up and returned to Greece in disillusion?

1

Of those that remain, do the parents feel that their children are becoming too Canadianized, or do the Greeks strictly maintain their own language, food, dress, customs and beliefs? What about their politics, religion and education? And, of course, what is the future of the Greeks in Canada?

The reader will judge whether these and other questions have been satisfactorily answered. However, since some of the answers required more data than exist at present, the author hopes that there will be further research carried out into the Greek situation in Canada. Until then the reader must tolerate some hypotheses and conjectures where firm data do not exist.

In this study several sources of data were employed. From the 1971 Canadian Census information was obtained on occupational status, educational achievement, age, sex, provincial distribution, periods of emigration, family size, marital status and marital dissolution of Greek immigrants. Information regarding the immigrants' participation and social integration in Canadian life was obtained from recent inquiries.[4] Studies on modern Greece have also provided valuable information on Greek institutions and social values.[5] Other useful historical information came from the National Archives of Canada.

A great deal of information dealing with the organization and historical development of the Greek church, ethnic organizations, and ethnic schools and with internal conflicts was obtained through personal interviews with influential individuals in the Greek communities of Canada. A set of informal questions dealing with various aspects of the community was used. The semi-structured interview allowed the interviewee to express his feelings, and provided a more insightful account than a formal interview. The conversations took place under various conditions in the workplaces, homes and offices of the respondents. The personal contacts of the author were useful in extending the number of interviews, and the author's fluency in Greek was an asset for those respondents not fluent in the English language.

Being both a Greek immigrant and a sociologist enabled the author to use the method of participant observation as well. For this study he participated in and observed Greek activities in several Canadian cities, including Calgary, Thunder Bay, Toronto, Montreal and Vancouver. In all cases the people he met were aware that he was conducting research, and no deception was involved. He could also draw on 13 years experience as a Greek Canadian, including participation in activities ranging from dances to church services, from community council meetings to chats with restaurant workers.

Historical documents of the ethnic communities such as constitutions, minutes of meetings, and histories of organizational activities also provided information. The Greek-Canadian communications media (newspapers, radio and television) were additional sources of information about the community's social organization and activities.

2

NOTES

1. According to Statistics Canada, Greek immigrants comprised only 0.6% of the population in 1971. In the same year there were approximately 180,000 Greek Canadians accounted for, including second and third generations.

2. Although the term "Greek Canadians" refer primarily to immigrants, it also includes those individuals who were born in Canada of Greek parents, the second and later generations, who identify themselves as Greeks.

3. Examples of such sociological inquiries include: Judith Nagata, "Adaptation and Integration of Greek Working Class Immigrants in the City of Toronto, Canada: A Situational Approach," *International Migration Review*, 4 (Fall, 1969); Peter D. Chimbos, "A Comparison of the Social Adaptation of Dutch, Greek, and Slovak Immigrants in a Canadian Community," *International Migration Review*, 6 (Fall, 1972); Peter D. Chimbos, "Ethnicity and Occupational Mobility: A Comparative Study of Greek and Slovak Immigrants in Ontario City," *International Journal of Comparative Sociology*, 15 (March-June, 1974); Constantina Asimopoulos, "The Relationship Between Social Mobility and Integration of Immigrants in Montreal," Ph.D. dissertation (Montreal: University of Montreal, 1975); Efrosini Gavaki, *The Integration of Greeks in Canada* (San Francisco: R and E Research Associates, 1977).

4. For example: Paul Larocque *et al.*, "Operationization of Social Indicators of Multiculturalism," Discussion Paper for Fourth Departmental Seminar of Social Indicators (Ottawa: Department of the Secretary of State, 1974); K.G. O'Bryan *et al.*, *Non-official Languages: A Study in Canadian Multiculturalism* (Ottawa: Minister of Supply and Services Canada, 1976), Efrosini Gavaki, *op. cit.*

5. For example: Irwin Sanders, *Rainbow in the Rock: The People of Rural Greece* (Cambridge, Mass.: Harvard University Press, 1962); and John K. Campbell, *Honour, Family and Patronage* (Oxford: Clarendon Press, 1968); Scott G. McNall, *The Greek Peasant* (New York: American Sociological Association, 1974).

ONE

The Political and Socio-economic Aspects of the Home Society

THE LAND AND THE PEOPLE

Modern Greece comprises the mainland – a peninsula jutting out into the eastern Mediterranean at the southeastern corner of Europe – and the Greek islands in the Ionian and Aegean seas. The total area of the country is 50,942 square miles or 131,944 square kilometres, which is about one-eighth of the size of Ontario, or equal to the size of England and Wales.

Greece is bounded by three seas, on the east by the Aegean, on the west by the Ionian, and on the south by the Cretan Sea. The land frontier on the north totals 755 miles or 1,215 kilometres, and is bordered by four countries: Albania, Yugoslavia, Bulgaria, and Turkey. Mountains cover more than two-thirds of the Greek mainland, and more than half of the population lives on the plains and the coastal stretches along the north or the Peloponnesus (the southern part of the mainland separated by the Corinth Canal). The islands of Greece, too, are mainly mountainous. They are mostly barren, with the exception of Crete, the major Ionian islands, and Rhodes, which in parts are as fertile as the plains of Thessaly, Macedonia, and Peloponnesus.

Approximately 30% of the land is arable and under cultivation, and the remainder is rough pastureland used for grazing goats, sheep and cattle. The timber resources of the thin forests are limited, having been reduced by centuries of felling, forest fires and grazing. However, some use has been made of the pine forests (the Aleppo pine) which produce resin used for industrial purposes and firewood.

The principal flatlands of the country are the plains of Boeotia, Thessaly, central and eastern Macedonia and Thrace, which are also the

---

*This chapter was prepared by Dr. Christos Jecchinis, Department of Economics, Lakehead University, Thunder Bay, Ontario.

main wheat-producing areas. Rice is grown in certain flat alkali lands of Peloponnesus near the sea. The rest of the arable land is found in the foothills where the soil is well suited to the growing of tobacco, grapes, olives and fruit. Cotton of competitive quality is grown both on the plains and the low hills wherever there is adequate irrigation.

The barrenness of a considerable portion of the country is compensated for by a peculiar beauty which has always attracted the artist, the poet, the historian and the archaeologist, as well as the tourist, who are entranced by the special quality of light and landscape. The clear light of the eastern Mediterranean pours down on mountains, undulating coastlines and the many whitewashed islands, contrasting attractively with the deep blue waters of the Aegean Sea. Nothing in the landscape is ever quite repeated: the contours and masses of the mountains and hills, the small valleys and gorges with olive groves and pine trees, the rocky peninsulas and the rugged coast all differ from place to place. Colours, heights, and distances change so rapidly that the traveller never wearies of the scenery. It is this kind of beauty that with history, tradition, and family ties provides the essence of the Greeks' affection for their country, and which explains the desire of some Greek emigrants for frequent visits and even for retirement in Greece when there are no close family ties in the adopted country.

There has been some debate over the purity of modern Greek ethnicity. The "pure race" of classical times has to some extent been diluted by Albanian, Slavic, Turkish and Western European (mainly Frankish and Venetian) migrations. However, "the view of Fallermayer so fashionable a century ago, that the modern Greeks have not a drop of classical Greek blood in their veins, has long since been discredited."[1]

The popular language now spoken by the people of Greece is known as *demotiki*, and it contains a number of Turkish, Italian, and other Western European words. It is based on the language of Hellenistic times that followed the Macedonian Empire established by Alexander the Great, although most Greeks have no difficulty in understanding *katharevousa*, the more formalized language still being widely used.

Greece has enjoyed considerable social harmony in modern times despite foreign infusions from immigration and conquest. World War II diluted and decreased the minorities in Greece, but even the pre-war census of 1928 reported a total of only 300,000 persons in the minority groups: Turks (86,000), Macedo-Slavs (82,000), Sephardin Jews (70,000), Vlachs (18,000), Bulgarians (18,000), Pomaks (17,000), and Armenians and others (9,000). Most members in the minority groups were and still are Greek citizens, and in general the social and religious minorities have not constituted a problem since the major exchange of populations between Greece and Turkey in 1923.[2]

In 1928, about 96% of the population professed to be members of the Greek Orthodox Church, but this percentage increased to 98% after World War II when many Greek Jews were eliminated by the Nazis during the occupation. The remaining two per cent of the population are Roman Catholics, Moslems, Jews and Gregorian Armenians. Since 1833, the Church of Greece has been autocephalous under the Holy Synod (the council of the Greek Orthodox bishops), though the divorce of the church in Greece from the rest of the Eastern Orthodox body has never been accepted by the Patriarchate of Constantinople (Istanbul).

Although the Greek Church does not possess the strong spiritual force and political influence it had in Byzantine times, it still has much influence in the countryside and among the Greek communities abroad. Every village has its priest, and it was mainly because of the clergy that the language and the traditions of Hellenism were kept alive during the long Ottoman rule and during the more recent Axis occupation. It is this tradition and influence that the Church and its representatives have carried out of the country to Greek immigrant groups in many parts of the world.

Social distinctions in modern Greece are based on education, occupation and ownership of land. Certain Corfu and other Ionian island families bear titles derived from Venetian times, but the granting of new titles is prohibited by the Greek constitution. Few large landowners have survived the reforms which took place between the two world wars. Some descendants remain of the men who organized the Greek War of Independence against the Turks in 1821, and these families are still highly respected. Most Greek leaders, however, in government, the armed forces and business, are drawn from peasant background or from the bourgeoisie which acquired wealth with the development of Greek capitalism in the last quarter of the nineteenth century. Origins are not important, however, in a country where the sense of equality, individualism and pride are highly developed. These qualities, and a passionate interest in politics, business and adventure, are the most outstanding characteristics of modern Greece.[3]

Social status in Greece, especially in rural areas, may also depend upon the recognition of honour. The family's honour lies in the good reputation and integrity of its men and the chastity and faithfulness of its women. Thus honour is equated with acceptable social status. It is through unspoiled honour that a poor person maintains respectability in the eyes of friends and the community at large.[4]

The rural people have been the most stable population element of the country. They live in compact villages and are mainly dependent upon land, and some are found in isolated peasant villages where most wants are supplied locally. In such agricultural settings the family is the main economic unit. The peasants produce enough to feed themselves, provide seed for harvest and have some surplus to sell for cash with which to pay taxes and purchase necessities from nearby towns or cities.

On the other hand one can find modern farmers who own larger plots of arable land and have adopted modern techniques. They grow little of their own food, but put their energy into crops which they sell.[5] Modern farmers are likely to specialize in one crop. Such is the case with most of the raisin producers of Peloponnesus, the tobacco growers of Macedonia, the vegetable and fruit growers of Attica and the wine producers of the islands of Samos and Leukas.[6]

One of the major problems faced by rural Greece is the limited supply of land and its distribution and redistribution through the dowry system. Dowry refers to the economic resources a young woman brings to her marriage. It is the dowry system which has caused farm land to be divided into small plots in strips around the villages, making it difficult to increase agricultural productivity. Because of the fragmentation of arable land, much of the farmer's working day "is spent simply travelling with implements to and from dispersed plots situated generally in different directions from the village."[7]

Another deficiency in the rural areas is the lack of adequate capital for agricultural investment. The desire to send children to urban centres for higher education, traditional investment habits, and the need to provide dowry land for daughters discourage the farmer from applying his savings to the improvement of farm land. Instead he relies on loans from the Agricultural Bank of Greece for the little improvements he may make.[8]

The life of rural Greece is also characterized by traditional patterns of mutual aid between families. These may include harvesting wheat and olives, taking turns in using animals to pull a plow, pruning vineyards and the like. The women help each other with such household tasks as cording wood, baking bread, cornhusking and weaving. Villagers also help each other in family crises when sickness, death and crop failures occur.[9] However, with the introduction of modern technology and the increasing availability of factory-made products after the 1960s, certain forms of mutual aid are becoming less frequent.

Despite mutual aid and the sense of community, Greek village life is not always harmonious. Disputes arise occasionally over the fragmentation of property, political ideologies, insults to family honour, and disagreements between siblings over inheritance.[10] Most hostilities, however, are between unrelated families and are based on competition for resources and wealth.[11]

THE HISTORICAL BACKGROUND

Modern Greek history (since the War of Independence in 1821) has been dominated by a series of wars which were conducted to defend the Motherland or to liberate territories and Greek populations from foreign rule. Imperialism and colonialism were not the objectives pursued, for all the territories gained had been originally Greek in classical and Byzantine times and contained Greek populations; few of these offered any important economic advantages.

The motives behind such expeditions were therefore historical and cultural, since the Greek people believed for a long time "that the *raison*

7

d'être of independent Greece was not the welfare of her citizens, but the liberation of the much larger irredenta beyond her borders from alien rule."[12] Furthermore, the apparent gains derived from victories were vitiated to some extent by the losses suffered from considerable human and material destruction, and it took, in fact, a long time to utilize the regained territories and turn them into sources of further development.

The external wars in which Greece was engaged adversely affected social development and contributed to the desire and/or need for emigration. The costly wars also contributed to discontent and unrest, resulting in the political instability, military coups and dictatorships that Greece has experienced since independence, and especially during the pre- and post-World War II periods. From 1919 to 1940 there were 25 changes of government, eight revolts and coups, and three dictatorships. From 1944 – after the liberation from the Nazis – to 1975, there were more than 30 changes of government, two phases of civil war, two military coups, and a dictatorship.

The wars and territorial expansion of modern Greece began in 1821 with the War of Independence against Turkish rule. This, in combination with other events and developments outside Greece, marked the beginning of the end of the Ottoman Empire. The revolution or War of Independence lasted for nearly 10 years, and although Greek independence was formally recognized in 1830 by the Three Protective Powers – Great Britain, France, and Russia – the new Greek state was not formally established until 1832. The frontiers of independent Greece were drawn just north of the town of Lamia in the southern Greek mainland.

In 1864, Great Britain ceded to Greece the Ionian islands, which had been British protectorates since 1815, and which had for four centuries previous to British rule been a dependency of the Republic of Venice. Thessaly in central Greece was annexed from the Ottoman Empire (Turkey) in 1881. In 1912-13, the First Balkan War (Greece, Serbia and Bulgaria against the Ottoman Empire) was won by the Balkan allies. Greek armies captured the towns of Tessaloniki, Preveza and Yannina; Crete, Samos and other islands were also liberated. The Second Balkan War (1913) ended in the defeat of Bulgaria by Greece, Serbia and Rumania. As a result of both Balkan Wars, western Macedonia, Epirus, Crete and the Aegean Islands became part of Greece.

In both world wars, Greece fought on the side of the Western allied powers against Germany and her allies. In 1919, Bulgaria was forced to cede western Thrace as a result of her defeat on the side of Germany during World War I. Greece received a temporary mandate from the Entente powers to occupy part of western Asia Minor and eastern Thrace, but had to evacuate these territories in 1922 after she was repulsed by the Turkish nationalists led by Mustafa Kemal.

In order to put an end to the continuous friction between Greece and Turkey, a friction due in large part to the presence of substantial Greek and Turkish minorities in both countries, the Treaty of Lausanne provided for an exchange of populations in 1923. Under this treaty, some 400,000 Turks had to leave Greece and over one million Greeks were compelled to leave Turkey. The bulk of the emigrants were resettled on lands which had been left vacant as the result of this wholesale transfer of populations.

In the years immediately following this exchange, the refugees from Asia Minor were a burden to the Greek economy. However, they were eventually assimilated successfully and became an asset to the socio-economic development of modern Greece as a result of their skills in commerce, trade, industry and agriculture. However, an estimated 150,000 Greeks emigrated to the United States, Egypt and a number of British colonies during the late 1920s and the 1930s.

On October 28, 1940, the Italian Fascists forced Greece into World War II by attacking the northwestern part of the country from Albania. The Greek army drove back the invaders and even occupied a quarter of Albania, forcing the German Nazis to assist the Italian forces. The Nazis advanced through Bulgaria and Yugoslavia in April, 1941, and overran Greece after two months of fighting. The German-Italian-Bulgarian occupation lasted until October, 1944, and was marked by appalling suffering and heroic resistance. After the end of the war, the Dodecannese Islands (since 1911 under Italian occupation) were ceded to Greece. However, after such a destructive war and three-and-a-half years of enemy occupation, the Greek economy was nearly destroyed.

The Paris Restoration Conference estimated the war devastation in Greece at $8,500,000,000. Over 1,300 localities and one-fourth of all the country's buildings had been destroyed, and there were one million homeless and displaced persons. Three-quarters of the Greek merchant marine was lost, as well as two-thirds of the country's motor vehicles and nine-tenths of its locomotives. Most railway tracks, stations, switching yards, and rolling stock were in a state of ruin. The roads were in complete disrepair, and all of the larger road and rail bridges were destroyed. Port installations and harbours were badly damaged or blocked, as was the Corinth Canal. Telecommunications had been rendered inoperative throughout much of the country. Vast areas of olive groves, orchards, vineyards, cornfields, and forests had been devastated, and the number of cattle and sheep had been greatly reduced. Worst of all, one Greek in every fifteen had died as a result of fighting, air raids, executions, starvation or disease.[13]

The efforts of successive post-war Greek governments to carry out the socio-economic recovery of the country with Allied aid were frustrated by the civil strife which followed liberation. The work of reconstruction and rehabilitation was seriously hampered by two attempts, in 1944 and from 1946 to 1949, at Communist takeover. These attempted revolutions by the Greek Communist Party, actively supported by the Communist Bloc, failed only after prolonged warfare. The road to recovery did not begin in reality before 1950, and it took at least another ten years to attain any significant development. As well, the civil war conditions of the 1944-49 years, and their adverse effect on social development, resulted in another exodus of Greeks and established a pattern of Greek emigration which was followed from 1951 to 1972.

The available statistics on post-war Greek emigration indicate that the annual volume of temporary and permanent emigration did not vary much from 1955 to 1961, from 1967 to 1968, and from 1971 to 1972, but it rose considerably from 1962 to 1966 (especially in 1963-65), and again in 1969 and 1970.[14] The first sharp rise was a result of the expansion of the West German labour market to Greece and other temporary emigrants from southern Europe, and the second rise in emigration from Greece was a result of the repression and uncertainty in the country following the establishment of a military dictatorship between 1967 and 1974.

THE MODERN POLITICAL SITUATION

Politics in modern Greece have been affected by the diverse factors of national history, the people's character, the natural poverty of the land, and the strategic position of the country at the crossroads of three continents (Europe, Africa and Asia), the latter situation resulting in the attraction of international rivalries.

In spite of the adverse cultural, social and economic effects of four centuries of Ottoman rule, Greece has had parliamentary democracy since 1864, interspersed periodically by a constitutional monarchy. However, the particular character of Greek politics, combined with foreign influences and interventions, have weakened the political system and left it defenceless against the imposition of occasional unconstitutional governments that have ruled at the expense of human rights and social progress. The problem has been accentuated by the lack of a defined political ideology and concrete socio-economic programmes. With the exception of the Communist Party, and to lesser extent the smaller social democratic parties, political parties in Greece have grouped themselves around a powerful personality rather than a dominating principle. Only two major debates have dominated Greek politics in the last one hundred years – the extension of social and structural reforms in the Greek economic system (including the communist upheaval), and the long drawn-out issue of whether Greece should be a monarchy or a republic.[15]

In the years after World War II, political stability and effective government policies were of primary importance to the social and economic recovery of Greece and to plans for long-term development. Any effort at reconstruction required the full co-operation of all political and social forces in the country. Such co-operation proved elusive. Sharp divisions within social institutions, especially trade unions, reflected deep

10

political and ideological differences. This sectarianism, along with the inherent weaknesses of modern Greek socio-economic structures and public administration, made the task of reconstruction extremely difficult. International rivalries and the civil war of the immediate post-war years exacerbated the problem. The adverse political developments in Greece during the 1944-74 period could not but cause, *inter alia*, an increase in the volume of emigration.

The emotions of the Greek people following their liberation from the Nazis in October, 1944, were mixed. There was jubilation and relief over the end of Nazi occupation and the forthcoming Allied victory, but apprehension as well about the political and economic future of the devastated and confused country. In the political field it was uncertain whether national unity could be maintained in the face of the sharp ideological divisions in the country, divisions which had been accentuated during the Nazi occupation between the various armed groups in the Greek mountains who had been fighting both the Nazi oppression and each other.

The worst fears of the Greek people over their country's fate in the immediate post-liberation period were realized. In two bloody rounds of civil war, one which pitted communist forces against nationalists from December, 1944, to February, 1945, and another from the autumn of 1946 to the autumn of 1949, the country suffered further human and material destruction. Although the civil strife ended with the defeat of the communist forces in 1949, political stability was not achieved until the end of 1952. The governments that were formed in the meantime were made up of the liberal and 'left of the centre' parties. Because it had twice tried to overthrow the elected government by force, the KKE (Communist Party of Greece) was not permitted to operate, but the ban did not apply to the communists as individuals. They were allowed to form another political party, the EDA (Union of the Democratic Left), not officially connected with the KKE. Furthermore, the government soon began the gradual release of rebel prisoners and others who had been sent to preventive exile in the islands. The authorities maintained their vigilance, but had strict orders this time to refrain from excesses.

Nevertheless, the defeat of the communists marked the beginning of another round of repressive activity and intimidation by the extreme right wing. This created social discontent, resulting in the Communists making considerable progress in both politics and the trade unions in the ensuing years. In the general elections of May 11, 1958, the pro-Communist EDA party received 24% of the vote and became the offical opposition in Parliament with 79 seats, an increase of 69 seats over the results of the general elections in 1951.[16]

Significantly, the communists had improved their position during a period of relative stability and economic progress, which Greece had been enjoying since 1956 under the leadership of Prime Minister K.

Karamanlis, leader of the National Radical Union (ERE). Social development, however, did not accompany economic progress. The new government failed to improve and expand social services, and took little or no action to correct the considerable disparities in income distribution. These government failures, as well as the inability of the progressive non-marxist opposition forces to unite and provide an effective alternative, had disillusioned and angered the lower income farmers and workers. It was, in fact, the protest vote of the dissatisfied non-communist lower income groups that gave the Communist party its electoral success in 1958.

The continuation of unsatisfactory social conditions on the one hand and the eventual unification of the progressive political forces on the other brought about the resounding defeat of the ERE government in the elections of February, 1964. The Centre Union (a united force of all the "centre" and the "left of centre" political groups under G. Papandreou) won by one of the highest percentages of the vote in modern Greek political history. The Centre Union received 53% of the vote and 174 seats in Parliament to 35% and 104 seats for the ERE; the pro-communist EDA dropped back to 12% and only 22 seats in Parliament. The protest vote which the EDA had received in previous years now went to the Centre Union.

The Centre Union government continued the policies of the earlier ERE government, but paid more attention to the needs of the lower income groups and to the democratization and improvement of social and economic institutions. However, internal weaknesses, external disruptive influences and serious disagreements between King Constantine and Prime Minister Papandreou resulted in the resignation of the Centre Union government in 1965. This marked the beginning of a new round of instability and confusion that lasted for two years.

In 1967, a group of medium-rank army officers under the leadership of Col. George Papadopoulos organized and executed a successful coup on the night of April 21, a coup which overthrew the constitutional government and established a military-civilian dictatorship. The seven-year dictatorship which followed was characterized by general repression and the suppression of human rights, including imprisonment and torture of political opponents, administrative corruption, high inflation, disorganization and a weakening of morale in the armed forces, and interference in Cyprus. Serious internal weaknesses and the engineered coup against President Makarios of Cyprus – which resulted in the Turkish invasion, the partial destruction of the island and the near-war situation between Greece and Turkey – brought about the downfall of the Greek Junta and its government in July, 1974. Former Prime Minister Karamanlis was brought back from self-imposed exile in France to head a coalition government.

Greece returned to democracy after the fall of the Junta, but many political and socio-economic problems continued to confront the country. Taking advantage of his popularity as the only political leader to lead the country in the difficult times of transition, Mr. Karamanlis and his government held general elections on November 17, 1974. Karamanlis's political party of New Democracy won 220 seats in the 300-member Parliament, capturing 54.5 % of the vote; the Centre Union (New Political Forces) Liberals and Social Democrats led by former Deputy Prime Minister George Mavros won 60 seats with 20.4% of the vote; the Panhellenic Socialist Union led by Andreas Papandreou took 12 seats with 13.6% of the vote; the United Left (Communist Front) won 8 seats with 9.3% of the vote; and all others, including a pro-Junta right wing party, had 1.2% of the vote with no seats in Parliament.

In December, 1974, the Greek people voted in a general plebiscite against the return of King Constantine and the Greek monarchy, and Greece was again declared a republic. A new constitution, approved and ratified by Parliament, specified *inter alia* the rules of electing the president of the new Greek Republic and the terms of his authority. In June, 1975, the Parliament elected Professor Constantine Tsatsos as President.

The government of Prime Minister Karamanlis quickly moved to fulfill some of its promises, not only by establishing a viable and democratic republic but also by uniting politically and economically with the European Economic Community. With the support of Parliament, including the major opposition faction, the Center Union-New Political Forces, the government applied for full membership in the European Economic Community (EEC). If Greece's membership is accepted and approved by the EEC partners, she will become a full member in 1980. It is generally agreed that this membership may have considerable favourable effects on the political and economic future of the country.

In the meantime, the Greek government has been facing the challenge of a transition dominated by a variety of serious problems. The first challenge involved the reorganization of the armed forces and the stabilization of the government's relationship with the military leaders. By commuting to life imprisonment the death sentences passed by the court against the top Junta leaders in August, 1975, the government was guaranteed smoother relations with the armed forces, while heavy sentences passed against the military police of the dictatorship placated popular resentment against the Junta.

On the other hand, other problems continue to pose a threat to the government's stability. These include student and labour unrest, the Cyprus crisis, Greek-Turkish relations, the need for reforms in the higher education system, the improvement of social services and technical training, reorganization of public administration, and the modernization of industry. Whether the current government can bring about the reforms necessary to propel Greece into the mainstream of Western European development is open to conjecture.

MODERN SOCIO-ECONOMIC CONDITIONS

With the endorsement of a new constitution in 1864, post-revolutionary Greece was to enter a period of territorial expansion and industrial development. The first factories in Greece were established in the early 1890s to process surplus currants into wine.[17] During the late 1890s economic advancement was reflected by the full operation of factories and the appearance of new buildings, hotels and business blocks in the cities of Athens and Piraeus. This upward swing in the Greek economy was brought to a temporary halt in late 1899 by drought, crop failures and the decline in the value of the drachma.[18] In a short time the economy recovered, however, and by 1917, 282 large factories and 2,000 small ones employing 35,000 workers were operating in Greece.[19] Political stability and improved communication encouraged Greek and foreign investors to pour capital into Greece and to enhance the country's economic development:

> Small industries were established all over the country and commercial and industrial centres developed gradually. In major cities such as Athens, Piraeus, Patras and Ermoupolis flour mills, tanneries, spinning mills, ship-repairing yards, ironworks, soap factories, small paint and dye plants, wine and alcohol distilleries, printing works and a few less important industries formed the nucleus of Greek industrialization.[20]

Most of Greece's economic growth, however, occurred after World War I with the territorial expansion of the country and the influx of refugees from Asia Minor. In the period between the two world wars, the first serious attempts were made to expand existing manufacturing and to develop new industries. In one decade (1928-1938) the volume of industrial production increased by 70% and the number of industrial workers before World War II was estimated at approximately 400,000. These developments were accompanied by a corresponding growth of trade unionism, especially in the tobacco industry, which had become of prime importance to the national economy.[21]

The effort to improve the Greek economy continued after World War II, notably after 1950 when civil strife had ended. However, the acceleration of industrialization was hampered by the lack not only of effective industrial organization but also of adequate sources of energy and raw materials. Hydro and lignite (brown coal) energy were not readily available before the late 1950s and the discoveries of modest offshore oil reserves in the north Aegean did not occur until the late 1960s.

Enemy occupation (1941-1944) and the civil strife that followed created longstanding adverse effects on post-war economic recovery and social development. The initial inertia was in large part due to extensive physical war damage and disruption. The Nazi policy of denuding the country of its raw materials, rolling stock and other economic resources also contributed to a disrupted economy after the liberation. With industrial production and trade nearly at a standstill, mass unemployment was common. The cost of living had risen enormously while money had lost its value. The inflationary circulation of currency had soared from 11,200 million drachma in 1940 to 604,570,000 million drachma by October 31, 1944. Had it not been for the relief provided by British Military Liaison (BML) and United Nations Relieve and Rehabilitation Agency, (UNRRA) the privations and famine would have continued.[22]

Although the Greek economy experienced a relatively high growth rate (six per cent) during the 1950s and 1960s, the traditional socio-economic structure did not change significantly. The Greek economy continued to be characterized by a relatively low degree of industrialization and wide disparities in regional development and income.[23] On the other hand the importation of technological know-how, the improvement of industrial skills, the effective utilization of energy resources, and the gradual improvement of tourism have contributed to the expansion and increased role of manufacturing industries in the industrial development of the country. Meanwhile agricultural production was hindered by problems identical to those in classical times: the inability of the land to provide enough food. This agricultural situation, in the absence of adequate exports, contributes to an imbalance of trade and payments. In terms of value, the imports of food commodities have always exceeded exports by a considerable margin. These adverse characteristics of agricultural production and the import-export imbalance have driven the Greeks further into commerce, the merchant navy, and emigration. They also have rendered Greece dependent on foreign capital, external income (remittances and emigrant gifts), profits, salaries from ocean-going merchant shipping, and tourism.

The national income of Greece remains small, and the standard of living of most citizens is low. In the years immediately before and after World War II it was difficult to ascertain the national income and its distribution. However, the ILO estimated that the national income of Greece, even in the best pre-war years, never reached 700 million drachmas ($658 million). Since the population in that year was estimated at 7,109,000, the per capita income was about $90. But even this figure gives a distorted picture of living standards because of the distribution of the national income among the various population groups.[24]

As a result of the war and enemy occupation, Greece "suffered more than any other country, with the possible exception of the Soviet Union."[25] Four years of civil war impeded reconstruction, and per capita incomes remained lower than in the pre-war period for at least three years after the war. Some modest improvement was registered before 1963 when an income of $531 per head was attained, rising to $1,760 by 1973.[26]

The disruption of the economy during the war and its adverse effects on society as a whole are understandable, but the persistence of wide

15

discrepancies in income distribution supports the contention that government policies (or the lack of them), as well as weaknesses in public administration, were also partly responsible for Greece's slow economic growth. The traditional social, cultural and economic distinctions that had existed since 1828 between the rural areas and the big city centres, especially Athens, persisted in spite of marked improvements in transport and communications and the economic uplift of the village economy after 1949. One important factor in the continued slow progress of agricultural production in the countryside is to be found in the centralization of the administration in the capital, and in the appointment of regional administrators (nomarchs) by the central government in Athens. Private industry also concentrated near the big ports and administrative centres, to the detriment of the rural economy. Thus the disparities in per capita income between the Athens region and the rest of Greece persisted long after the end of World War II.[27]

Sharp income disparities also remain among the various social groups across the country, notably between the wage earners and small farmers. Nearly all economic policies of the government between 1953 and 1963 ignored the need for social development. For example, a liberal credit policy intent on fostering private enterprise and industrial development, and the expenditure of large sums for the improvement and expansion of infra-structure and tourism, did little to improve social welfare or meet claims for wage and salary increases. The IKA (The National Social Security Institution) services deteriorated in the same period due to inadequate funding, organization and administration. As a result, neither living conditions nor incomes of the workers improved in the period of the National Radical Union government from 1956 to 1963. It was evident that only the middle and upper-middle classes were reaping the fruits of economic progress, and the income distribution was becoming increasingly inequitable.

Judging from the available official data, the wage and salary earners did not receive a fair share of the increased productivity in that period. The total average annual rate of growth of real GNP at market prices in 1950 to 1960 was six per cent and between 1960 and 1964 it rose to 8.5%. Industrial production had been increasing by an average of a little more than 7.5% per annum from 1958 to 1963, and agricultural production by an average of about five per cent in the same period. It is evident, therefore, that the Greek economy in that period could have provided higher incomes for the wage earners; but average earnings for male and female workers in the same period remained at a near subsistence level.

The government's policy of economic expansion involved holding labour costs at a minimum by holding wages down. In a system where the labour market and industrial relations were controlled by the government, wages and salaries could only be raised by ministerial decrees, even in cases where government-approved agreement was reached between employer and employee organizations.

16

Some argue that part of the blame for the failure of Greek wage earners to improve their lot lies with the trade unions for not representing the workers more strongly. However, even in this, the government was partly responsible because it could have helped, for instance, to solve some of the labour movement's constitutional and administrative problems since it was through legislation that many of the trade union rules and regulations in Greece were established. Instead of helping the movement to acquire a place in the scheme of national socio-economic planning and development, the government did everything in its power to undermine the trade unions through direct interference and by promoting dissension and factionalism among their leaders.[28]

Following the elections of 1963, the Center Union Government continued the development policies of the previous National Radical Union Government, but it paid special attention to the needs of the lower income groups. Social services were improved and expanded to include complete free education at all levels, and efforts were made for more equitable income distribution. As a result, social conditions improved considerably in 1964 and 1965, benefiting not only the small farmers but also the low-paid wage and salary earners.

Another factor contributing to adverse social conditions and the need for migration is that for existing levels of economic development Greece has had a substantial manpower surplus. This was reflected in unemployment and underemployment, and has resulted in depressed living standards. Greece, in fact, has always been an exporter of labour. "The point is important, for the existence of a manpower surplus has strongly influenced Greek thinking and Greek legislation on employment matters and accounts in large measure for the *eleemosynary* aproach which has been adopted to these questions."[29]

As late as 1971, and in spite of increased temporary and permanent emigration, considerable unemployment and underemployment persisted. Across the country, there was a considerable number of employable males and females who were not working.[30]

Social conditions and disparities were affected also by established educational standards. Although Greece has had a better record than her Balkan neighbours in the field of educational achievement, standards have been lagging behind Western Europe, especially among the rural population. Compulsory primary education was introduced after World War I, but various forms of school interruption led to a considerable percentage of illiterates, especially among females and ruralites. High school attendance up to the age of 15 became compulsory in the post-World War II period and in 1963 free education at all levels was offered. However, free tuition was not enough to attract and produce adequate numbers of college or university students and qualified graduates, since the institutions of higher education are few, overcrowded, and located mostly in large cities. The inadequate facilities and the small number of instructors create serious problems of enrolment size and teaching standards. Post-secondary education in Greece, therefore, is far from satisfactory, although the standards of secondary education can be compared favourably with those in other developing countries.

Educational and cultural disparities between the rural areas and the major urban centres have been aggravated by the fact that light as well as sophisticated entertainment has concentrated heavily in the urban centres. At least 80% of the country's cinemas, theatres, concert halls, exhibitions, galleries, sports centres, and libraries are in the Athens-Piraeus area. Festivals, international conferences and tourist attractions are mainly found in this area as well.

EMIGRATION FROM GREECE

Forced and voluntary emigration from Greece has occurred throughout the 3,000 years of its history. Emigration during the first 1,500 years included some planned colonization in neighbouring and distant regions under Greek control or influence. This was especially so during the Athenian and Macedonian conquests and expansions in the fifth and fourth centuries B.C. and in the expansion periods of the Byzantine Empire from the fourth to the sixth centuries A.D.

The considerable Greek exodus throughout history may be attributed to a variety of factors, including socio-economic and political conditions in Greece, the many and destructive wars, and the occasional oppression by domestic and foreign tyrants, especially the lengthy Ottoman occupation from 1453 to 1828. However, the causes of voluntary emigration may also be found in the long-established traditions of the Greek nation and the character of its people. This included curiosity, and a passion for travel, change, and self-improvement. It was not need and circumstance alone that drove the Greeks across the seas in search of other lands and new fortunes, but also their spirit of adventure. This, in combination with their business acumen and skilled seamanship, has helped them become one of the greatest maritime nations of the world.

Greek immigrants were partly responsible for the success of the War of Independence against the Ottoman Empire, and contributed to the rebirth of the nation after its liberation in 1828. These contributions came about despite a deterioration in conditions during the Ottoman domination. The Greek immigrant communities in parts of the empire and in some of the free nations of Europe progressed and prospered. Those immigrant communities outside Greece were able to play an important part in preserving the national spirit of the Greek people and in preparing and organizing the Greek revolution. After the War of Independence, they helped to set the pace for the political and cultural life of the new state.

Greeks did not begin to emigrate to the New World as early as did Western Europeans, not only because of the greater distance from the mother country, but also because Greeks tended to move first to established communities in such places as London, Paris, Marseilles, Vienna, Trieste, Odessa, and Varna, in the Middle East, especially in Smyrna and Alexandria, and in north and northeast Africa. Direct Greek emigration to North America did not start in earnest until the twentieth century. In the United States Greeks tended to concentrate in New York, Philadelphia and Chicago, and in Canada they settled in Montreal, Toronto and Vancouver.

Low wages, inflation, unemployment and the slow economic and social development in Greece during the 1950s and 1960s were decisive factors in the exodus of much of the Greek labour force. The emigration increased by a considerable 20% per annum. During the five-year period 1959-63, 315,000 workers left Greece, seeking better futures elsewhere.[31]

Despite a sharing of general characteristics and a common desire to better themselves and contribute to whatever place they are in, the rural-urban differences among Greeks are reflected in education, wealth, occupations, outlooks, accents and tastes. When Greeks emigrate, such differences affect their likelihood of success and happiness in their adopted homes.[32]

The numbers and characteristics of Greek emigrants in modern times have varied with the changing socio-economic and political conditions in Greece, as well as with the changing conditions and immigration policies of the recipient countries. Permanent Greek immigration in the last 30 years has been concentrated in Canada, the United States, Brazil, Venezuela, Australia, South Africa and Britain (mainly Greek Cypriots). Temporary Greek immigration has concentrated mainly in West Germany, but there has been some temporary immigration also to Austria, the Benelux countries, Sweden and Switzerland.

According to the Statistical Service of Greece, permanent and temporary Greek emigration from 1951 to 1971 totalled 1,178,000 persons. It is estimated that about 1,500,000 Greek citizens emigrated to foreign lands in the 30 years between 1945 and 1975, which is equivalent to 17% of the 8,768,641 total population of Greece in 1971. This post-World War II emigration has not only benefited the recipient countries but also the Greek economy as well. The exodus has eased the unemployment situation and the demand for arable land and social services, especially in rural areas. It has also contributed substantially to the balance of payments and development plans, by means of the monetary remittances by emigrants to their relatives in Greece, and the transfer of some of their savings to Greek financial institutions. Greek emigrants have also invested profits in Greece which have been gained from property and business enterprises abroad.

In conclusion, the long tradition of Greek immigration can be mainly attributed to socio-economic hardships and instabilities of the Greek society. It was mainly the socio-economically deprived Greek peasants and those prosecuted for their political beliefs who left their homeland seeking fortune and freedom abroad. Canada has become a favourite new home for many Greeks because of its democratic institutions and economic opportunities.

NOTES

1. Bickman Sweet-Escott, *Greece: A Political and Economic Survey 1939-53* (London: R.I.I.A., 1954), p. 2.
2. *Ibid.*, p. 3.
3. *Ibid.*, pp. 4-5.
4. Constantina Safilios-Rothschild, *Toward a Sociology of Women* (Toronto: Xerox College Publishing, 1972), p. 84.
5. Irwin Sanders, *Rainbow in the Rock: The People of Rural Greece* (Cambridge, Mass.: Harvard University Press, 1962), pp. 308-309.
6. *Encyclopedia Americana*, 1966, Vol. 13, p. 371.
7. John Campbell and Philip Sherrard, *Modern Greece* (London: Ernest Benn Limited, 1969), p. 330.
8. *Ibid.*, p. 331.
9. See Sanders, *op. cit.*, pp. 194-197.
10. Campbell and Sherrard, *op. cit.*, p. 344.
11. J.K. Campbell, *Honour Family and Patronage* (Oxford: Clarendon Press, 1964), p. 204.
12. N. Kaltchas, *Introduction to the Constitutional History of Modern Greece* (New York: Columbia University Press, 1940), p. 4.
13. "*Greece-Basic Statistics*" Greek Office of Information (London, 1949).
14. Statistical Service of Greece (Athens, 1973).
15. Sweet-Escott, *op. cit.*, p. 7.
16. "Post-War General Elections in Greece," Prime Minister's Office, Press and Information Department (Athens, 1964).
17. *Encyclopedia Britannica*, 1966, Vol. 13, p. 371.
18. Theodore Saloutos, *The Greeks in the United States* (Cambridge, Mass.: Harvard University Press, 1964), p. 2.
19. *Encyclopedia Britannica, op. cit.*, pp. 371-372.
20. Christos Jecchinis, *Trade Unionism in Greece* (Chicago: Roosevelt University Press, 1967), p. 6.
21. *Ibid.*, pp. 50-51.
22. Sweet-Escott, *op. cit.*, pp. 93-100.
23. *Collier's Encyclopedia*, 1966, Vol. II, pp. 394-395.
24. ILO, *Labour Problems in Greece* (Geneva, 1949), p. 27.
25. *Ibid.*, p. 25.
26. *United Nations Statistical Yearbook* (New York: United Nations, 1974).
27. Ministry of Coordination, Regional Development Services (Athens, 1963).
28. See Jecchinis, *op. cit.*
29. OECD Economic Survey, (Greece, Paris, 1966) and ILO Yearbook of Labour Statistics (1966).

30. Statistical Services of Greece (Athens, 1973).
31. Statistical Services of Greece (Athens, 1966).
32. It is difficult to determine what percentage of Greek immigrants come directly from rural communities because of the steady movement of ruralites toward urban centres during the 1950s and 1960s. Thus many of the rural people who immigrated to Canada and other parts of the world had lived and worked, at least for a short time, in cities such as Athens, Salonica and Patras.

TWO

Settlements and Demographic Aspects

THE EARLY EXPLORERS

No one knows exactly when the first Greeks came to North America. Some writers believe that Christopher Columbus was a Greek: for example, Demetrius Sicilianos in his book *The Greek Background of Christopher Columbus* claims that "Christopher . . . the discoverer of America and named Columbus, is not an Italian, but a Byzantine Nobleman, whose real name was Dispatos."[1] Another author, Malafouris, recounted the exploits of Greeks who in the middle and late eighteenth century reached the shore of Florida.[2] George Vlassis in his book *The Greeks in Canada* has indicated that Greek seamen had visited Canadian shores prior to 1800. In 1592, Juan de Fuca (whose original name was Yannis Phokas) and who was born on the island of Cephalonia in the Ionian Sea explored the coast of what is now British Columbia while navigating for the Spanish navy;[3] the strait which divides Vancouver Island from Washington State was named after this explorer. Juan de Fuca's visit to the west coast of Canada is corroborated by the narrative of an Englishman, Michael Lok, who met the famous navigator in Venice in 1596.[4]

Greek immigration to Canada, however, began with the arrival of adventurous Greeks who left their homeland after the revolution (1821-1827) against the Turkish conquerors. Most of the first Greek immigrants came from the Islands and Peloponnesus (peninsula of southern Greece), especially the most unproductive provinces of Arcadia and Laconia. The Peloponnesians were followed by economically deprived villagers from mainland Greece.

Other early Greeks known to have settled on Canadian soil were Panayotis Nonis and Theodore Lecas. Both men were born in Krandion, Crete, and took part in the siege of the City of Nafplion during the revolution. They immigrated to Montreal in 1843.

It has also been said that around the year 1850 "a number of Greek sailors who had sailed up the St. Lawrence River had deserted their ships and remained in Quebec, married French-Canadian girls and evidently all traces of them have been lost."[5] This argument derives from a story told by two Greek Canadians from Montreal, Bill Dranidiotis and Nicholas Tagaras, who in 1908 met a 70-year-old farmer from St. Antoine, Quebec, who claimed to be of Greek descent. The farmer, whose name was Eustrat Thaquene, called himself a Greek Canadian and said his father had sailed from Greece.[6]

In 1851, two-and-a-half centuries after the visit of Juan de Fuca, another Greek arrived in British Columbia. He was George Kapiotis, a native of Kyme on the Island of Eubeoa. Kapiotis served in the British Navy, took part in the Crimean War and sailed around the world seeking fortune and adventure. He joined the great gold stampede to California in 1849 and later the gold rush of the Cariboo, B.C., where he made a fortune. After he settled in Victoria, Kapiotis married a young Indian girl named Mari-Ann, the daughter of the Indian Chief of the Songees tribe. Vlassis notes that the couple was married by a Russian bishop according to the Greek Orthodox ritual. Kapiotis died in Victoria on November 15, 1916, at the age of 93. His granddaughter Orsa married John Douglas, grandson of Sir James Douglas, the first Governor of Victoria, and the first white man in the territory. Kapiotis' grandson George Athans, a physician, represented Canada in the 1936 Olympic Games in Germany. He held a number of championships, including the Canadian springboard and Pacific Coast diving championships.[7]

Another outstanding pioneer was Dr. Petros Constantinides, the son of a professor at the University of Athens. Constantinides obtained his medical degree from the Royal College of Physicians in Edinburgh, Scotland, and came to Toronto in 1864. As far as can be determined, Constantinides was the first Greek physician to emigrate to Canada. He has also been considered one of the first operating surgeons in Toronto, and amongst the oldest general practitioners of Ontario. His family is one of the oldest recorded Greek-Canadian families in Toronto. Dr. Constantinides' children Ianthe and Charles received Masters' degrees from the University of Toronto in 1902 and 1903 respectively.[8]

John Giannaris (Yannaris) was a sailor and adventurer from the Greek Island of Syros. Born in 1859, Giannaris arrived in Vancouver in 1878. He and a companion deserted their ship *Struan* in order to stay and make their fortune in the new country. It wasn't long before Giannaris bought his own boat and started a salmon fishing business. Although Giannaris was naturalized as a British subject and changed his name to John Stevens, he became known as "Johnny the Greek." In 1887 John married a girl named Emma, the stepdaughter of Joseph King. John, who had seven children, died on October 8, 1938, in British Columbia at the age of 79.[9]

Prior to 1900 Greek immigration to Canada was sporadic. In 1871, only 39 persons of Greek origin were known to be living throughout

Canada, and by 1900 the Canadian Census recorded approximately 200 persons of Greek descent. Many of these pioneers who landed on Canadian soil, and who usually ended up in Toronto or Montreal, were sailors from the Greek Islands. Other commercially-minded Greeks first emigrated to the United States but subsequently moved to Montreal and other areas of Canada such as Nova Scotia, New Brunswick and Ontario.[10] They usually entered the street trades, selling cigars, flowers, sweets and peanuts. Within a relatively short period of time many graduated from street vending trades into small businesses of their own. By the beginning of the twentieth century a number of Greeks owned confectionaries, restaurants and miscellaneous stores in Montreal, Toronto and Vancouver.

GROWTH AND ORGANIZATION: 1900-1945

With the discovery of new economic opportunities in North America, the exodus of Greek peasants to Egypt, Russia and the Balkan states almost ceased, while the movement across the Atlantic assumed greater proportions.[11] Greek immigration into Canada increased considerably after 1900. From July 1, 1900, to December 31, 1907, approximately 2,540 Greeks entered Canada,[12] most of whom were peasants from Peloponnesus, while a few were Macedonian fur traders who carried on the trade of their native town Kastoria. Emigration to Canada was spurred by repeated crop failures, oppressive taxation and increasing poverty. Others had emigrated from the Ottoman Empire for political reasons. Effective in 1908, the new Turkish constitution required Greeks in Macedonia and other Turkish-occupied Greek regions such as Epirus, the Island of Lesbos and the Dodecanese to render military service,[13] and a number of prosperous individuals left their homeland to avoid conscription into the Turkish army. Some of them had college degrees from American schools in the Near East.[14]

Two additional factors increased the flow of Greek and other immigrants to Canada during the early twentieth century. The Canadian government instituted a policy of importing cheap labour from Europe for economic development (notably in the freight transportation industry) and the United States imposed quotas on aliens. Although Canada did not adopt formal quotas it controlled immigration by establishing a list of "preferred" and "non-preferred" countries from which to select immigrants. British, French and Americans were preferred while the Chinese and Asians were restricted.[15] The flow of various ethnic groups into Canada undoubtedly created anxieties for those who feared that the influx of immigrants from southern and eastern Europe "would affect the pioneer spirit . . . on which the progress of Canada depended."[16]

The arrival of the early Greek immigrants was not a completely happy event. They came at the time when ethnic prejudice and discrimination, especially against southern Europeans, was strong in Canada. The majority of the early immigrants were villagers who had little previous contact with urban communities. As newcomers they had no access to credit, and possessed only rudimentary knowledge of the host society's language and social institutions. Some cursed their fate on finding themselves in a foreign land among inhospitable strangers, far from their friendly villages and loved ones. Being cut off from their families, friends and church, they felt lonely and alienated. Some who could not make the adjustment worked for a short period of time, saved money for their passage and returned to Greece to start over again.

From their early days of immigration to Canada, Greeks concentrated in urban centres. There were two reasons for this. First, many of the pioneers were sailors who visited the ports of Montreal and Vancouver, liked the surroundings and decided to stay. Subsequently a chain of Greek immigrants followed their compatriots. Many of the later arrivals came through the port of New York, which is geographically close to Montreal and Toronto. A second factor in immigration to urban areas was their distaste for farming, a way of life they had rejected in their homeland and did not want to adopt in Canada. Farming in Greece was not only an occupation of low prestige but one of "short crops, debt, despondency and little hope for the future."[17] Thus urban communities were attractive to the Greeks who wanted to work hard, make their fortunes in a relatively short time and eventually start their own businesses or return to Greece to pay off family debts and make life more comfortable. In businesses such as shoeshine parlours and restaurants Greek Canadians employed those who followed them from their homeland, many of whom were relatives or compatriots from their home village. Thus the concentration process continued with the arrival of more Greeks who preferred to settle near and work with their countrymen.

The overwhelming majority of Greeks who settled in Canada during the early 1900s were young males without families, including adolescents who came to work and support their poor families in Greece. They were mainly labourers with little formal education who were "often defrauded and deceived by fake employment bureaus usually run by their own countrymen."[18] Some of the young immigrant boys "were under the padroni – that is, men who brought them over and control their earnings."[19]

Because Greek immigration in the early years consisted mainly of males, large numbers of men lived together keeping house in some co-operative arrangement and forming what may be called primary groups of Greek extraction. Some lived in crowded boarding houses near the railroads and other job sites, because they saw themselves as sojourners and wanted to save as much money as possible either for returning home or for bringing over relatives.[20] Greek restaurants and coffeehouses were the places where the lonely immigrant men could meet after work and on Sundays to socialize with compatriots. In Vancouver, for example, the

25

early Greek immigrant men have been described by Lambrou as "having no organized social life except for the coffeehouse which was established in 1906. . . . This was the early place where the men could relax, drink coffee and talk."[21]

Because of the absence of eligible Greek women, many of the Greek men married non-Greek girls. Thus an undisclosed number of the early Greek-Canadian families were of ethnic admixture. The more traditionally-oriented Greek men returned to Greece in search of a wife or arranged marriages through the exchange of photographs with eligible girls in Greece selected by their parents. Arranged marriages among Greek males "should not be understood in the context of the Greek kinship system in which mate selection was an affair that goes beyond the immediate parties concerned. It was a matter of economics, for many Greek male immigrants could not afford to travel to Greece searching for a bride."[22]

With the arrival of women and children from Greece after 1905 and the increase in marriages, the family became the centre of social activities for many Greek Canadians. Leisure-time activities and holidays were spent with related and non-related Greek families. Namedays were special occasions where friends and relatives extended good wishes and celebrated with folk music and a variety of food and sweets. Christmas and Easter were important religious holidays observed with much festivity and zeal, especially in cities with large Greek settlements. Greeks also enjoyed picnics where they could roast lamb outdoors, drink Greek wine and dance to live music. Such social occasions fostered the preservation of ethnic traditions.

In 1911 there were 3,614 persons in Canada of Greek origin and in 1912 the number had increased to 5,740.[23] The majority of them, 67%, were in the provinces of Ontario and Quebec. With the growth of Greek immigration, Greek settlements in large Canadian cities began to develop a sense of ethnic community and solidarity. The two decades from 1900 to 1920 may be considered as the period of establishment for the first ethnic institutions concerned with the preservation of the Greek language and culture.

The founding of the first Greek churches in Montreal (1906) and Toronto (1909) signified the beginning of Greek ethno-religious communities in Canada. The church became the centre of the Greek community, for many important social and cultural functions had to be blessed or administered by the church. But the social and cultural organization did not come from their religious institutions alone. The ethnic associations were as essential as the Greek Orthodox Church. In fact the establishment of the churches in the various Canadian cities was often preceded by Greek associations. These included the *Patris* (Motherland) in Montreal; the Saskatoon Greek Society in Saskatoon, Saskatchewan; the Panhellenic Union in Ottawa; the Annunciation Benevolent Greek Society in Winnipeg; the American Hellenic Educational Progressive Association (AHEPA) in London, Ontario; and the Hellenic Patriotic Association in Vancouver. These organizations were designed to remind the immigrant of his Hellenic heritage and obligations to the homeland, and to promote a better understanding of the Greek people in Canada.

In 1912 and 1913 the settlement process of many Greek Canadians was interrupted by war in Greece. During the Balkan Wars numerous young men returned to Greece to join the Greek army and fight against the Turks. Among the volunteers was Father Paparaschakis, the first parish priest of St. George Greek Orthodox Church in Toronto, who was killed in action.[24] Meanwhile, the Greek-Canadian communities of Montreal, Toronto and Ottawa became scenes of preparation and ethnic solidarity. The Panhellenic Union played an important role in mobilizing potential Greek soldiers in various Canadian cities. Upon their arrival in Greece the volunteers were sent to military camps in Athens and Nauplion and eventually to the battle front along with thousands of Greeks from the United States. After the war many of the volunteers returned to Canada.

During World War I an undisclosed number of Greek Canadians joined the Canadian army to fight for their adopted country. Among them were 20 Cretans from Montreal. The Cretans were hopeful that such an enlistment would mean their eventual assignment to the Macedonian front where they could fight on the side of the Cretan Division within the Greek armed forces. Instead they were sent to the Western Front. Three of the 20 were killed in action and seven others were wounded.[25] As soon as the war was over most of the surviving volunteers came back to Canada with the intention of resettling permanently. Among those who came and established their own businesses were Yannis Apostolakis and Michael Ntoulis of Montreal.[26]

It should be noted that during World War I Canadian military leaders were reluctant to enlist Greek immigrants into the Canadian armed forces. In October, 1917, the Major General of Canadian Military District No. 6 in Halifax asked the General Commanding Officer in Ottawa whether or not it would be in order to enlist Greeks for the Canadian Expeditionary Force. In reply, the Adjutant General of the Canadian Militia in Ottawa stated that "in individual cases, Greeks who appear suitable may be enlisted. No special effort, however, should be made to recruit them."[27] The "unsuitable" Greeks at that time were the supporters of the neutralist and German sympathizer King Constantine of Greece.

Despite the hardships of settlement and adjustment to a new society, Greek Canadians continued to contribute to the economic and cultural growth of Canada with decisiveness and loyalty. The stream of Greek immigration to Canada continued steadily. In 1931 the population of Greek origin in Canada had risen to 9,450 persons. Over one-half (5,579 or 59%) of them had been born in Greece.[28] By this time Greek Canadians had gained a reputation for being honest and industrious, and were responsible for the operation of many of the finest restaurants, hotels, theatres and recreation clubs in Canada. A few had become successful farmers in Ontario, the Prairie Provinces and in Galiano Island, British Columbia. A number from the Aegean Island of Scopelos became successful in the fishing business of Deas Island, near Ladner, British Columbia.[29] Others ventured into salmon fishing in Vancouver and Victoria. Those unable to enter the fishing business opened Oyster Bars where they catered to their fellow Greeks.[30] Those who did not venture into their own businesses found employment in restaurants, factories and railroad construction gangs.

Between 1920 and 1940, other Greek churches were founded in Halifax, Quebec City, Ottawa, Edmonton and Vancouver. More Greek societies and associations of various kinds appeared in conjunction with the growth of the Greek communities. Greek youth organizations such as Sons of Pericles, Greek Boys' Club and Greek Girls' Club also made their appearance in large cities such as Montreal and Toronto. The young were admonished by their parents and community leaders to learn and maintain the Greek language in Canada. For example, the Greek Canadian Thomas Kapelos, in a commentary published in *The Greek Year Book* (1934), advised young Canadians of Greek parentage:

> Having learned Greek you will come closer to the more intellectual people of your father's country. You will be able to read in the original not only the works of your immortal ancestors, but also the works of the contemporaries. . . . You, young Canadians of Greek extraction, have a good opportunity to increase your knowledge – grasp it – make it a good start – start with Greek.[31]

In the later 1930s hundreds of young immigrants and second-generation Greek Canadians were attending high schools and universities throughout Canada. Many of the graduates entered high status occupations, with favoured professions being engineering, economics, law and medicine. High status occupational achievement was perhaps due to the "prodding of parents who remembered only too well that these were the professions that counted in Greece."[32] Other young Greek Canadians became teachers, lecturers, artists and business managers. Many parents, motivated by their own hardships, encouraged their children and helped them financially to obtain university educations.

The young Greek Canadians began integrating socially and economically into the dominant English-speaking society. During World War II a considerable number served in the Canadian armed forces and distinguished themselves at the battle front. According to Vlassis, there were 68 young men of Greek descent from Montreal alone who enlisted in the Canadian Army and fought during the war. Many more volunteers came from the various Greek communities throughout Canada, a number of whom were killed in action.[33] In 1946 the Hellenic Branch of the Royal Canadian Legion was organized in Montreal by war veterans of Greek descent, with Dr. Arthur Kalfas as its first president.[34]

The patriotic spirit of Greek Canadians during World War II was also manifested in their response to Canadian Red Cross Society appeals. For example, the Greek Canadian Ladies Society of Montreal organized two groups with a total membership of 125 persons to work for the Red Cross in making hospital supplies and comforts for the Canadian troops.[35]

GROWTH AND ORGANIZATION AFTER WORLD WAR II

The Canadian government adopted a more liberal immigration policy in the years following World War II. This change was due to various factors including the need to populate and develop Canada, pressures by ethnic groups and individuals to rescue relatives from the socio-economic catastrophies of Europe and the large number of displaced persons and orphans who had failed to meet admission requirements of other countries.[36] The admission of more immigrants was considered cautiously by the Canadian government, because of racial and ethnic biases and the conditions of the Canadian labour market which was experiencing recessions, high unemployment and demands for certain occupational specialties. Some of the opposition to immigration derived from unskilled Canadian workers who perceived the newcomers as competitors for scarce jobs. Resentment against unskilled workers tended to increase during periods of high unemployment.

Canadian immigration regulations of the early 1950s emphasized the sponsorship of relatives and friends and the admission of agriculturalists, domestics, nurses' aids and other workers specifically nominated by Canadian employers.[37] Greek Canadians sponsored and nominated relatives, friends and even co-villagers who wanted to come to Canada.

Immigration policy changes in the early 1960s emphasized selection of unsponsored immigrants from anywhere in the world, with selection based on education and occupation skills. This policy provided opportunities for professionals and skilled workers but excluded many unskilled labourers. To circumvent this, many Greeks "were entering Canada as visitors, making contact with influential individuals or bodies, and then applying to stay permanently."[38]

The post-World War II immigration policies placed Greece among the most important sources of Canadian immigration, surpassed only by the United States, Britain, Italy and Portugal.[39] From 1945 to 1971 no fewer than 107,780 Greek immigrants entered Canada.[40] During the years 1946 to 1964, 4,597 (7.8%) of the 58,536 Greek immigrants did not come directly from Greece, but from other countries where unsatisfactory political and socio-economic conditions forced Greek minority groups to

TABLE 1

Distribution of Greek-born Population in Canada, by Province and Chronological Period (1901-1951)

Province	1901	1911	1921	1931	1941	1951
CANADA	213	2,640	3,769	5,579	5,871	8,584
Alberta	1	97	217	270	190	244
British Columbia	59	683	483	532	511	573
New Brunswick	4	24	42	41	33	40
Newfoundland	—	—	—	—	—	1
Nova Scotia	4	36	83	96	108	129
Manitoba	3	64	133	135	137	158
Ontario	73	1,119	1,147	2,936	3,570	5,731
Prince Edward Island	—	—	3	—	2	4
Quebec	56	545	1,115	1,294	1,112	1,559
Saskatchewan	1	40	221	272	202	154
Yukon and Northwest Territories	12	12	2	3	6	1

Source: George D. Vlassis, *The Greeks in Canada* (Ottawa: Leclerc Printers Limited, 1953), p. 93.

TABLE 2

Population of Greek Ethnic Origin in Canada by Age and Sex, 1971*

Age	Males Number	%	Females Number	%	Total Number	%
0-19	23,190	30.0	23,005	39.0	47,200	37.9
20-39	26,890	41.0	23,380	40.0	50,275	40.5
40-59	11,500	17.5	9,125	15.0	20,615	16.5
60 +	2,895	4.5	3,585	6.0	6,385	5.1
Total	65,475	100.0	59,010	100.0	124,475	100.0

Source: "Ethnic Groups by Age Groups," 1971 *Census Canada Catalogue* 92-731, Vol. I (Part 4), January, 1974.

*The discrepancy in the totals is due to rounding.

GRAPH NO. 1

Greek Immigrants to Canada

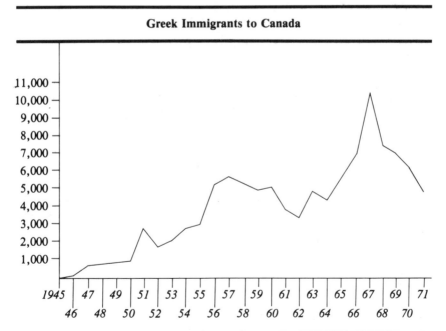

Source: Canada Department of Citizenship and Immigration: Immigrants by ethnic origin.

remigrate.[41] The available data indicate that during the same period 1,697 Greek immigrants with Greek passports had not been born in Greece.

A notably moderate volume of Greek immigration to Canada began in 1951 immediately after the Greek Civil War (1946-1949). A steady increase, however, did not occur before 1964 and reached its peak in 1967. Immigration remained fairly high in 1968 and declined gradually in the following years. The relatively high Greek immigration to Canada during 1967-1968 was due in large part to unstable politico-economic conditions in Greece and the new Canadian immigration policies of the 1960s. On the other hand, the steady decline of Greek immigration since 1968 has been attributed to the improvement of the Greek economy, the temporary emigration of Greek workers to Germany and the changes in Canadian immigration regulations.

Although the number of Greek male immigrants in Canada has always been larger than the number of females, the ratio has been decreasing steadily since the early 1940s. In 1941, according to Vlassis, 26% of the immigrant Greek population were females.[42]

In 1971, 47.4% of the Greek immigrant population were females (See Table 3). The high ratio of males, especially in the earlier periods of immigration, is attributable to the custom of the Greek males (whether married or single) to emigrate to foreign lands either to make their fortune and return to Greece or to settle and bring their relatives at a later date.

According to 1964-71 statistical information – among Greeks female immigrants are more numerous than males in the 15 to 24 age group, as the Greek government does not permit young males in that age bracket to leave the country without having served in the armed forces. The majority of the Greek immigrants, however, are in the 20-24 and 25-29 age groups. It seems then that both male and female immigrants migrate after they finish school if they are unable to find satisfactory employment in their homeland.

Greek Canadians are thus a young group with 57% belonging to working and productive age categories (20-59 years of age). At least 78% of the total Greek-Canadian population in 1971 was under the age of 39 (See Table 2). The mass emigration of young Greeks to Canada and other countries in the 1950s and 1960s contributed to the low birth rate, zero population growth and shortage of agricultural labour in Greece in the 1970s.

When post-war Greek immigrants arrived in Canada, they tended to settle in the cities of Montreal, Toronto, and Vancouver and to a lesser extent in other Canadian cities such as Edmonton, Winnipeg and Thunder Bay. The main concentration of settlement, however, has been in the large urban communities of Ontario and Quebec. Since 1911 Ontario has been the most popular destination. During the period 1964-71, 55% of all Greek immigrants gave Ontario as their intended destination, while 46%

TABLE 3

**Population of Greek Ethnic Origin
in Canada by Sex, 1971**

Sex	Number	%
Males	65,475	52.6
Females	59,000	47.4
Total	124,475	100.0

Sources: "Ethnic Groups," 1971 *Census of Canada*, Catalogue 92-723, Vol. 1 (Part 3) October, 1973.

intended to go to Quebec, four per cent to British Columbia, and two per cent to Manitoba. According to the 1971 Census of Canada, approximately 84% of Canadians of Greek origin were residing in cities with populations of 500,000 and over (See Table 5). At least 98% of Greeks were residing in Canadian communities classified as urban, with the highest concentration in the cities of Montreal and Toronto.[43]

The heavy concentration of post-war immigrants in metropolitan centres may be explained by the attraction of Greeks to already-established Greek communities. When the immigrant is transplanted from one society to another he prefers to be where he can speak his native language and associate with those having similar beliefs, values and traditions. Thus the ethnic community with its religious and educational institutions, and its recreational, commercial and cultural facilities, had a strong attraction for new immigrants. In large urban cities the immigrant could also work in industry, accumulate money quickly and start a business of his own. When this concentration started it continued because new immigrants were sponsored by relatives and friends, as well as because that there were strong family ties and ethnocentrism among Greeks.

The following case history is an example of the sponsorship patterns commonly found among Greeks in Canada:

In 1953 Marina left her village in southern Greece at the age of 17 and came to Canada to work as a domestic. Upon her arrival to London, Ontario, she was able to obtain a job in a factory and thus avoid the degrading job of a domestic servant. Two years later she sponsored her oldest brother Nikos who came and started as a dishwasher in a Greek-owned restaurant. A few months later Marina sponsored her parents, two brothers and a sister.

The following year (1956) Marina sponsored her fiance George, a young man from a nearby village whom she married as soon as he arrived in Canada. The same year George sponsored his sister Dena who came to London and started her first job in a dry cleaning

33

TABLE 4

**Percentage Distribution of Greek Ethnic Origin Population
for Canadian Provinces in Rank Order, 1941, 1971**

| | 1941 | | 1971 | |
Province	%	Cumulative	%	Cumulative
Ontario	50.5	50.5	53.8	53.8
Quebec	23.3	73.8	34.4	88.2
British Columbia	9.5	83.3	5.3	93.5
Alberta	5.2	88.5	2.6	96.1
Manitoba	3.4	91.9	1.7	97.8
Nova Scotia	2.9	94.8	1.0	98.8
Saskatchewan	4.2	99.0	.7	99.5
New Brunswick	.9	99.9	.3	99.8
Newfoundland, N.W.T.	.1	100.0	.2	100.0
Yukon, P.E.I.	—	—	—	—
Canada	100.0		100.0	

Source: *The Canada Yearbook,* 1945, p. 105; Ethnic Groups, 1971 *Census of Canada,* Catalogue 92-723, Vol. 1 (Part 3), October, 1973.

store. A year later (1957) Dena sponsored her fiance John who was from Marina's home town. The same year John sponsored his sister Eleni who came and got a job in a dry cleaning store. In 1958 Eleni sponsored her fiance Petros who obtained a job as a dishwasher in a Greek-owned restaurant. In 1959 Petros sponsored his brother Stavros who also started as a dishwasher. Three years later (1962) Stavros sponsored his fiancee, a girl he had met in Greece.

In 1971 Marina's younger sister Rena visited Greece where she met a young man from a nearby village, and became engaged to him. Late in 1971, Rena sponsored her fiance, whom she married in London, Ontario.

All the above-mentioned immigrant men who came through sponsorship and started with menial jobs, by 1978 had owned their own restaurants in London, Ontario, and considered themselves successful Greek Canadians. Although they came with the hope of making their fortunes and returning to Greece, they stayed in Canada.

The availability of social services which support new immigrants has also played a role in reinforcing urban concentration. In the early 1950s, for example, the Canadian Red Cross brought more than 200 young Greek refugees into Canada from Iron Curtain countries and reunited

TABLE 5

Percentage Distribution of Population of Greek Origin by Sex and Size of Canadian Community, 1971

Size of Community	Male	Female	Total
500,000 and over	83.2	84.5	83.9
100,000 – 499,999	9.6	9.3	9.4
10,000 – 99,999	5.0	4.3	4.7
9,999 and under	2.2	1.8	2.0
Total	100.0	100.0	100.0

Source: "Ethnic Groups", 1971 Census Canada, Catalogue 92-725, Vol. 1 (Part 3), April, 1973.

them with relatives in Toronto. These Greek nationals had been retained following the 1946-49 civil war in Greece. The Canadian Red Cross was instrumental in co-ordinating the services of various social agencies, among them the Neighborhood Workers Association, the Welfare Council of Toronto, and the Ontario Welfare Council. The already-established relatives made great efforts to plan and finance the refugees' passage and helped them find employment, especially in Greek-owned businesses.[44]

The preference of many rural Greeks for an urban lifestyle, apparent in Greece as well as abroad, can be seen as a reflection of rising expectations for better financial and educational opportunities. However, in Canada the concentration of Greek immigrants in the metropolitan centres in some respects impedes adaptation. Since the majority of Greek immigrants come from rural areas, upon arriving in Canadian cities they not only have to adjust to Canadian culture in general and the English language, but also to an urban industrial setting. The rural immigrant must therefore cope with future shock as well as culture shock in the fast-paced urban milieu.

The newly arrived Greeks tend to cluster in specific neighbourhoods, usually characterized by older and cheaper housing. Two factors account for this: the low wages which force them to rent cheap housing, and their preference for being near relatives and those of the same ethnicity. Being close to those who speak the same language and have the same culture provides the new immigrants with a sense of security and belongingness, and minimizes cultural shock.

The mass settlement of Greek immigrants in large urban communities during the 1950s and early 1960s was characterized by many hardships. For example, many immigrants experienced lack of privacy in their homes, since it was not uncommon for two or three families with young children to share the same household because of economic necessity. The families involved were usually related or came from the same town or village in Greece. Some parents and children had to sleep in the same

TABLE 6

Distribution of Population of Greek Origin By Type of Community, 1971

Type of Community	Number	%
Urban	122,670	98.6
Rural non-farm	1,265	1.0
Rural farm	540	.4
Total	124,475	100.0

Source: "Ethnic Groups," 1971 *Census of Canada*, Catalogue 92-731, Vol. 1 (Part 4) January, 1974.

room, and families had to take turns with the cooking and eating facilities.

As the years passed and the immigrants improved their economic status, they were able to buy their own homes and to move out to better residential areas. Many of those who bought houses in suburban areas tended to select an area where Greeks had already established their residences. Surveys conducted by the Survey Research Centre at York University in the early 1970s indicated strong residential clustering of the Greeks in Toronto (as well as of other ethnic groups), and even the casual visitor to the city comments on commercial areas where many of the store signs are written in Greek, and bouzouki music emanates from restaurant and coffeebar juke boxes.[45]

Despite "upward mobility" to the suburbs, clusterings of Greek immigrants in the older sections of the city are not on the decline. Such culturally unique areas are still present in Montreal (Park Avenue), Toronto (Danforth Avenue) and Vancouver, and their existence depends to a large extent on the continuous influx of new immigrants. Greek restaurants, grocery stores, theatres and other places of entertainment are located in these areas.

In a recent sociological study Gavaki has claimed that sections in the City of Montreal where Greek immigrants are highly concentrated can be considered as "ghettos," characterized by low income, unemployment, low level of schooling and physical deterioration.[46] Very little family disorganization and crime is found in these areas.

ACCEPTANCE BY THE HOST SOCIETY

Some prejudice and discrimination towards Greeks by the host society were perhaps inevitable, especially in the early years of immigration. Greek immigrants can recall days when they could not walk through the downtown areas of cities or speak their native language in public, even in their own restaurants, without being accosted or assaulted.[47] The Greek immigrant, with his foreign clothes and manners, unusual name and speech, was eccentric to established Canadians of British or French ancestry and aroused their hostility. Many immigrant men were typically swarthy and moustached and bore the sweat and strain that results from toiling long hours in factories, restaurants and shoeshine parlors. It was thus inevitable that they would be conspicuous to white collar clerks, businessmen and similar elements of the comfortable, cosmopolitan society around them.

On the other hand, the Greek immigrants themselves contributed to the animosity and resentment. Ethnocentric, apprehensive and distrustful of the unfamiliar new environment, they kept to themselves and resisted assimilation. They preferred their traditional norms and values and resisted those Canadian. Meanwhile, established Canadian businessmen found themselves confronted by aggressive, ambitious competitors. Happily for all, the Greeks proved through mutually acceptable means that they could adapt to the host society and contribute to its economic and cultural enrichment. Some Greeks went as far as to change their names to achieve acceptance in Canadian business circles.

In the early 1900s even Canadian immigration policies were biased against Greeks. According to Woodsworth, Greeks as well as others who came from the eastern Mediterranean constituted one of the least desirable classes of immigrants.[48] Avery, in his analysis of early Canadian immigration policies, has noted that "generally the immigrants from southern Europe fell into the non-preferred category: Armenians, Greeks, Turks, Italians, Bulgarians, etc. However, immigrants from France, Belgium, Holland, and Scandinavian countries, Germany, Finland and Switzerland were constantly encouraged to immigrate."[49]

Canada's immigration policies were influenced by racist and environmental (climatic) theories popularized by writers such as Madison Grant in the United States and George Parkin in Canada. The belief in a hierarchical structure of racial types which associated southern Europeans with anarchy, radicalism and socialism is commonly expressed in the writings of these writers.[50]

Let us now examine a few reported incidents of discrimination against Greek Canadians during the early years of settlement. In 1907 the Canadian Pacific Railway (CPR) refused to hire Greeks as freight handlers in Port Arthur, Ontario, since Greek immigrants were known for taking the initiative in organizing strikes and defying the company's exploitative working conditions.[51] On December 22, 1913, eight Greeks from Vancouver sent a signed petition to Mr. H. Stevens (MP) complaining of the delay in obtaining their Certificates of Naturalization. Although these immigrants swore that they had three years of residence and took an oath of allegiance, Judge Grant was reluctant to grant their Certificates of Naturalization.[52] In January, 1918, a naturalized Greek Canadian from

Edmonton filed a complaint to the Deputy Minister of Justice that Canadian authorities declined to allow him to vote in the Dominion election and on the question of prohibition in Alberta.[53]

In Toronto there was hostility on the part of many who believed that Greek immigrants, and especially those from Asia Minor, were pro-German. This, according to Greek immigrants, was a misjudgement. On March 1, 1918, Mr. J. C. Walsh, the acting Consul-General of Greece, visited Toronto from Montreal in order to promote more amiable feelings towards the Greek Canadians. Mr. Walsh and leaders of the Greek community in Toronto made an effort to convince the Canadian authorities that although many Greek immigrants had been born in Turkey, yet they were not alien enemies and their loyalty and sympathy lay with the allies. Mr. E. Kilismanis, the Secretary of *Karteria* (an association composed of Greek-Canadian immigrants born in Turkey), further indicated that Greeks from Turkey intended to remain Greeks and their loyalty and sympathy was with Canada and her allies. According to Kilismanis, more than 40,000 Greeks from Turkey were fighting against the Bulgarians.[54]

Perhaps the most publicized instances of hostility against the Greeks in Canada were the anti-Greek riots in Toronto in August, 1918. It is said that on August 2, a Canadian soldier had been assaulted in a cafe owned by a Greek and a group of his fellow soldiers raided the cafe. Several raids which resulted in property damage were later made on other cafes owned by Greeks, some of whom were naturalized British subjects. One Greek-owned restaurant located on Yonge Street escaped assault when its owner placed the Union Jack at the front door. On August 3rd a group of Canadian rioters clashed with Toronto policemen who were making an effort to protect Greek Canadians and their property. A number of policemen and rioters were injured.

An aroused Greek-American journalist lost little time in protesting the riots. On August 5, 1918, Petros Tatanis, the founder of the Greek-American newspaper *National Herald* in New York, sent a telegram to the Lieutenant-Governor of Ontario requesting the protection of innocent Greek Canadians. According to Tatanis's telegram, Greek Canadians had shown indisputable loyalty to Canada and her allies, were faithful to the tradition of their native country through their support of the Greek liberal government of Eleftherios Venizelos, an ally of Great Britain, and they did not deserve such treatment.[55]

Fortunately, the Greek immigrants did not generally experience longlasting prejudice and discrimination. With the prestige of Hellenic culture, the arrival of highly-educated immigrants, the visits of many thousands of Canadians to modern Greece, and the continuous appearance of Greeks in business, many Canadians began to show an appreciation for the Greek presence in Canada. In 1934, Fred I. Malone, as Assistant Crown Attorney, described the Greeks of Toronto as being law-abiding, industrious, honest and respectable citizens.[56] The Canadian historian John M. Gibbon cited the teachings of Greek theologians of the Byzantine era as having had vital influence upon the growth of Christianity in Western civilization,[57] and the works of ancient Greek philosophers, artists, architects and poets as other contributions to Canadian culture.

An important historical event which created positive attitudes toward Greek Canadians was Greece's firm and heroic position on the side of the Western allied powers during World War II. According to Saloutos, this was the period when Greeks in the United States gained respectability as an ethnic minority.[58] In Canada, admiration for Greece's resistance to Fascist forces has been expressed by Eric F. Gaswell, former National Secretary of the Canadian Author's Association, in a Forward to Vlassis's book. He writes:

> There are many references in literature to "the Glory that was Greece," but this is a time to grasp realities and bestow honour where honour is due. We have all thrilled at the spectacle of a gallant people making desperate resistance against hopeless odds, stemming the advance of a barbarian invader in the storied streets of Athens and among the islands of the Aegean Sea . . . we owe it to the Canadians of Greek origin to show our appreciation of what their European kinsmen are doing in the cause of freedom by developing a closer contact with them in the relationship of community living. There is need for an intimate knowledge of these splendid citizens, their individual talents and traditional aspirations.[59]

Other favourable remarks about the gallant and courageous Greeks during World War II were made by Canadian political leaders on July 4, 1942, at the United Nations Day Army Week in Ottawa. On this date, King George II of Greece was warmly received by the Canadian government and speeches containing words of praise and admiration for the Greek people were made by Prime Minister Mackenzie King, the mayor of Ottawa, Stanley Lewis, and various radio broadcasters. During the late 1940s and early 1950s Greece was favourably mentioned in the House of Commons by political leaders like A. M. Stuart, L. B. Pearson, D. M. Fleming and G. A. Drew.

Canadian appreciation for the Greeks was not limited to speeches and praise, but was also manifested in financial assistance. At the beginning of the Italian attack on Greece the Canadian Red Cross shipped $30,000 worth of food and surgical supplies to Greece. Later wheat and other supplies were sent by the Aid-to-Greece Fund operating in conjunction with the Allied War Relief Fund and the Canadian Red Cross. The Greek War Relief Fund contributed over $6 million worth of food and other supplies.[60] Many outstanding Canadians in the religious, political and business life of the country offered their prestige and energy for the success of the campaign.[61]

The tourist trade during the 1960s and 1970s has also contributed its

39

share to the appreciation of Greece and Greek Canadians. Hundreds of Canadians, many of them students, visited Greece annually and were inspired by the culture of the country and the friendliness and hospitality of its people. In Canada many Canadians patronize Greek restaurants, pastry shops, food markets and places of entertainment. One is not surprised to see Canadians entertaining themselves in Greek night clubs, in Montreal, Toronto and Vancouver where bouzouki music plays and Greeks dance the zembekiko dance, the typical dance of "Zorba the Greek."

The remarks by Canadian writers and politicians, and the social contacts between Canadians and Greeks reflect changes in attitudes and increased tolerance for the Greek presence in Canada. It must not be assumed, however, that Greek Canadians of the 1970s are fully accepted or treated equally in the Canadian social structure. In heterogeneous and economically competitive societies like Canada, prejudice and discrimination against ethnocultural groups is probably inevitable.

NOTES

1. Demetrius Sicilianos, *E Helliniki Katagogi tou Christoforou Kolombou* (Athens: 1950), p. 3. See also Seraphim G. Canoutas, *Christopher Columbus: A Greek Nobleman* (New York, 1943).

2. Bambis Malafouris, *Hellenes tis Amerikis, 1528-1948* (New York: 1948), p. 26.

3. George Vlassis, *The Greeks in Canada* (Hull: Leclerc Printers Ltd., 1953), p. 79.

4. This narrative is contained in a book by Samuel Purchas entitled *Pilgrims*, published in London in 1625.

5. Vlassis, *op. cit.,* p. 92.

6. *Ibid.,* p. 137.

7. *Ibid.,* pp. 83-84.

8. *Ibid.,* pp. 84-85.

9. *Ibid.,* pp. 85-91.

10. See Takis Petritis, "The Greek Immigrants in Canada," in *Afieroma* (Montreal: Cretan Association of Montreal, 1972-1973), pp. 5-23.

11. Mary Antoniou, *Welfare Activities Among The Greek People in Los Angeles* (San Francisco: R and E Associates, 1974), p. 8.

12. J.S. Woodsworth, *Strangers Within Our Gates* (Toronto: University of Toronto Press, 1909), p. 24.

13. Theodore Saloutos, *The Greeks in the United States* (Cambridge, Mass.: Harvard University Press, 1964), p. 33.

14. Vlassis, *op. cit.,* p. 92, 139.

15. *Report of the Royal Commission on Bilingualism and Biculturalism:* "The Cultural Contribution of the Other Ethnic Group," Book IV (Ottawa: Queen's Printer, 1970), p. 25.

16. R.H. Coats, *The Immigration Program of Canada* (Newton, Mass.: Pollak Foundation For Economic Research, 1926), p. 184.
17. Saloutos, *op. cit.,* p. 60.
18. Woodsworth, *op. cit.,* p. 122.
19. *Ibid.,* p. 138.
20. Robert F. Harney and Harold Troper, *Immigrants* (Toronto: Van Nostrand Reinhold Ltd., 1975), p. 24.
21. Yanna Lambrou, *The Greek Community of Vancouver: Social Organization and Adaptation,* Unpublished M.A. Thesis, University of British Columbia, 1975, p. 61.
22. George A. Kourvetaris, "The Greek American Family," in Charles H. Mindel and Robert W. Haberstein, eds., *Ethnic Families in America* (New York: Elsevier; 1976), p. 175.
23. Vlassis, *op. cit.,* p. 93.
24. P. Exacoustos, "St. George's Church and the Greek Community in Toronto," *Greek Year Book* (Toronto: The Greek Orthodox Church of St. George, 1934), p. 23.
25. Petritis, *op. cit.,* pp. 18-19.
26. *Ibid.,* p. 19.
27. *Public Archives of Canada*, R.G. 24E, Vol. 436.
28. Vlassis, *op. cit.,* p. 93.
29. *Ibid.,* p. 122.
30. Lambrou, *op. cit.,* p. 58.
31. Thomas Kapelos, "Why Should a Young Canadian-Greek Study Greek," *Greek Year Book* (Toronto: The Hellenic Church of St. Georges, 1934), p. 49.
32. Saloutos, *op. cit.,* p. 324.
33. Vlassis, *op. cit.,* pp. 155-161.
34. *Ibid.,* pp. 155-156.
35. These were organized under the leadership of Mrs. Pota B. Salamis and Mrs. N. Tseperis, both from Montreal.
36. *A Report of the Canadian Immigration and Population Study: The Immigration Program,* Vol. 2 (Ottawa; Information Canada, 1974), pp. 17-18.
37. *Ibid.,* p. 21.
38. *Ibid.,* p. 30.
39. Canadian Manpower Statistics (Ottawa, 1971).
40. Canada Department of Citizenship and Immigration, (1945-1971).
41. In 1951, for example, the Greek Government requested the admission to Canada of 200 Greek citizens residing in China. The majority of these Greek nationals were given permission to enter Canada as landed immigrants after consideration of their ages, occupational qualifications and experiences and the available assistance of the Greek communities of Toronto and Halifax in accommodating refugees. The majority of the re-migrated Greeks, however, came from Australia, Brazil and West Germany.

42. Vlassis, *op. cit.* (first edition, 1942), pp. 13-14.
43. It can be estimated that at least 75% of the total Greek-Canadian population in 1971 was residing in the cities of Montreal and Toronto, with the latter having at least 40% of the total Greek population.
44. See *Report of the Neighborhood Association to the Advisory Committee of the Canadian Red Cross Society on the Adjustment of Greek Immigrant Children from Iron Curtain Countries* (Toronto: Canadian Red Cross), July 7, 1956.
45. In suburban districts of metropolitan American cities we find that the "first and second generation groups have patterns of segregation from each other and from the native white population and that are frequently similar to those of their central city neighbours." See Stanley Lieberson, "Suburbs and Residential Patterns," *American Journal of Sociology*, 67 (May, 1962) p. 681.
46. Efronsini Gavaki, *The Integration of Greeks in Canada* (San Francisco: R and E Research Associates, 1977), p. 36.
47. Such incidents were described to the author by Greek immigrants in Calgary, Montreal, Toronto and London, Ontario.
48. Woodsworth, *op. cit.,* p. 138.
49. Donald H. Avery, Canadian Immigration Policy and the Alien Question 1896-1919: The Anglo-Canadian Perspective. Unpublished Ph.D. Thesis, University of Western Ontario, 1973, p. 104.
50. *Ibid.,* p. 107.
51. Jean Morrison, "Ethnicity and Violence: The Lakehead Freight Handlers Before World War I," in Gregory S. Kealey and Peter Warrian eds., *Essays in Canadian Working Class History* (Toronto: McClelland and Stewart, 1976), pp. 143-160.
52. Public Archives of Canada, R.G. 13A2, Volume 185.
53. Public Archives of Canada, R.G. 13A2, Volume 219.
54. *The Globe,* Toronto, March 2, 1918, p. 8.
55. Public Archives of Canada, R.G.C. Al, Volume 10.
56. Fred I. Malone, "An Appreciation of a Greek Citizen," *Greek Year Book* (Toronto: The Greek Church of St. George, 1934), pp. 37-38.
57. John M. Gibbon, *Canadian Mosaic* (Toronto: McClelland and Stewart, 1938), pp. 324-327.
58. Saloutos, *op. cit.,* pp. 362-386.
59. Vlassis, *op. cit.,* pp. 9-10.
60. Florence Macdonald, *For Greece a Tear: The Story of the Greek War Relief Fund of Canada* (Fredericton, New Brunswick: Brunswick Press, 1954).
61. Vlassis, *op. cit.,* p. 67.

THREE

Occupational Status and Social Mobility

OCCUPATIONS OF EARLY IMMIGRANTS

From the early years of immigration to Canada, Greeks have displayed an affinity for hard work and socio-economic advancement. Despite the fact that they came from rural backgrounds and lacked capital, they were able to meet the challenges of the new society. Their experiences with harsh socio-economic conditions in the homeland and their willingness to get along with little of a material nature in a foreign land enabled them to survive, and to overcome prejudice, discrimination and ignorance of their new society's language and culture.

Because of their low academic achievement in the homeland and their lack of skills, the first Greeks who came and settled in Canada were forced into some of the most gruelling and menial jobs in the private sector of the economy. When they had learned the English language and accumulated enough money, many of them ventured into small businesses. According to the available information, some Greek immigrants in Montreal became actively involved in small businesses during the early 1860s. The first included the tobacco shop of Kyriakos Kritikos (1864); the Confectionery Co'y, a pastry shop run by A. Zervoudakis (1876); and the Gerasimo Restaurant of G. Gerasimos (1880). In the 1877 Provincial Exhibition of Quebec, A. Zervoudakis took part in the Confectionery Products Competition and was awarded a diploma for the quality of his pastries.[1] On the west side of Canada the pioneer Greeks also were venturing into businesses, notably commercial fishing and restaurants. In 1895, John Nicholas Giannaris, along with other Greek fishermen, built the Colonial Cannery in Vancouver. Unfortunately the ambitious venture failed after one year of operation and Giannaris returned to fishing.[2]

Other entrepreneurs among the early Greek pioneers were pushcart peddlers, shoe-shiners and fruit stand owners. Like other immigrants, the Greek pioneers initially chose such vocations because they required little investment and a minimal command of the English language. Lambrou, for example, wrote of the early Greeks of Vancouver:

> They aspired to start their own jobs and saved money for that purpose. As soon as they had enough capital, they invested it by buying a stand or a cart for selling fruits, or flowers in the streets. . . . By saving small amounts of capital they expanded as small merchants.[3]

By 1910 many restaurants, cafes, confectioneries and hotels had been established by Greek immigrants in the cities of London, Montreal, Ottawa, Winnipeg and Vancouver. Greek immigrant entrepreneurs also became the owners of theatrical businesses, notably in Montreal. The first cinemas which appeared in Montreal in 1910 were owned and operated by Greek immigrants. One of the proprietors, George Ganetakos, became the President and Managing Director of the United Amusement Corporation. By 1953 this corporation was in control of 42 movie theatres in Quebec. The Brown Brothers opened their theatrical business in Edmonton about 1910, becoming the first Greek Canadians to start such a business in Western Canada.[4]

Thus from the beginning of their settlement the competitive-minded Greek Canadians showed strong involvement in the business world. It was through this process that they acquired wealth and status and became independent. This process of economic emancipation has been classically described by Professor Edward A. Ross who viewed the early Greek immigrant in North America as thrifty and commercially minded.[5]

But not all Greek immigrants experienced upward mobility. Many remained in jobs with long hours of work and low pay. Jean Morrison describes the exploitation of early Greek immigrants and other ethnic freight handlers in the Lakehead cities of Port Arthur and Fort William, Ontario, in the early 1900s. At the CPR freight sheds it was the Greek and Italian workers who took the initiative in strikes for better wages and regular hours of work. The Greeks fiercely opposed strikebreakers and the company's private police force.[6]

There is no accurate information regarding the occupational status and social mobility of Greek Canadians prior to 1950. However, according to Vlassis's account, in 1951 there were 1,066 small businesses throughout Canada owned by Greek Canadians, of which at least 680 were restaurants. Other businesses included candy shops, bowling alleys, ice cream parlours, theatres, hotels, and shoeshine parlours. The overwhelming majority (70%) of these businesses were concentrated in Ontario and Quebec, and at least 35% were in Toronto and Montreal alone.[7]

Of course not all of the successful Greek Canadians of this period were involved in small businesses. Many who had received their university degrees in Greece or Canada entered such professional occupations as law, medicine and teaching. During the period 1920-1952 more than 450 immigrant and second-generation Greek Canadians had completed or were in the process of completing their degrees at institutions of higher learning.[8]

Vlassis's data cited above are the more impressive when one considers that in 1951 the population of Greek origin in Canada numbered only about 14,000 persons, of whom 8,000 were landed immigrants.[9] The reason for the high number of Greeks in business, perhaps, was the remigration of low status Greek immigrants from Canada to the United States between 1910-1950.

WORK AND OCCUPATIONS OF RECENT IMMIGRANTS

In 1951 the Greek government brought to the attention of the Department of Canadian Citizenship and Immigration the fact that 50,000 Greek workers, farm labourers, fishermen, female domestics and other occupational categories could be available for emigration to Canada.[10] Leaders of Greek-Canadian communities and ethnic organizations such as the AHEPA requested that the Canadian government initiate liberal immigration policies for Greek immigrants. Greek-Canadian leaders also indicated that employment and transportation for the new immigrants could be arranged by Canadians of Greek origin.

Despite the requests and Canada's labour scarcity at that time, the Canadian Department of Citizenship and Immigration was reluctant to approve the large-scale entry of Greek nationals into Canada. Instead the Department decided to institute a trial immigration movement in order to ascertain the suitability of Greek workers under Canadian conditions. In August, 1951, the Deputy Minister of Immigration, Mr. Laval Fortier, proposed to the Deputy Minister of the Department of Labour, Dr. A. MacNamara, that 1,100 Greek immigrants be admitted, including 500 female domestics, 200 restaurant workers and 400 agriculturalists and miners, for 1952.[11] In July, 1952, the admissible occupational categories were extended to include close relatives, nurses and nurses' aides. Revisions to the list of admissible categories continued to occur almost yearly.

The trial period for Greek workers lasted for at least four years (1952-1956) without restrictions on large scale immigration being lifted. Many Canadian employers complained about the difficulty Greek immigrants had in learning English or French and their unwillingness to work on farms and under Canadian climatic conditions. The majority of outdoor workers left their first jobs to seek employment in restaurants, shoeshine parlours and factories.[12] On December 6, 1957, the Acting Deputy Minister of Citizenship and Immigration, C. S. Smith, in a memorandum to the Acting Minister of Immigration, suggested that importing farm labourers from Greece be discontinued:

Throughout the past decade we have had a sympathetic attitude toward immigration from Greece, mainly because Greece is a member nation of NATO and also because of the economic situation there. . . . But invariably those workers who came from Greece would not be considered suitable due to their unwillingness to live in rural areas and the difficulties in learning English or French. . . . Greek immigrants have a strong tendency to move to the Greek communities, accept employment with Greek Canadians, usually in non-productive industries at depressed wages and therefore never really contribute very much to Canada. . . . Therefore, I believe the movement should not be continued in 1958. In view of our past experiences with unskilled or otherwise unsuitable workers, I do not believe we should undertake a movement of farm or railway track workers from Greece.[13]

The suggestions made by Acting Deputy Minister Smith were not carried out and the proportion of Greek immigrants who entered Canada as farmers and farm workers during the 1960-1970 period remained about the same as before (13%).[14] The pressure on the Canadian government to accept a greater number of workers from Greece and the Greek immigrants' ability to find jobs led to toleration of the Greek immigrants' movement to urban communities. Thus, Greek immigrants continued to enter Canada allegedly to work on farms but instead to work in the cities in restaurants, factories, construction and other unskilled occupations.

One may ask why Greek immigrants coming from rural backgrounds were unwilling to work at rural jobs in Canada. The Greek immigrant's lack of experiences with mechanized farm equipment, methods of Canadian farming and cold climatic conditions had, to a certain degree, influenced this attitude. Furthermore, city life offered more social and economic opportunities. In the city the ambitious and enterprising Greek might have steady employment, and even the chance of extra jobs to supplement his salary and increase his savings. In the city, moreover, he could associate with other Greeks, and familiarize himself with financial opportunities and trades requiring small initial investments, before venturing into business on his own. It was not uncommon to hear the new immigrants refer to Montreal or Toronto as *ptochomana* (a provider of the poor people), but it was also true that the majority of the economically unsuccessful Greeks could be found in these two metropolitan centres.

In the 1960s Canada became more receptive to immigration from Greece. The number of Greek immigrants who entered Canada from 1960 to 1970 increased by 84% over the previous decade (Table 7). Moreover, Canada received a higher percentage of skilled Greek workers. From 1950-1960 nine per cent of the Greek workers who entered Canada belonged to the skilled categories, compared with 44% from 1960-1970. Twenty per cent of all Greek immigrant workers[15] and 46% of all skilled workers who entered Canada in the 1960s belonged in the occupational category of tailors and furriers. The increase of skilled immigrants during the 1960s is attributable to Canada's immigration

TABLE 7

Intended Occupations of Greek Immigrants to Canada by Chronological Period

Intended Occupation	1950-1959		1960-1970		Total	
	Number	%	Number	%	Number	%
Domestic servants	7,106	25.0	3,665	7.0	10,771	13.4
Cooks and food workers	403	1.4	2,015	3.9	2,418	2.9
Waiters, porters	—	—	1,008	1.9	1,008	1.3
Farmers and farm workers	2,292	8.1	3,045	5.8	5,337	6.6
Carpenters and electricians	838	3.0	2,399	4.6	3,237	4.0
Tailors and furriers	427	1.5	5,323	10.2	5,750	7.1
Machinists and mechanics	230	.8	3,940	7.5	4,170	5.2
General labourers	6,254	22.0	5,081	9.7	11,335	14.0
Wives and children	9,398	33.1	22,172	42.3	31,570	39.1
Other non-workers	1,463	5.1	3,698	7.1	5,161	6.4
Total	28,411	100.0	52,346	100.0	80,757	100.0

Source: Canada Department of Citizenship and Immigration, Statistics Division 1950-1970. The above figures do not include the many hundreds of Greek nationals who entered Canada illegally, such as deserting seamen.

policy and an increase in the number of qualified workers in Greece as a result of improvements and expansion of apprenticeship training programmes and corresponding changes in the amount of domestic labour. The number of domestic servants, at its peak in the 1950s, dropped sharply in the 1960s due to the availability of such jobs in Greece and West Germany.

Generally, the Greek immigrants who entered Canada in the 1950s were overrepresented in the unskilled occupational categories and thus contributed heavily to the bottom layer of the Canadian stratification of that period. The low occupational status of new immigrants in Canada has been described by Porter as "entrance status."[16]

According to the 1971 Census of Canada, Greek immigrants were in a relatively low occupational status compared to the total active Canadian population. Only six per cent of the employed Greek immigrants were in managerial and professional positions, compared with 17% of the total employed Canadian population. The majority of the Greeks, 63%, were found in service, recreation, manufacturing, mechanical and construction jobs, whereas only 32% of the total Canadian work force was found in those occupational categories (See Table 8).

The minimum educational attainment of the Greek immigrants in their homeland and their limited knowledge of the English language were important factors affecting their level on the socio-economic ladder. As Table 9 indicates, Greek immigrants in Canada had a lower academic attainment than the Canadian-born population, and less than other ethnic groups such as the British and Dutch. In 1971, 54% of Greek immigrants aged 15 years and over had less than eight years of schooling completed, compared with 33% of the Canadian-born population. Only three per cent of Greek immigrants had university degrees as compared with five per cent of the Canadian-born population.

The low level of schooling among Greeks is mainly due to the lack of opportunities in the homeland, especially during World War II and the Civil War of 1946-1949. Regional disparities in the quality of and opportunity for education in Greece is another important factor. Children in rural Greek communities not only attend grade schools inferior to those of urban communities, but also have less access to education. High schools (*gymnasia*) in Greece are mainly located in big towns and cities, and are almost nonexistent in the villages. However, during the 1960s and 1970s the Greek educational system had been improved and the academic achievement of Greek youth is much higher than in previous generations.

The academic attainment for men is higher than women for both Greek and Canadian born. However, the level of schooling is higher for Canadian-born women than Greek immigrant women. In 1971, 77% of the Greek women aged 15 years and over had completed less than 11 years of schooling as compared to 70% of Canadian-born women. Only 1.6% of Greek women had university degrees as compared to three per

TABLE 8

Occupational Distribution of Employed Greek Immigrant Population (Identified by Ethnic Group) by Sex Compared to the Total Active Canadian Population, 1971 (per cent)

Categories	Greeks			Canadians		
	Males	Females	Total	Males	Females	Total
Managerial	1.5	.6	1.2	5.5	2.0	4.3
Professional	5.0	5.0	5.0	10.0	17.8	12.8
Clerical	4.1	12.4	6.9	7.7	31.7	15.9
Service-Recreation	37.5	24.0	33.0	9.2	15.1	11.2
Transport-Communication	2.8	.1	1.9	5.8	.3	3.9
Commercial-Financial	6.8	3.7	5.8	10.1	8.4	9.5
Agricultural	.7	.6	.5	7.1	3.6	5.9
Manufacturing, Mechanical Construction	27.7	33.7	29.7	27.4	7.7	20.6
Labourers, n.e.s.	2.1	3.1	2.4	4.6	1.8	3.6
Fishing, Logging, Trapping, Mining, etc. Non-Stated, Not Elsewhere Classified	11.8	16.8	13.6	12.6	11.6	12.3
Total	100.0	100.0	100.0	100.0	100.0	100.0

Source: 1971 *Census of Canada*, Catalogue 94-788 (AE-4), March 1974; Information for Greeks processed for P. Chimbos by Statistics Canada, September 1974.

cent of the Canadian-born women (See Table 9). The lower academic attainment of the Greek female immigrants is attributed to the lower expectations for female scholastic achievement, especially in the Greek rural areas.

The occupational distribution of the employed Greek immigrant population presented by the 1971 census (See Table 8) should be viewed with some caution. The occupational categories of the census are not based on income or prestige, and some self-employed occupations such as restaurant ownership are classified under the category of "service and recreation." Neither can these categories be equally applied to all Greek-Canadian communities throughout Canada. A study in Thunder Bay, Ontario, in 1969 showed that in the small Greek community there Greek immigrants not only improved their socio-economic life in the new society, but of the 71 Greek immigrants in the sample the majority, 37, were restaurant owners or managers of small businesses. At least 60 had entered semiskilled and unskilled occupations when they first arrived in Canada. At the time of the survey only 18 of the respondents stated that there had been no change in their occupational status.[17]

A more recent (1976) survey in London, Ontario, provides additional information concerning the Greek immigrants' movement to small businesses. Of the 636 family heads, 176 (25%) were proprietors of small businesses, such as restaurants and stores, and only 15 (2.3 per cent) were professionals. Approximately 40% were in the occupational categories of "food services" and "general labour."[18]

In large metropolitan communities, then, we expect to find a relatively high proportion of Greek immigrants in the unskilled occupations and unemployed categories. The large numbers of new immigrants who came to the large cities in the 1950s and 1960s were likely to be "trapped" in factory work or chronic unemployment. In 1970 researchers studying the development of the Greek community in Montreal concluded:

> Although it is true that some of the Greeks who have immigrated to Montreal since 1950 are extremely wealthy individuals with standards of living frequently far surpassing those of the resident Greeks, they constitute a small minority. The vast majority of the new arrivals, coming as they do from small villages, are poor and consequently are obliged to accept lower standards of living and are among the first to suffer during difficult times such as we are experiencing now.[19]

Like working-class people in general, Greek immigrants have found their income determined by their occupation. Coming to Canada with low academic attainment and no skills meant that their earnings have been below the Canadian mean. According to the 1971 Census of Canada, 76% of the 85,025 Greek-Canadians aged 15 and over had an average income of $4,680 as compared to nine per cent of all Canadians. The average income in Canada in 1971 was $5,043. On the other hand,

TABLE 9

Greek Ethnic Group and Canadian-Born Population Aged 15 and Over, by Sex by Highest Level of Schooling, 1971

	Greeks						Canadians					
	Males		Females		Total		Males		Females		Total	
	Number	%	Number	%	Number	%	Number	%	Number	%	Number	%
Less than Grade 5	3,610	8.0	6,520	16.3	10,130	11.9	509,215	11.9	454,215	6.8	963,430	6.3
Grades 5-8	17,635	39.2	17,850	44.6	35,485	41.7	2,103,710	41.7	2,014,185	27.9	4,117,895	27.1
Grades 9-11	7,980	17.7	6,230	15.6	14,210	16.7	2,607,900	16.7	2,875,690	34.6	5,483,590	36.1
Grades 12-13	5,300	11.8	3,970	9.9	9,270	10.9	1,323,000	10.9	1,656,970	17.5	2,979,970	19.6
Some Post-Secondary Education or Training	5,800	12.9	3,360	8.4	9,160	10.8		10.8				
Some University	2,890	6.4	1,430	3.6	4,320	5.1	504,040	5.1	420,725	6.7	924,765	6.1
University Degree	1,780	4.0	670	1.6	2,450	2.9	492,605	2.9	227,255	6.5	719,860	4.8
Total	44,995	100.0	40,030	100.0	85,025	100.0	7,540,470	100.0	7,649,035	100.0	15,189,510	100.0

Source: 1971 *Census of Canada*, Catalogue 94-786 (AE-2), January 1974; Information for Greeks processed for P. Chimbos by Statistics Canada, August 1974.

only 1,565 or two per cent of the Greek-Canadians earned an average of $23,506 per year.[20] Furthermore, the Greek immigrant earned between $1,500 to $3,000 less than other Canadians in the same kind of work.[21]

In recent years several dozen Greek immigrants have entered professional positions. Greek immigrant professionals in Canada, as well as in the United States, tend to enter teaching positions, especially at the college and university level.[22] Professions such as law, medicine and accounting have also attracted Greek immigrants. However, most of the clientele of these professionals continue to be Greek immigrants, mainly for linguistic and cultural reasons. There are also many Greeks who work in the federal and provincial public service and as engineers for private companies.

Although a relatively high proportion of Greek Canadians have remained in unskilled and semi-skilled occupations and receive low wages, their standards of living have been improved considerably by immigrating to Canada. Generally the Greek immigrant workers have been able to enjoy cars, TVs, modern home appliances and better medical services and to accumulate personal savings. Their economic improvement in Canada has also contributed to better educational opportunities for their children and financial aid for relatives in Greece. In a research project Greek Canadians received one of the highest scores on "being generally satisfied" with their life in Canada.[23]

THE RESTAURANT BUSINESS

The so-called "ethnic specialty" as an avenue to upward mobility has been observed in the occupational structure of certain ethnic groups in Canada as well as in the United States. Ethnic specialties are "occupations for which those of a particular ethnic origin are thought to have a special affinity and in which they thus have an advantage in attracting clients or customers and in developing skills and connections."[24] The restaurant as an ethnic specialty has been an important avenue of upward mobility for many Greek Canadians. The Vlassis inquiry shows that in 1953 at least 64% of the businesses owned by Greek Canadians were restaurants and cafes.[25] In Thunder Bay, Ontario, 31 (44%) of the 71 Greek immigrants interviewed in 1969 were restaurant owners.[26] In 1972, 125 (71%) of the 176 small businesses owned by Greeks in London, Ontario, were restaurants. Leaders of Greek communities in Montreal and Toronto also claimed that most of the Greek proprietors are in the restaurant business. According to Saloutos:

> The restaurant business represented the first stable economic base on which many ambitious immigrants built their fortunes. The restaurant was important for other reasons as well. It brought the Greek businessman into closer contact with the general public, which in many instances found him to be a hard-driving and in-

dustrious person. Commercial, patriotic, and fraternal agencies solicited his services or sought contributions from him for a wide variety of causes.[27]

One of the main reasons why so many Greek immigrants entered the restaurant business was that an immigrant could enter the business with a small investment, no academic training and little knowledge of the English or French language. It was an enterprise where the ambitious, talkative and hospitable Greek had the opportunity to interact with his patrons, work hard to satisfy them and become economically successful. The cohesiveness and co-operation commonly found in the Greek kinship system is perhaps a related factor accounting for the attraction of the restaurant business. Porter points out that when ethnic groups are closely knit, their cultural milieu will encourage certain kinds of occupational choices and discourage others.[28]

Some of the restaurants owned by Greek Canadians have been enterprises of related families. When two brothers or cousins learned the trade of cooking they invested their small savings in a restaurant. Their wives and adolescent children could help in serving food or washing dishes. When additional help was needed some friend or relative could be hired. This kind of business setting "had an advantage over competitors who were forced to rely on hired help."[29]

The Greek immigrants who ventured into restaurants and other businesses were not unfamiliar with enterprises of a competitive nature. Historically, the Greek in eastern Mediterranean areas has been pictured as an individualistic, foresighted, competitive trader.[30] Furthermore, Greek immigrants coming from agricultural areas of Greece had experienced a private enterprise economy by owning and managing their own small farms. Some of them were merchants of livestock and farm products such as olive oil, oranges and wheat. Such economic values and experiences influenced the immigrant's saving and investment practices in the host society. And entering the business world in the host society was one of the surest routes to upward mobility for many Greek immigrants.[31]

The following case histories are typical of the Greek immigrant's upward mobility through hardships and involvement in the restaurant business:

Case One
Anastasi was born in a Greek peasant family, the oldest of four children. Being born in a poor family and small rural community he was able to complete only the fifth grade of primary school. In 1906 at the age of 16 Anastasi immigrated to the United States with the hope of making his fortune, helping his family financially and eventually returning permanently to Greece.

In 1910 Anastasi . . . emigrated to Canada. He settled in London,

53

at age of 70, George was still managing his restaurant, and was actively involved in the socio-economic and cultural affairs of the Greek community.

Considering their low socio-economic status upon arriving in Canada, many Greek immigrants can be proud of their success in small businesses. From their local competitors they quickly learned the Canadian method of doing business. Greek businessmen usually express admiration for the North American business system, referring to its efficiency, cleanliness and organized character.

Although there are no empirical data on the occupational status of second-generation Greeks in Canada, it appears that the children of immigrants are unlikely to enter the restaurant business. Although Greek restaurateurs take pride in their economic achievements, they view the restaurant as a place of low prestige and long hours of hard work where the owner and the worker become alienated from family life and the intellectual world. Restaurant owners often complain of not being able to take a vacation, attend church on Sundays, or even visit friends or relatives on religious holidays and namedays. Because of these hardships, Greek-Canadian business parents encourage their children, and help them financially, to obtain higher education.

Achievement motivation is commonly observed among Greek Canadians. Members of the second generation are expected by the family and ethnic community to move upward socially. In small Greek communities where Greek families are acquainted with each other, the academic achievement of children receives the approbation of the entire Greek community, and affects the family's status and prestige. The relationship between parental aspirations and the academic achievement of second generation Greek Canadians as compared to other ethnocultural groups will have to be demonstrated by future sociological inquires.

ADJUSTMENT TO CANADIAN WORKING CONDITIONS

Although many Greek immigrants have succeeded in the Canadian labour market, some experienced a decline in occupational status here as compared to their homeland. A number of school teachers, college students, and junior level public servants left Greece seeking higher monetary rewards in Canada, but since they did not speak English or French or were not accredited by Canadian authorities, they were forced to take menial jobs. Some were able to improve their situation by entering such businesses as travel agencies and restaurants while others were absorbed by the institutions of local Greek communities (radio, newspapers, ethnic schools).

Many Greeks who emigrated to Canada, especially those from villages, found some difficulty in adjusting to the regularized work schedule of Canadian society. Those who had worked long and irregular hours on their own farms had to adjust to the rigid schedule of the factory or restaurant in Canada. In the home society field work was broken by the large midday meal, the early afternoon siesta during summer months, folk singing, story telling and gossip. Monotonous work was also broken by religious holidays, especially the celebration of namedays, weddings, baptisms, and village feasts (*panigyria*). There are at least 60 religious holidays in Greece which faithful Orthodox Christians are expected to observe.

The most unusual occupational adjustment, however, had to be made by men who were forced to take jobs as cooks and dishwashers. In Greece men considered these to be feminine tasks and thus a threat to a man's masculine self-image. But when they arrived in Canada they found out that learning to cook and wash dishes was the first step in their upward mobility. It was through this "degrading" occupational process that many Greek immigrants became restaurant owners and improved their socio-economic status.

Some of those who could not adjust to the relatively harsh working conditions in farming, lumbering and restaurant and factory work returned to their homeland within a short time. Others stayed for several years, made their small fortunes and eventually returned to Greece where they could invest their savings. Many sold their business, houses, cars and furniture before leaving Canada. But upon their return to the motherland they experienced problems of readjustment. They soon found out that business competition was just as relentless as it had been in Canada and that the politico-economic situation was more uncertain and fragile. Although Greek life was more culturally rewarding it lacked many of the comforts, amenities, material possessions and medical and educational facilities that were available in Canada. Being unable to re-establish themselves in their native land, some returned to Canada. The case history of Tony typifies the Greek immigrants who tried but could not re-establish themselves in the homeland:

> Tony was born and brought up in a small village of southern Greece. He came from a large family of eight children. His father was a small tavern proprietor who during the Nazi occupation lost his business. After this the family continued to work on small farms for their economic survival.
>
> Tony's education was interrupted during the war and thus he was able to complete only grade 6. At the age of 16 he decided to leave the village and seek a better future in the city. He moved to Athens where he worked as a clerk in his brother-in-law's food market. After several years of hard work and thrift Tony was able to open a small fruit stand in suburban Athens. Since the profit was very small, Tony decided to emigrate to Canada for a few years, make a certain amount of money and return to Greece and open a better and bigger business. In 1956 at the age of 29 Tony emigrated to

Canada. He was only six days in Toronto when, with the help of relatives, he found a job in a small factory. Although his salary was low, Tony was able to save a portion of his weekly pay. In 1958 he married a Greek immigrant girl who at the time was working as a dressmaker in a downtown Toronto factory. Tony's wife also had hopes of returning to Greece permanently.

In order to make money quickly Tony invested his family's savings in a small food market on the west side of Toronto. The business went well and within a few years Tony was able to buy his first house. By 1968 he had accumulated the desired amount of money to return to Greece. In 1969 Tony sold his business, house and car and with his wife and two children returned to Athens where they hoped to establish their permanent residence. However, it did not take long for Tony and his family to find out the difficulties of readjusting to the socio-economic life of their homeland. As Tony put it: "You know when you go there then you realize how difficult it is to start a new life in Greece. My son who had finished grade 6 in Canada could not easily adjust to the Greek educational system. He found the curriculum completely different. My wife, on the other hand, started complaining about the inconveniences of the homes and the shopping centres. Myself, I found it difficult to open a new business in Athens. The competitors there are very shrewd businessmen. So we stayed there for about five months and then we packed our suitcases and returned back to Toronto. I am so glad to be back in Canada. It is true that here we work hard, but we enjoy so many good things. And I know that my children will have a brighter future in Canada."

Although there is no empirical evidence concerning the extent of exploitation suffered by Greek immigrants, thousands of Greek workers had to take any available jobs, often those the native-born Canadians did not want. Like other non-English-speaking immigrants, Greeks accepted jobs with long hours and low pay. Here we will discuss a few examples of exploitative employment.

As noted earlier many Greek immigrants found difficulty adjusting to certain types of hard labour and the environmental hardships of such occupations. For some of them the hardships of lumberjacking were so intolerable that they made a formal request to Greek authorities in Canada for better employment. In August 26, 1951, twenty Greek lumberjacks, working for the Abitibi Pulp and Paper Company in Regan, Ontario, sent the following letter to the Consul General of Greece in Toronto:

Dear Mr. Consul,

We would ask that you excuse our illiteracy and incoherence found in the composition of our letter, as it is written by people who were farmers and had the misfortune not to learn their native language properly. Many days have passed since we started working. We were all hoping that few would have been the days that we would have suffered owing to our lack of knowing the work of a lumberjack. But all of us are slowly seeing how we were fooled because as the days passed things got worse.

Thousands of mosquitos await every morning twenty of us so they can get their fill with our blood. Our bodies are full of growths from their bites. From the time we came we drink water from holes found under the roots of tree trunks. Most of the time the water is yellow in colour and full of small insects. We have no clothes left and we are forced to get some from the supply house signing and paying for them with our future earnings. They told us that after four weeks of work we could be working on straight piece work basis and not as the immigration authorities told us that we could be getting an increase in wages.

We are poor people who came here to work and we really want to work. However, we do not want to die under these conditions. This is the land (place) of our work and we beseech you as a representative of the Greek nation, which we happen to be citizens of, to try for the betterment of our lives and the rewarding of our toils.

We are hoping because we are aware in advance of your good intentions and your energetic activities that you should place us soon in jobs that our toils will be justly rewarded and our health be protected.

We are submitting our respects to the Father (priest) and request that he too take up our cause and both of you act together.[32]

Respectfully,
E.X. and all the fellow Greek workers.

Two months later a similar letter signed by 23 Greek immigrants was sent to the Consul General of Greece in Toronto describing their hardships in northern Ontario and asking for improvement of their working conditions. At that time the 23 labourers were working as lumberjacks in Minnipuka, Ontario, for the Abitibi Pulp and Paper Company.[33]

Greek men were not the only ones to suffer hardships and exploitation upon arriving in Canada. Shortly after World War II thousands of young Greek women emigrated to Canada with the intention of working as servants for wealthy Canadian families. From 1950 to 1970, 10,771 Greek women entered Canada to work as domestic servants. At least 5,950 of them came during the five-year period 1956-1960.[34] Many of these prospective domestic servants were vocationally trained in Greece by the International Committee for European Migration (ICEM). The two-month training included instruction in the English language, in the operation of modern household appliances and in other phases of household work which could enable the girls to keep a modern home in Canada. Some of the girls were working as domestics in Greek cities while attending training classes in the evening.[35]

The young domestics (mainly between the ages of 20 and 30) came from poor Greek families, had little education, and saw little or no opportunity for improving their economic status in the home society. Some were refugees from Iron Curtain countries who entered Greece during the Civil War of 1946-1949. By emigrating to Canada as domestic servants the young Greek women could obtain landed immigrant status and eventually sponsor other family members. Thus, economically-deprived Greek parents reluctantly and out of desperation sent their daughters to Canada to open the way for their families' economic opportunities. For the majority of these girls, moving far away from home on their own was their first major and most painful social experience.

Another important reason why many single girls decided to leave their homeland was to reduce the burden of dowry for their families. By emigrating they would have the opportunity of either getting married without dowry or building up a dowry and returning to Greece. The economic pressures of the dowry system also caused many Greek fathers and brothers to emigrate to Canada, Germany or the United States in order to help the young women in the family accumulate dowries.[36]

Although many Greek girls entered the Canadian work force as domestic servants at weekly salaries as low as $15.00[37] others refused to enter such menial jobs. As soon as they arrived in Canada they were helped by Greek friends or distant relatives to find jobs in a factory or restaurant. Even those who started working as servants did not remain in their jobs for long. Since the Canadian Department of Citizenship and Immigration did not strictly require a specific period of service in domestic employment, the girls moved out as soon as they found other jobs. The following case history is typical of the Greek domestic servants who entered Canada:

> Maria lived with her parents, two brothers and three sisters in a small village in southern Greece. They farmed a small plot of nearly barren land which could only produce the wheat needed for the family's bread.
>
> Since Maria was the oldest child, her parents decided to send her to Canada as a domestic servant, and she was expected to sponsor her brothers later. In 1959 at the age of 26 Maria left her village and went to Athens to take a special course in home economics offered to prospective domestic servants. Although Maria had only completed Grade 6 she was able to meet the requirements of her home economics course by demonstrating adequate knowledge of reading and basic arithmetic. During her six-months training Maria took basic courses in English and familiarization with Canadian electrical appliances.
>
> After the completion of her home economics training, Maria successfully completed a test of "good deportment" administered by a

Canadian female examiner. But before she could obtain her visa Maria was required to sign a statement indicating that she would not sponsor a relative to come to Canada for at least one year. After all these procedures Maria was permitted to enter Canada as a landed immigrant.

In the fall of 1959 Maria came to Toronto to work as a domestic servant in a wealthy Canadian family as prearranged by the Canadian authorities. According to Maria all the family members were nice to her and expended much effort in teaching her good English. Maria's monthly salary was $75.00. From this salary she helped her poor family in Greece.

After being a domestic servant for a year Maria sponsored her older brother to come to Canada as a landed immigrant. As soon as her brother arrived in Canada Maria left her domestic job and through the Manpower Office she found another position as a cleaning woman in a downtown Toronto hotel. Her starting salary in 1961 was 65¢ per hour but with the tips, Maria made fairly good pay.

At the end of 1962 Maria visited Greece where through matchmaking she became married to a man from her village. He was a labourer who was anxious to come to Canada and improve himself economically. After their marriage Maria and her husband went to Toronto where both obtained jobs in a factory. Within a few years they were able to sponsor other relatives to come and work in Canada.

By 1977 Maria and her family were happily settled in Toronto and did not intend to return to Greece permanently. As Maria put it: "We went through many hardships but now we are happy. Our two children are doing well in school and we are so proud of them. We are so lucky to leave our poor village and come to Canada where we improved our lives."

In the 1950s and early 1960s many Greek immigrants entered unskilled or semiskilled occupations in Canadian factories. Although their salary was more satisfactory than that of the average worker in Greece, many factories were still paying low wages relative to Canadian standards of living. The majority of the new immigrants who entered these underpaid jobs were women. In 1957 the Canadian immigration authorities had received complaints that the "Dress Manufacturer's Guild did not live up to its agreement concerning accommodation and employment for seamstresses brought from Greece. Some workers complained to the effect that the Guild was not paying them the agreed wages."[38] In certain factories, notably clothing factories, the workers were threatened with dismissal if they joined unions. Even in the early 1970s Greek women working in clothing factories could recall incidents where they could not ask for union or legal intervention because they feared dismissal. For example, on April 14, 1972, forty female Greek-Canadian factory workers in Montreal were fired for joining a labour union. Although on April 7th these women signed union applications, on the 11th of the same month the factory management asked them to sign a statement indicating that they would not join a union for at least a year. Failing to comply with the demands of the management, the women were fired on the spot. After taking their grievances to the Quebec Ministry of Labour the 40 workers were reinstated 10 months later and compensated for salary losses.[39]

Even in 1976 many of the restaurants in Montreal were reported to be paying Greek immigrant waitresses $25 for a 60-hour work week and threatening to blacklist them if they complained or attempted to join the Association of Greek Waitresses. At that time the minimum wage in Quebec for workers receiving tips was $2.50 per hour for the first 45 hours and $3.75 for overtime. Such exploitation, however, resulted in formal complaints and the intervention of the Quebec Labour Relations Board and the Hellenic Canadian Labour Association.[40]

As noted earlier, low wages inevitably forced many new immigrants to live in overcrowded and deteriorated housing areas of large Canadian cities. For example, Park Avenue and Park Extension in Montreal (the city's most depressed area which is inhabited mainly by Greek immigrants) has been characterized by inadequate heating, plumbing and sewage systems, and health standards below the average for the metropolitan area. In 1961, 23.2% of the families of this area had an annual income of less than $3,000 as compared to 20% for the Montreal metropolitan region.[41] Low economic standards had also resulted in little political power.[42]

Exploitation of Greek immigrant workers has been reduced in recent years because of the minimum wage standards imposed by the provinces and the development of ethnic labour associations. For example, the Greek Canadian Labour Association of Montreal has helped thousands of Greek workers to familiarize themselves with Canadian labour legislation and has encouraged them to join local labour unions. The Labour Code of Quebec has also been translated into Greek and made available to all Greek Canadians of the province.

Some exploitation of Greek immigrants had been carried out by established Greek-Canadian businessmen, in many instances relatives of the newcomers. This type of exploitation has been referred to as the *padrone* system. Padronism has been a common phenomenon in the history of North American immigration, especially among Italians. The *padrone* is a businessman who provides the new and insecure immigrant with a job and helps him to find a place to rent, with the understanding that the immigrant must retain this particular job for a reasonable period of time. The *padrone* or boss system was mainly confined to the shoeshine trade. In certain instances a small loan (passage money) would also be forwarded to prospective immigrants. Through this process the new immigrant employee became "morally" obligated to his employer. Because of this "favouritism" and his ignorance of the English (or French) language and Canadian labour legislation, the new immigrant was perhaps less likely to leave a job in which he was exploited to search for better employment conditions elsewhere.

Unsponsored Greek immigrants who could not speak English or French and were desperate to obtain their first jobs in Canada were also potential victims of exploitation at the hands of Greek employers. The following case is typical:

> Petros emigrated to Canada in the summer of 1968. He had been in Montreal for about a week and he was looking for his first job. He was an unskilled labourer and spoke only the Greek language. Petros was told by his Greek friends in Montreal that jobs for Greek immigrants were more likely to be available in factories or restaurants. Being occupationally unskilled and insecure in a foreign land, Petros decided to find a job in a restaurant owned by a Greek where at least he could speak his native language with his employer and co-workers. Petros was only five days in Montreal when he walked into a restaurant in downtown Montreal and asked the man standing at the cash register: "You Greek?" The man says: "Yes." Petros replied in Greek: "I am a Greek too. I have been in Canada for a few days and I am looking for a job. I'll do anything." The boss said to Petros: "What job were you doing in Greece?" Petros replied: "I was a farmer. My wife and two children are still in Greece. I will bring them over as soon as I make enough money for their passage." Then the boss said to Petros: "The only job I can give you is a dishwasher. We pay the dishwashers 90¢ an hour. Maybe that is not much for you but as you know here you have two free meals a day." Then Petros said to the boss: "I'll take it."

There is a general belief among many Greek immigrant workers that Greek employers are more exploitative than Canadian employers of Anglo-Saxon background. In a study of Thunder Bay,[43] 150 Greek immigrants in the sample were asked the following question regarding their preference for employers: "Suppose you were offered two jobs with similar pay: one is to work for an employer of your own ethnic group and the other is for a Canadian employer. Which one would you prefer?" At least 64 (43%) of the respondents stated they would prefer to work for a Canadian employer. The chief reason given by the interviewees for this preference was the feeling that he could be less demanding and less likely to take advantage of them. As one interviewee put it, "A Greek boss always expects you to work hard, put extra time but without extra pay. He thinks he is doing you a favour. A Canadian boss is more systematic. If you work extra, he will pay you extra." On the other hand, 32% of the interviewees preferred to work for a Greek employer: the most common reasons were "speaking the same language" and "being more at ease with a Greek employer."

OCCUPATIONAL GROUPS AND SOCIAL POWER

As we note in Chapter Four the individuals who constitute the loosely organized Greek community in Canada share certain social characteristics such as cultural values, language and religion. However, within this ethnic collectivity are social groups differing from each other in occupation, wealth and power. "Power" is the ability to influence decision-making within the administrative structure of the ethnic community. Based on the observations of class structure within the Greek community in Montreal by Stathopoulos,[44] the Greek community of Vancouver by Lambrou,[45] and the writer's own observations and research, the following general groups are suggested:

1. *The professionals:* This group consists mainly of first and second generation Greeks with high academic achievement. These are the doctors, lawyers, teachers and artists and they have the most prestige within the Greek community. Their fellow Greeks look upon them with admiration and pride. From this group are recruited some of the community council members and leaders of the ethnic associations. The Greeks usually call them the *morfomeni* (the "educated ones"), those who theoretically are seen as examples of the ethnic group's opportunities for upward mobility. In small Greek communities the professionals do not constitute a large power group.
2. *The entrepreneurs:* These are the business proprietors. In their ranks are included a few of the very wealthy "old timers" who came to Canada prior to World War II. Traditionally they have been active contributors and participants in the establishment of the church and the ethnic associations. From this group are recruited the majority of the Greek community board of trustees.[46] Generally they are conservative and support church authority. Competition for administrative positions within the ethnic community is common among these business proprietors. The most successful are well known to many Canadian businessmen, politicians and city officials. Many of these upwardly mobile Greek Canadians can be classified economically as middle or upper middle but lack the attitudes, manners and values of the Canadian middle class or even of the middle class in Greece. A rural background in Greece and a lack of higher academic training have not allowed them to become fully familiar with middle class values.
3. *The workers:* This, the largest group, consists mainly of recently arrived immigrants who are employed in the lower socio-economic occupations. In large Canadian cities like Montreal many live in areas

predominately populated by Greek immigrants. They are under-represented in the administrative council and their membership in the church and its sectarian associations is relatively lower than the other groups.

In spite of their low academic attainment the entrepreneurs, especially the wealthy ones, have most influence on policies, largely because of their generous contributions and proportionately high representation on the community council. Their power is usually challenged by young, politically liberal Greek Canadians (usually students and professionals) who demand change. Because of such demands these intellectuals have been labelled "agitators" or "radicals" and their entrance to administrative positions is viewed with suspicion by the conservative elements in power.

The influence of the wealthy Greek entrepreneurs upon important decisions and their consequences have been described by Lambrou in her study of the Greek community in Vancouver:

> The desire to build the new church away from the residential area left a lot of people dissatisfied. Many objected that the new area (Kerrisdale) was chosen in order to satisfy the wealthier segments of the Greek populations who perhaps felt awkward with the unpretentious small church in Kitsilano, a less prestigious district. . . . Many parents objected that the distance was too great for their children who attended the Greek-language school in the church hall. . . . There was a lot of bitterness. This resulted in the formation of independent Greek-language schools supported totally by parents' funds.[47]

In the cities of Montreal and Toronto a relatively small faction of economically successful and professional Greek Canadians have succeeded in establishing their own independent churches. These independent parishes do not seem to be in direct contact with the larger Greek community and the working classes. Since they attract many of the more integrated Greek Canadians of the second and third generation, the English language is commonly used in church services and Sunday schools.

SURVIVAL OF ETHNIC IDENTITY AND SOCIAL MOBILITY

Can Greek Canadians experience upward mobility and still maintain their distinctive identity and some degree of cultural autonomy? There are two views on this question.[48] One is that an ethnic group either assimilates or remains in a low status. Greek Canadians, according to this view, will not be able to share equally in Canada's social and economic rewards as long as they resist assimilation into the dominant Anglo-Saxon or French cultural values. The other view is that upward mobility does not necessarily depend on assimilation or loss of ethnic identity. Those who hold this view claim that there are groups in North American society that show high social mobility without being assimilated.[49]

One may argue that the somewhat limited socio-economic status of the Greek minority in Canada, together with its low rate of assimilation, supports the first view. However, in one particular Canadian city Greeks have shown a lower degree of assimilation than the Slovaks, but a higher degree of occupational mobility.[50] Also, successful Greek-Canadians not only have maintained their ethno-religious identity but also are strong supporters of the ethnic institutions. They have been active contributors to the establishment of the church as well as secular and non-secular Greek associations. These individuals are likely to serve in the administrative councils of the Greek community and the large Greek-Canadian associations.

Vlassis lists as prominent Greeks those who are economically successful and who have been active participants in and financial contributors to the Greek community. Most of these Greeks had come to Canada prior to World War II, especially from 1910 to 1930. Frank Bazos, for example, who was the president of the Devon Dairy Company (a principal ice cream company in Ontario), had also been the chairman of the Building Committee of the Greek Orthodox Church in Toronto, a Mason, and president of the AHEPA Chapter of "Lord Byron." The successful restaurateur Peter Bassel, owner of the Bassel Restaurant in Toronto, also had served as the president of the Greek community of Toronto and the order of AHEPA. Another wealthy Greek immigrant who contributed money and time to the Greek community of Toronto was Constantine Apostolakos (Charles Brown) the owner of one of the most successful mushroom farms in Ontario. He served as a president of the Greek community in Toronto in the early 1950s and contributed much of his wealth to the building of a new Greek church and the Hellenic Cultural Centre in Toronto. The successful Greek physician Dr. Leonidas Polymenakos served as president of the Greek community in Toronto during the mid-1970s and has contributed financially to the Greek community and devoted much of his time to organizing programs for the maintenance of Greek schools and cultural activities in Toronto.

Similar patterns of participation have been observed in Montreal. According to Vlassis,[51] the 23 presidents of the Greek community in Montreal (from 1925-1952) were successful immigrants who had contributed to the social and economic welfare of the Greek community. For example, Phrixos Papachristidis, graduate of the University of Lausanne in economics and successful proprietor in the shipping business, served as president of the Greek community in Montreal in 1941 and financially supported the Church and other Greek institutions. George Ganetakos, who owned and operated many theatres in Montreal and district, had also supported the Greek church in Montreal and the Greek associations. During World War II Ganetakos became the chairman of the Greek War Relief Fund in Canada. Among other successful immigrants and staunch supporters of the Greek community in Montreal were Spyros Colivas, George Grivakis, Nick Lazanis and Nicholas Sclavoudakis.[52]

Yet another example is Ernest Cholakis, the Broadway Florist of Winnipeg. Ernest, who became a successful businessman, had no formal education and knew little English. He and his Canadian-born children (who have also been economically successful) have been strong financial supporters of the Greek church and schools in Winnipeg and he has served in the Greek community council. Ernest had also contributed financially to the institutions of his home village Varvitsa in the Province of Laconia.

Jimmie Condon of Calgary, a native of the village Hora in northeastern Greece, is another successful Greek-Canadian businessman. His "Palace of Sweets" and "Palace of Eats" were well known to Calgarians during the 1920s and 1930s. Jimmie has given generously in many ways to his adopted country and directly contributed large amounts of money for the establishment of the Greece Orthodox Church in Calgary. In 1963 Jimmie was named Calgary's Sportsman of the Year in recognition of his active involvement and encouragement of youngsters in sports including hockey, soccer, bowling and basketball. In 1977 at the age of 88 Jimmie commissioned an Athenian sculptor to create a white marble statue of Hippocrates and a grouping of Socrates and two students for the University of Calgary campus. This gift was an expression of Jimmie's appreciation for his cultural heritage. As he put it, "I have a deep respect for learning and a great desire to encourage it, and I have reverence for the cultural legacy which my Greek forefathers gave the development of western culture."[53]

Still another example is Yannis, a recent immigrant and successful restaurateur in the City of Vancouver.

> Yannis who climbed from a waiter to a successful businessman (co-owner of three well established restaurants in Vancouver), is a regular church member, contributes financially to the Greek community, and has served in its administrative council. Yannis and his family associate mainly with Greek-Canadians, especially relatives, and attend Greek dances and cultural activities. His young children attend the Greek afternoon school regularly and speak the Greek language fluently. Yannis as a successful businessman belongs to a few Canadian clubs and associations. Although he claims to be more Greek than Canadian, he wants his children to grow up in Canada, which he considers to be the country of opportunity.

Examples such as these tend to disprove that assimilation is a prerequisite to upward mobility. By no means do the above-mentioned names constitute an exhaustive list of Greeks who have been prominent within the Greek-Canadian minority. These names are given only as examples.

The Greek Canadians who have proudly retained their ethnic identity and supported the institutions of the ethnic community are likely to be active participants in the socio-cultural life of the host society as well. They belong to Canadian associations such as the Masons and the Kiwanis, they associate with non-Greek businessmen, support local politicians and contribute to charitable drives. Some of them have "Canadianized" their long and difficult-to-pronounce Greek names. They have adopted enough of the host society's culture to function and be accepted, and not enough to endanger their ethnic identity.

The general conclusion to be reached concerning the occupational status of Greek immigrants is that the overwhelming majority of them have improved their standard of living by coming to Canada and many have moved out of their entrance status. However, in the mid-1970s Greek Canadians are relatively powerless politically and have a low status in Canadian society. Their mobility is generally not great and since they start low they do not usually get past the middle-class level. Although Greeks have been a part of the Canadian mosaic for more than 80 years, they are not represented in high economic and managerial (corporation) positions. The reasons for this may be the barriers raised by the charter groups and the relatively low academic attainment of the majority of Greek-Canadian immigrants.

With the passage of time the status of the Greek minority is expected to improve. Second and third generation Greek Canadians are more likely to obtain professional and skilled occupations than were their parents because of higher educational achievement. We also expect that future upwardly mobile Greek Canadians will continue to maintain their cultural identity.

NOTES

1. George Vlassis, *The Greeks in Canada* (Hull: Leclerc Printers Limited, 1953), pp. 137-138.
2. *Ibid.,* p. 89.
3. Yianna Lambrou, The Greek Community of Vancouver: Social Organization and Adaptation. Unpublished M.A. Thesis, University of British Columbia, 1975, pp. 58-59.
4. See Vlassis, *op. cit.,* pp. 121, 207.
5. Edward A. Ross, *The Old World in the New* (New York: The Century Company, 1914), p. 184. Professor Ross said of the business-minded Greek, "From curb to stand, from stand to store, from little store to big stores, to the stores in other cities. Such are the stages of his "upward" movement."

6. Jean Morrison, "Ethnicity and Violence: The Lakehead Freight Handlers Before World War I," in Gregory S. Kealey and Peter Warrian eds., *Essays in Canadian Working Class History* (Toronto: McClelland and Stewart, 1976), pp. 114-160.

7. Vlassis, *op. cit.,* pp. 221-254.

8. *Ibid.,* pp. 103-119.

9. *Ibid.,* p. 96.

10. Department of Canadian Citizenship and Immigration, Ottawa, Deputy Minister's Records, 1952, File No. 3-51.

11. Department of Labour, Ottawa, Deputy Minister's Records, 1951, File No. 3-51.

12. Department of Canadian Citizenship and Immigration, Deputy Minister's Records, 1957, File No. 3-33-14.

13. *Ibid.,* File No. 3-33-14.

14. Canada Department of Citizenship and Immigration, Statistics Section 1950-1970.

15. The categories of "wives and children" and "other non-workers" are excluded from our calculation.

16. John Porter, *The Vertical Mosaic* (Toronto: University of Toronto Press, 1966), p. 63-64.

17. See Peter D. Chimbos, "Ethnicity and Occupational Mobility: A Comparative Study of Greek and Slovak Immigrants in Ontario City," *International Migration Review,* Vol. XV, 1974, pp. 58-66.

18. The data were obtained from *The London Greek Community Telephone Directory, 1976.* Our data should be considered as rough estimates since the occupations of 18% of the Greek family heads in London were unknown or not recorded.

19. Julius Metrakos, *et al., Commission for Community Development for the Greek Orthodox Community in Montreal,* Interim Report. (Montreal: Greek Orthodox Community, July 31, 1970), p. 19.

20. See Statistics Canada, "Greek Ethnic Group by Income, Education and Occupation," Catalogue No. 8917-13549A.

21. "Canadian Immigration and Population Study," *Three Years in Canada* (Ottawa, Information Canada, 1974), pp. 53-55.

22. Nicholas D. Iliopoulos, *Who is Who of Greek Origin in Institutions of Higher Learning in the United States and Canada* (New York: Greek Orthodox Archdiocese, Office of Education, 1974), p. x.

23. Paul Larocque, *et. al., Operationalization of Social Indicators of Multiculturalism,* Discussion Paper for Fourth Department Seminar on Social Indicators, Ottawa, November 26, 1974, pp. 62-63.

24. *Report of the Royal Commission on Bilingualism and Biculturalism* (Ottawa: Vol. 4, 1969), p. 51.

25. Vlassis, *op. cit.,* pp. 221-254.

26. Chimbos, *op. cit.,* p. 64.

27. Saloutos, *op. cit.,* p. 265.

28. Porter, *op. cit.,* p. 74.

29. Saloutos, *op. cit.,* p. 266.
30. Bernard C. Rosen, "Race, Ethnicity and the Achievement Syndrome," *American Sociological Review,* Vol. 24, (1959), pp. 47-60.
31. Saloutos, *op. cit.,* p. 258.
32. Archives of the Greek Consulate, Toronto, Canada.
33. *Ibid.*
34. Canada Department of Citizenship and Immigration, Statistics Section, 1950-1960.
35. Department of Citizenship and Immigration (Immigration Branch) File No. 553-33-5522, Ottawa, September 20, 1956.
36. Jane Lambiri-Dimaki, "Dowry in Modern Greece," in Constantina Safilios-Rothschild ed., *Toward a Sociology of Women* (Toronto: Xerox College Publishing, 1972), p. 77.
37. This information is based on interviews with domestic servants.
38. Department of Citizenship and Immigration (Immigration Branch) File No. 552-1-552, Ottawa, 1957.
39. See *The Greek Sun,* Montreal, November 28, 1972, p. 16.
40. Sheila Arnopulos, "Waitresses Paid $25.00 for Sixty Hours," *The Montreal Star,* Montreal, December 16, 1976, pp. 1-2.
41. Efrosini Gavaki, *The Integration of Greeks in Canada* (San Francisco: R. and E. Research Associates, 1977), p. 35.
42. Bambis Kiattipis, *The Organization of the Park Extension Citizens* (Montreal: Park Extension Community Corporation, 1973), p. 6.
43. Peter D. Chimbos, "A Comparison of the Social Adaptation of Dutch, Greek and Slovak Immigrants in a Canadian Community," *International Migration Review,* Vol. 6·(Fall 1972), p. 236.
44. Peter Stathopoulos, *The Greek Community of Montreal* (Athens: National Centre for Researchers, 1971), pp. 26-27.
45. Lambrou, *op. cit.,* pp. 79-82.
46. The selection of the board of trustees (community council) can be influenced by region of birth in the home society. In certain Greek communities the council members (mainly businessmen) recruit their support from regional compatriots. For example, Spartans (those coming from the Province of Laconia) have been predominately found in the Greek community councils of Montreal and London, Ontario.
47. Lambrou, *op. cit.,* pp. 134-140.
48. For a comprehensive discussion of the two theoretical perspectives on pluralism see William M. Newman, "Theoretical Perspectives for the Analysis of Social Pluralism," in *The Canadian Ethnic Mosaic: A Quest for Identity,* ed., Leo Driedger, Toronto: McClelland and Stewart, 1978, pp. 40-51.
49. Milton Gordon, Assimilation in American Life (New York: Oxford University Press, 1964).
50. Peter D. Chimbos, "Ethnicity and Occupational Mobility: A Comparative Study of Greek and Slovak Immigrants in Ontario City, *International Journal of Comparative Sociology,* 15 (1974), p. 66.

51. See George Vlassis, *op. cit.*, pp. 182-185.
52. *Ibid.*, pp. 136-146.
53. See the Greek Canadian newspaper *Action,* January 1978, p. 11.

FOUR

Community Organization and Intra-Ethnic Conflict

Whenever a stable nucleus of Greek immigrants settled in a Canadian city, they formed a community (*kinotis*). A Greek community may be defined as a grouping of people within a Canadian city who share the Greek culture and language, and have some form of ethnic and religious organization. The participants carry on their activities through this structure for the purposes of maintaining their ethnic identity, preserving the culture of the home society and obtaining spiritual guidance. The structural unity of the community is based mainly on the church, ethnic organizations and educational institutions. The Greek ethnic community does not necessarily have strictly geographical boundaries. However, in large Canadian cities such as Montreal, Toronto and Vancouver one may observe a heavy concentration of Greek Canadians in a particular area or neighbourhood.

THE CHURCH

Historically the Greek community in Canada has been organized around the church (*ecclesia*) which is its most powerful component. As with many ethnic minorities in North America, the church is dominant in almost all socio-cultural activities of the parish.[1] It becomes more than a strictly religious centre for immigrants in a foreign land.[2] The Greek Orthodox Church has kept the immigrant attached to his home country and helped him to preserve his faith, language and culture in the new society. The receptiveness of the Greek immigrant to these objectives of the church has been described by Saloutos, who writes of the Greek immigrant in the United States: "Absence from his ancestral home, the fear that he might never see it again, the thought of losing his nationality and of dying in a strange land, caused him, at least for a time, to embrace his religion with a fervor that he never had in Greece."[3]

The Greek Orthodox Church symbolizes nationality, and adherence to it nourishes ethnic identity. During the Turkish domination (1453-1828) the Greeks clung to their church as the only means of preserving their linguistic and cultural identity. As McNall points out, the "church, whose language was Greek, assumed the duty of preserving not only the faith, but the Greek 'nation' or Hellenism. Because there was no government to represent the Greek people, the church often became the center of social organization in the villages."[4] After Greece's liberation from the Turks the church extended its role of preserving Greek ethnicity to other countries where Greeks had emigrated. Clergymen were trained in theological colleges in Greece and then sent to foreign lands to serve in cities with large Greek communities. The first Greek Orthodox church in North America was founded in 1864 in New Orleans by Greek merchants, and by 1900 other churches were established in other American cities such as Chicago and New York.[5]

The Greek church in Canada is an offshoot of the church in the United States, and the two have shared a similar structure and problems in adjusting to North American society. Since its beginning the Greek church in Canada has been directed and controlled by the Greek Orthodox Archdiocese of North and South America with its headquarters in New York City. In 1906 the first Greek community[6] in Canada was organized in Montreal by about 1,000 Greek Canadians. On October 25 of the same year Father A. Papageorgopoulos arrived in Montreal and held the first Greek Orthodox Church service.[7] By 1909 a second Greek community, St. George in Toronto, was founded. Later other Greek communities were established around Orthodox churches in the cities of Winnipeg, Fort William and Ottawa.[8] By 1978 at least 40 Greek Orthodox churches had been established throughout Canada to serve the spiritual and educational needs of Greek Canadians. In certain cities where the Greek population was too small to support an organized parish, priests from larger Greek communities came periodically to perform religious services.

As indicated earlier, the establishment of Greek parish churches in Canada was usually preceded by some kind of ethnic organization and a sense of ethnic consciousness. Collective action was necessary in order to make the proper arrangements for the founding of the church, ethnic schools and the administration of the Greek community. For example, the Greeks of Montreal had formed ethnic associations before undertaking the establishment of the church in 1906.[9]

Although the Greek church is considered the centre of both religious and social activities in the ethnic community, the majority of Greek Canadians are not paid-up members of the parish.[10] They use the church for baptisms, weddings, funerals, and Sunday and holiday services, and attend sponsored dances and recreational activities, but do not pay dues and hence do not officially belong. Active church membership seems to be higher in small Greek communities than in large cities where anonymity is more prevalent, ethnic pressure is less, and where community leaders have less influence.[11] Apathy towards formal church membership is considered a serious problem by both civic and religious leaders of the ethnic communities throughout Canada, yet the absence of flagrant discrimination against recent Greek immigrants, the inability of poor families to pay membership dues, inefficient leadership and religious schisms are reasons why some Greek Canadians avoid membership in the church.

We do not imply that Greek Canadians ignore the church. In large Canadian cities the churches are usually crowded on religious holidays. When important community issues arise, such as whether to dismiss the priest or to elect a new board of trustees (community council), many non-members pay their dues in order to participate in the decision making. Even non-members make their voices heard in social gatherings and coffeehouses by criticizing the performance of the clergymen and the members of the community council. The voices of these outsiders may indirectly influence the policies and opinions of the decision makers of the ethnic community. A small percentage (approximately 5%) of Greek Canadians who belong to other religious denominations such as Jehovah's Witnesses show little or no interest in the activities of the predominantly Greek Orthodox community.[12]

COMMUNITY LEADERSHIP

The administrative body of a Greek community consists of an elected Board of Trustees (a council), headed by a president and vice-president. The officers are elected by the active members of the community and are responsible for its economic and social affairs. The duties and responsibilities of the community officials are mainly based on the Uniform Church Regulations drafted by the Greek Orthodox Archdiocese of North and South America.[13]

The members of the board of trustees are elected for a term of two years. In large Greek communities the candidates usually belong to a loosely organized coalition (*syndiasmos*). For example, in the 1976 elections of the Greek community of Montreal there were two coalitions each with its own platform for dealing with community issues, and only a few individuals ran as independent candidates. In smaller communities, the candidates usually run on their own and are not committed to a political party.

The coalitions or independent candidates who run for the administrative positions of large Greek communities usually inform the electorate about their objectives through the Greek communications media (TV, radio and newspapers). The programmes emphasize the preservation of Greek values and institutions in Canadian society and the unity of the Greek community. For example, in the Montreal community elections in 1976 the objectives of the two coalitions were stated in campaign leaflets[14] as follows:

Coalition 1
Greek community (*Kinotis*) signifies to us '50 Years of Action' for the preservation of our religion, conservation of the Greek language, the survival of our cultural tradition and service to the Greeks of Montreal.

Coalition 2
Co-operation of our community with the associations, federations and other Greek organizations; not isolation from our fellow Greeks. Our purpose is the unity of the Greeks in our community. Every Greek must become a member of our community and remain a member of the local Greek associations.

The coalitions also specified in their programmes the needs for a new community centre, more and better teachers for Greek schools, homes for the aged and day care centres. One of the coalitions included the issue of Cyprus in its platform, suggesting that Greek Canadians must remain united and harmonious in order to support effectively the independence and territorial integrity of Cyprus.

The two coalitions contesting the administrative positions do not seem to differ in their objectives. This indicates that those who disagreed were either apathetic or unable for some reason to compete for administrative positions within the Greek community at that time. Candidates usually attract votes from relatives, friends, business associates and compatriots from the same town, village or province in Greece.

An examination of the power structure of various Greek communities suggests that the governing officials consist mainly of the economically and socially influential members of that community (see Table 10). They are occupationally successful individuals who enter the power positions for challenge, prestige, publicity and status. Some of the officials, especially the "old timers," have been financial contributors to the establishment of the church. Prior to World War II the most powerful decision makers of the Greek community had a relatively low level of schooling but were successful small businessmen. However, after the war and especially in the late 1960s and early 1970s, new immigrants with more education and liberal views started to penetrate the administrative positions of the Greek communities. At least 19% of the members of the board of trustees who were elected in the Greek communities of London, Montreal, Toronto and Vancouver were professionals.

The president and members of the council are usually busy people working in their businesses or place of employment and contributing extra time for their administrative responsibilities in the Greek-Canadian community. They attend church services regularly, make appearances at community dances and ethnic celebrations, and deliver speeches at formal gatherings. Speeches are also given by the priest and when appropriate by honoured guests from the municipal or provincial government.

75

TABLE 10

Occupational Status of Elected Officials in Four Greek-Canadian Communities,* 1976

	Elected officials	
Occupational status	Number	%
Professionals	15	19.0
Small business proprietors	32	40.5
Skilled, sales and lower level managers	27	34.1
Semiskilled and unskilled	5	6.4
Total	79	100.0

*The Greek communities are those of Montreal, London, Toronto and Vancouver which constitute approximately 80% of the Greek-Canadian population in Canada. Information on the occupational status of the elected officials was obtained through personal communication.

Since early times Greek communities in Canada have been dominated by conservative leaders whose values were compatible with those of the church and the governments of both the home and the new societies. In the early 1970s, however, younger people with liberal views have been elected to powerful positions in the community. This reflects the impact of recent immigrants upon the traditional structure. For example, in 1975 in Toronto a group of liberal Greeks (many of whom were professionals) were elected to the board of trustees. These "new blood" individuals, as they have been called, challenged the old order, notably the influence of the clergy upon the elected officials of the community. This change inevitably created anxiety amongst high-ranking church officials. Demands for administrative changes are more likely to occur in Greek communities where there is a concentration of young and educated individuals willing to challenge traditional authority. However, some working class Greek Canadians who have experiences with reformist political movements in Greece during the 1940s or have been inspired to political activity by the democratic opportunities in Canada may also work for change.

ETHNIC ORGANIZATIONS

Greek societies and associations are numerous and their functions are primarily ethnocultural and philanthropic. Our analysis here will be concerned with those parish organizations which historically have been essential components of the Greek community and thus have played an important role in reinforcing the traditional power of Greek Orthodoxy within the community structure. These organizations are under the supervision of the parish priest and their local by-laws must be approved by the Greek Orthodox Archdiocese.

An important church organization is the Philoptochos Society for married women. The name of this organization is derived from the Greek words *philos* (friend) and *ptochos* (poor). It sponsors drives and bazaars in order to secure money for the church and other philanthropic purposes. This particular society mainly attracts devout women whose families are regular supporters of the ethnic community. The majority of the married women, especially in Montreal and Toronto, are not members of the Philoptokos Society, as membership seems to be higher in small Greek communities where ethnic group pressure for membership is more effectively applied.

A youth organization known as the Greek Orthodox Youth Association (GOYA) is also important in the Greek community. It is directed by the Greek Orthodox Archdiocese for the purpose of bringing young adults closer to the Greek culture and religious life. Active participation of young people in the Greek community encourages the persistence of Greek values and language, and also ethnic endogamy. In fact GOYA arose out of the fear that interethnic marriage among young Greeks in the United States and Canada was on the increase and something had to be done to "save" them from getting "lost" to another ethno-religious group.

Wherever GOYA has been well organized, its members have become active in teaching Sunday Schools, assisting in philanthropic tasks and serving as administrative assistants to the community council. However, the organization has been unable to attract large numbers of young Greek Canadians in the metropolitan communities. This seems to be mainly due to the failure of GOYA to provide programmes attractive to contemporary youth, problems of communication between youth and parish priests, and the availability of non-sectarian associations.[15]

Generally speaking, efforts by parish organizations to deal with important issues of the ethnic community are ineffectual. Because such organizations are directed by conservative leaders they have been unable to redefine their original objectives and philosophies and thus are not prepared to deal with current problems. For example, no parish organization had ever attempted to use its resources to combat exploitative labour conditions and unemployment among Greek working class immigrant women in the cities of Montreal or Toronto.

NON-SECTARIAN ORGANIZATIONS

Greek Canadians began to organize societies and associations independent of church influences prior to World War I. Being in a foreign land far away from their loved ones, the early Greek immigrants organized associations in order to maintain a sense of security and community life. In the associations they could meet their compatriots, speak their native language, entertain themselves with the folk music of the home society, and decide how best to preserve their culture and ethnic identity.

The first associations were patriotic in nature and their membership consisted of immigrants from various parts of Greece. By 1905 the first two patriotic associations were organized in Montreal – *Patris* (Motherland) with president Demetrios Pergantis and *Anagenesis* (Regeneration) with president Athanasios Spyridakos. The main objectives of these associations were to preserve Greek culture and identity and provide solidarity among the immigrants. One of the best known patriotic organizations was the *Panhellenios Enosis*, an offshoot of the Panhellenic Union in the United States.[16] It was first organized in Montreal under the leadership of a Greek lawyer named Demetrios Nikolakakos. As a patriotic organization the Panhellenic Union played an important role in mobilizing Greek immigrants in Canada and the United States to fight for Greece in the Balkan Wars (1912-1913). Although the organization was short lived it demonstrated that Greek immigrants were still dedicated to the mother country and willing to give their lives for its freedom and ideals.

After World War I the largest and most powerful Greek association in North America was founded. The American Hellenic Educational Progressive Association (AHEPA) was first organized in Atlanta, Georgia, in 1922 by Greek immigrants who believed that such an organization could "unite their fellow countrymen, inculcate in them an aggressive national conscience, educate them in the fundamental principles of Americanism and aid them to adapt themselves to the social and commercial climate of the country."[17] The first objective of AHEPA was to combat prejudice and discrimination against immigrants, but later "its scope was broadened to include educational, social, political, cultural and benevolent activities."[18]

Like the parish and other patriotic associations, AHEPA expanded its influences in Canada. In 1928 the first AHEPA Chapter (Lord Byron Chapter) was organized in Toronto under the leadership of Evangelos Kilismanis. In 1929 the second Chapter (Lord Nelson Chapter) was organized in London, Ontario, and subsequently other chapters appeared throughout Canada. By 1976 there were 15 AHEPA chapters with approximately 800 members. The main objectives of AHEPA were to promote a mutual understanding of the two cultures (Greek and Canadian) and encourage members to participate in the civic and commercial life of the host society. Other constitutional objectives were to champion the cause of education, repel the interference of any religion in governmental affairs, and encourage loyalty to Canada and reverence for its traditions.[19]

AHEPA primarily attracted businessmen and professionals, and appealed little to the average Greek worker. This can be explained by AHEPA's failure to provide the new immigrant workers with assistance and direction in dealing with problems of employment and adjustment in the host society. On the other hand many ideologically liberal Greek Canadians considered the organization to be conservative and pro-

American. Although AHEPA claims to be non-partisan, its political influence has been observed in certain historical events. For example, in 1967 when colonels of the Greek Army staged a military coup, the leaders of AHEPA not only failed to protest such action but justified its objectives. The coup, according to AHEPA leaders, did no injury to the Greek people and was necessary to restore political stability and prevent a Communist takeover. Five months later the American AHEPA urged the United States government to continue its military and economic aid to the military regime of Athens, on the grounds that the colonels were determined to keep Greece in NATO and a faithful ally of the United States.[20] The support of AHEPA for the military Junta of Athens has been described by Vournas:

> Ahepans seeking to justify their organization's aberrations have pointed to the fact that since the Junta was recognized and actively supported by the United States Government, the AHEPA was duty-bound to follow official policy. They point to the constitution of the order – an oath each member is required to take: "Loyalty to the United States; allegiance to its Flag; support to its constitution; obedience to its law and reverence for its history and traditions."[21]

Another important non-sectarian Greek association is the Daughters of Penelope, a women's auxiliary of the AHEPA. Its members are mainly wives of men who belong to the AHEPA. The main functions of the Daughters of Penelope are to promote the social, ethnic and intellectual interests of its members, to help AHEPA sponsor conventions and dances, and to raise money for philanthropic purposes in Canada and abroad. The Maids of Athens is a junior women's auxiliary of AHEPA whose objectives are also philanthropic and patriotic in nature. The Maids of Athens society has been active primarily in the Greek communities of Montreal, Toronto and Vancouver.

The Sons of Pericles is a junior men's auxiliary of AHEPA whose main objectives are to provide means of stimulating the spiritual, intellectual and physical growth of its members, to promote the ideals of both Canadian and Greek cultures, to provide an understanding of Greek family life, and to provide leadership opportunities. Any male between the ages of 14-23 of Greek descent or whose father is a member of AHEPA is eligible for membership. The Sons of Pericles has been active in Montreal, Toronto, Edmonton, Saskatoon and Vancouver, but it has failed to attract the masses of young Greek Canadians. Like the Greek Orthodox Organization (GOYA), the Sons of Pericles has failed to provide programmes which appeal to many young Greek Canadians. Also, like other Greek associations, the Sons of Pericles has been dominated by Greek-American leadership in the United States.

One association popular with post-secondary Greek-Canadian students is the Greek University Students Association. It is found on several campuses and has both first and second generation Greek immigrants in its membership. This organization is both social and political in nature, but is primarily a social network for its members.

An important post-World War II Greek-Canadian association is the Hellenic Canadian Cultural Society (HCCS). It was founded in January, 1961, in Toronto by physicians and professors, with Dr. L. Polymenakos as its first president. By 1977 two other chapters of the HCCS were organized in Montreal and Ottawa. Any individual of Greek descent who holds a university degree is eligible for membership. In 1977 the society had approximately 120 members. Its main objective is to further Greek ideals and culture in Canada by education in the Greek-Canadian communities. The society has sponsored many public educational lectures and provided financial assistance for philanthropic purposes.

The HCCS has been criticized as an elitist organization which has ignored the needs of the working class. Some critics further claim that the organization is too ideologically conservative since it remained silent during the military dictatorship in Greece (1967-1974). However, immediately after the invasion of Cyprus (1974) by the Turks, the HCCS voiced disapproval of the Greek military Junta and criticized its interference in the internal affairs of Cyprus. The HCCS blamed the invasion of Cyprus on the dictators and the conflicting interests of the superpowers who were seeking control of the area. On August 17, 1974, the following telegram was sent to Prime Minister Trudeau by members of the HCCS of Toronto: "You are respectfully requested to use the power of your office to the effect that a permanent ceasefire is established in Cyprus, that the Turkish invaders are withdrawn from Cyprus, and that the territorial integrity and independence of Cyprus are restored."[22]

During the Cyprus crisis the HCCS also worked with various Greek organizations to provide Greek Cypriots with funds, medical supplies and clothing. More importantly, the HCCS supported the formation of the Committee for Justice in Cyprus in order to inform the Canadian public about Cypriot refugees' problems and to support the independence and territorial integrity of Cyprus. Thus the HCCS has fulfilled political as well as educational, cultural and philanthropic functions within the Greek community.

LOCAL ORGANIZATIONS

With the mass settlement of Greek immigrants in large Canadian cities during the 1950s and 1960s, many local organizations arose.[23] They appeared as soon as a large number of immigrants from a particular Greek village, city or province had settled in a Canadian city. The main objectives of these organizations were to collect money for improvements in the poor villages and towns the immigrants had left behind. The direct aid given by such organizations has played an important role in the rapid reconstruction of many buildings, such as schools, electricity plants, and waterworks, which were destroyed during World War II and the Civil War of 1946-49.

In 1975 there were approximately 90 local Greek organizations in Canada, all within Ontario, Quebec and British Columbia. The majority were in Ontario and Quebec, mainly in the cities of Toronto and Montreal. Although such organizations reflect the Greek immigrant's attachment to his native land, they foster a local orientation which could impede solidarity among Greek Canadians. This problem of disunity has been seriously considered by leaders of large organizations in Montreal who in the early 1970s attempted to co-ordinate all small local organizations into a federation, the Federal Union of Greek Associations of Montreal. Such efforts were viewed by the various associations with reluctance and suspicion. As far as can be determined, the local associations have retained their strength but they will probably decline with the passing of the first generation of immigrants.

NEW PROGRESSIVE ORGANIZATIONS

Neither the parish nor non-sectarian organizations were structurally or ideologically capable of meeting the needs of the influx of immigrants who came to large Canadian cities. Most of the guidance and direction for the new immigrants in the Canadian milieu was provided by family and kin. It was relatives who helped the newcomers find employment, a place to stay or a family physician.

In 1969 the Hellenic Federation of Parents and Guardians of Montreal was organized by Greek parents to deal with the academic problems of their children. At that time more than 3,000 Greek-Canadian children were attending Canadian schools in Montreal. The basic objectives of the association were to improve the academic training of Greek children, inform parents about educational problems faced by their children, help Greek-Canadian children to make a better adjustment to the Canadian educational system, and ensure the teaching of the Greek language and culture by providing children with supplementary schools. In other words the association had to create programmes to deal with children's social adjustment to the Canadian educational system on one hand, and the need to maintain Greek language and culture on the other. By 1975 the association had achieved many of its objectives and had become an effective force for coping with problems of Greek-Canadian children in Montreal.

Another organization which has helped the new immigrants to deal with problems of adjustment was the Greek Canadian Labour Association (GCLA). It appeared in Montreal in September, 1970, and by March, 1971, its constitution was approved by the provincial government of Quebec. The main objectives of the Association were to inform Greek immigrants about Canadian labour laws and civil rights and thus help to combat exploitative working conditions, to help unemployed Greek immigrants find jobs, to encourage Greek workers to become members of Canadian labour unions, and to inspire among its members co-operation and devotion to Canadian institutions.[24]

The leaders of the association were young, educated and ideologically liberal Greek immigrants who had lived and worked among working-class Greek Canadians. They had observed the problems which immigrant workers were confronted with in the new society and decided to find possible solutions. The organizers of the GCLA felt that it was essential to emphasize causes rather than symptoms in order to deal effectively with the employment problems of Greek workers. Thus, the basic motto of the association since 1971 has been "Greek workers unite through the local labour unions." It was through proper organization and co-operation, the association felt, that the new immigrants could make important changes for the improvement of their socio-economic life.

The GCLA attracted its members mainly from unskilled labour, especially those who immigrated to Canada after 1950. By 1976, the association had 2,000 active members, but confined its activities to Montreal because it was in Montreal where most unskilled Greek immigrants were trapped in exploitative jobs.

Although the GCLA is supposedly apolitical it was directly concerned with human rights and civil liberties in Greece during the right-wing dictatorship (1967-1974). According to GCLA leaders, a strong protest against Greece's dictatorship was a moral obligation. Greek Canadians who sympathized with the dictatorship labeled the GCLA as a radical association.

In 1976 the Centre of Social Services for Greek-Canadians was established in Toronto, under the direction of the Greek Community of Metropolitan Toronto Inc. The main objective of the centre was to provide Greek immigrants (especially those who lacked knowledge of the English language) with essential social services, including family counselling, information on social and legal matters in the host society, and programmes for youth and retired people. The organizers of the centre, like those of the progressive associations in Montreal, were young and educated Greek Canadians.

Although parish and most nonsectarian organizations were primarily established for patriotic, philanthropic and cultural purposes, they also performed other functions for their members.[25] First, the ethnic organizations served as guides to immigrants in the transition from an agricultural community in Greece to a complex urban Canadian life by providing opportunities for interacting with familiar people and hearing the language and music of the homeland. Second, Greek organizations have served as agencies of acculturation. Members of the various associations and societies became accustomed to the democratic processes of Canadian organizations, and the leaders were given the opportunity to practise leadership techniques. They learned to handle problems involving complex co-operative efforts such as serving members and keeping them active, raising money and arriving at joint decisions acceptable to all social functions. Some immigrants who had leadership experience in small Greek associations were able to attain leadership roles in AHEPA and other middle-class Canadian associations.

THE ETHNIC SCHOOL

Since the early 1900s the ethnic school has been an important Greek community institution in Canada, providing the children of immigrants with instruction in Greek language, history and religion. This was essential to the immigrants who wanted to preserve their language and culture. The ethnic school appeared as soon as the Greek immigrants established a community. The first school, named Plato, was organized in 1910 in Montreal under the direction of Greek-born teacher John Dedaskalou. It claimed to be the first full-time Greek school in North America where Greek-Canadian children could receive primary education. Other full-time accredited Greek primary schools in Montreal were established later. The curriculum was that established and set down by the Protestant School Board of Montreal. After the completion of the Greek primary school the children could transfer to the Protestant schools where they were given full credit for their previous academic training.

Supplementary schools for Greek language and religion teaching appeared later in Montreal and other communities along with the establishment of the parish church. The parish priest usually served as the first teacher of the ethnic school. With the flow of Greek immigrants to Canada after World War II, professional teachers and laymen with some college training from Greece were hired to teach in afternoon schools. In large Greek communities like Toronto and Montreal, private ethnic schools appeared under the direction of qualified teachers from Greece. By 1976 dozens of church and privately-directed Greek schools were operating in various communities throughout Canada. They were held during late afternoon hours with a curriculum consisting of language subjects (reading, grammar, composition), history and geography of Greece, religion and music, subjects which contributed to the learning and cultivation of the Greek language and the patriotic education of children. These part-time Greek schools were supported mainly by fees by parents. They were partially subsidized by the municipal boards of education or the provincial government.

Greek community schools in Canada at first normally utilized texts published in *katharevousa* (formalized Greek language) and approved by the Ministry of Education in Greece.[26] Many teachers and parents complained that such reading materials were difficult and tiresome for children. *Katharevousa*, they argued, is much different than the *demotiki* commonly spoken in the homes; thus the children found themselves in contradictory and confusing learning experiences. After the fall of the

83

military regime in 1974 demotic texts started to become available in Greece and in Greek schools in Canada. In 1976 the Greek Parliament passed a law to replace the so-called "elitist" *katharevousa* and replace it with the *demotiki*, especially at the primary school level.

While Greek schools have experienced certain problems in finding funds and qualified teachers, they remain important vehicles for the transmission of Greek language and culture in Canadian society. Parents as well as leaders of the ethnic communities have shown a strong desire to keep the Greek school as an institution of ethnic pride and cultural importance. In a survey at least 77% of the Greek respondents felt that it was important to provide additional Greek schools in Canada as a means of language retention. This was the highest percentage among the ten ethnic groups included in the survey.[27] The importance of language retention has been described by the president of the Academic Committee of Greek Community Schools in Toronto: "The teaching of the Greek language in Greek schools is imperative and indispensable for two main reasons: the preservation and transmission of our cultural traditions and our gradual adaptation to the new society."[28]

There is no doubt the Greek parents (immigrants and even second-generation Greeks) are determined to provide their children with adequate knowledge of the Greek language and culture. In 1976 more than 12,000 children attended Greek afternoon schools (Grades 1-6) throughout Canada. Approximately 4,000 children were enrolled in 100 Toronto schools operated by the Greek Community of Metropolitan Toronto Inc. alone and a few hundred were enrolled in private Greek schools. The same year approximately 3,500 children attended afternoon schools operated by the Greek Community of Montreal Inc.[29]

THE COFFEEHOUSE

No analysis of Greek community life would be complete without considering the Greek coffeehouse (*kafenion*), one of the oldest Greek institutions in Canada. The coffeehouse appeared in Canadian cities wherever a sufficient number of Greek males had settled. In the coffeehouse the Greek men gather to drink their Turkish coffee or eat Greek pastry, meet compatriots, discuss Greek politics and community issues, play card games and listen to Greek music. It is a social and recreational centre where restaurant and shop owners, factory and restaurant employees, unemployed and amateur philosophers would gather after working hours and on weekends to experience a taste of the Old Country's social life.[30]

Although many other types of social outlets became available with the growth of the Greek communities, the coffeehouse has remained a centre of social interaction in large urban centres. It has been viewed by some Greek observers as an "evil" place where "lazy" men spend hours playing cards, gambling and ignoring their familial responsibilities. While some of the young single men may spend long hours in the coffeehouses, the vast majority of Greek men do not "hang out" or waste time in such places. The coffeehouses provide many lonely single immigrants with companionship and a familiar cultural setting. As Saloutos points out, the coffeehouses "were gathering places where men could meet and discuss a wide variety of subjects, where information and advice could be obtained, and where the otherwise lonely hours could be spent in the company of compatriots."[31]

In certain Greek communities the traditional coffeehouse has lost much of its appeal, as Greek men are becoming increasingly interested in other social outlets. According to Patterson, there were several coffeehouses in the 1920s and 1930s in downtown Vancouver, while today there are no Greek coffeehouses *per se*. Other places of business such as billiard halls, bakeries and restaurants serve as substitutes for this special Greek institution.[32] It is not uncommon, for example, to see several Greeks sitting in the rear of bakeries drinking coffee, gossiping about the community and socializing. Lambrou further indicates that in those new substitute coffeehouses in Vancouver the Greek immigrants

> usually discuss the latest political events in Greece, and have passionate arguments over the advantages and disadvantages of life in Canada. They read Greek newspapers and play the latest Greek music in the juke-box. . . . Newly arrived immigrants receive information from the owner regarding jobs with Greek employers, or directions on how to get a new job through the Manpower office.[33]

ETHNORELIGIOUS HOLIDAYS AND SOCIAL LIFE

There are certain cultural activities sponsored by the Greek-Canadian communities that reinforce the preservation of Greek customs and traditions. Important functions are the annual celebrations of Greek Independence Day on March 25th and the anniversary of Greece's resistance against Italy's aggression on October 28th. The celebrations include special church services, parades (in certain cities), speeches by community leaders and dances with Greek food and pastries. In such ethnic festivities participation of Canadian politicians from municipal and provincial governments is frequent, especially in large Greek-Canadian communities. In Vancouver, for example, Mayor Jack Volrich proclaimed the week of March 20-28, 1978, for Greek celebration and March 25th as Greek Independence Day. In his written proclamation the mayor praised the Greek people of Vancouver for assisting in the development and progress of the city.[34]

Religious festivities are also an important aspect of the ethnic community's social life. Easter is perhaps the most important. The joy of Easter symbolically begins at midnight mass on Saturday when the priest comes from the sanctuary with lighted candle and announces to the congregation "Christos Anesti" (Christ is Risen) and the faithful reply "Alithos Anesti" (He is truly risen). According to Greek Orthodox tradition, "the priest lights the candles to those nearest him, and they in turn light others, repeating the priest's words until the whole church is full of lighted candles. After the service, it is customary to try to carry the lighted candle home."[35] The blessed candlelight, according to the faithful, should bring peace and prosperity to the family.

Easter Sunday is usually celebrated with relatives and friends. Traditional food includes roast lamb, *mageritsa* (a ceremonial soup consisting of tender liver of the pascal lamb), feta cheese, salads, Greek wines and Easter bread. Easter eggs dyed in red symbolizing the blood of Christ are also a part of the festivity. Before the meal, members of the family and friends crack their eggs against each other's and the one whose egg best withstands the cracking is expected to have a good and prosperous year.

Another important Greek social occasion is the Vasilopita Feast, which is sponsored by the Philoptokos Society. Every January many Greek families and their guests gather to celebrate the New Year's Feast by cutting the Vasilopita (St. Basil's sweet bread or torte). This custom dates back to the fourth century of the Christian era when the first Philoptokos group was founded by St. Basil, Bishop of Caesaria in Cappodocia, Asia Minor. According to tradition the Vasilopita was served by St. Basil at his annual gatherings. As the climax of the occasion he would ask for bids to donate to orphans and to the poor. The highest bidder received the honour of cutting the Vasilopita. The ancient custom includes baking a coin in the Vasilopita, and whoever receives the piece with the coin supposedly will have good luck during the year.

Annual dances and picnics sponsored by the Greek-Canadian communities and ethnic associations are additional festive occasions. The spirit, pride and enjoyment of Greek Canadians is obvious in their dancing, as it is in their feasts and other celebrations. When the orchestra starts playing everyone catches the contagious spirit of the Greek popular music. Soon the dancers get in line holding hands and start moving to the rhythm of the lively music.

Various kinds of folk dancing are practised by Greek Canadians. The country dances (*vlachika*) are commonly danced by people from rural Greece "where often the foot-stamping dances were performed during the Ottoman domination as means of defiantly continuing Greek culture and asserting the Greekness of the dancers and performers."[36] One of the most popular country dances is the *tsamikos*, first danced by the *Kleftes* (Greek revolutionary warriors) who fought the Turkish conquerors. The dance is done in circular fashion with hands linked. It is usually led by men "who kick high in the air and slap their shoes as they kick, expressing their desire to fly away from the earth."[37]

Other popular dances include the *hasapikos*, first danced by the butchers of the Byzantine era, and the *hasaposervikos*, which involves staccato steps. Both dances originated in Greek taverns where men tradi-

James Condon family in Greece, 1895 or 1896. The Condons later settled in Calgary. (Glenbow-Alberta Institute)

Greek priests arriving at Quebec. (Public Archives Canada)

Greek immigrant arriving at Union Station, Toronto, in 1959, one of 300 Greek and Italian immigrants who arrived onboard the Olympia. *(Globe and Mail)*

ΧΑΡΑΚΤΗΡΙΣΤΙΚΑ
SIGNALEMENTS

Συζύγου — Femme

Ἐπάγγελμα / Profession

Τόπος καὶ χρόνος γεννήσεως / Lieu et date de naissance

Διαμονή / Domicile

Πρόσωπον / Visage

Χρῶμα ὀφθαλμῶν / Couleur des yeux

Χρῶμα κόμης / Couleur des cheveux

Ἰδιαίτερα σημεῖα / Signes particuliers

Φωτογραφία / Photo

Ὑπογραφὴ κατόχου
Signature du titulaire
καὶ τῆς συζύγου
et de sa femme

ΥΠΟΓΡΑΦΗ ΤΟΥ ΧΟΡΗΓΗΣΑΝΤΟΣ ΤΟ ΔΙΑΒΑΤΗΡΙΟΝ ΥΠΑΛΛΗΛΟΥ
SIGNATURE DE L'AGENT DELIVRANT LE PASSEPORT

ΤΕΚΝΑ — ENFANTS

Ὄνομα / Nom | Ἡλικία / Age | Γένος / Sexe

Passport of Peter Economopoulos, who emigrated to Canada in 1951. (Multicultural History Society of Ontario)

Like many Greek immigrants, Peter Economopoulos found work in a lumber camp while establishing himself in Canada. (Multicultural History Society of Ontario)

Interior of the Mount Royal Tea Room, Calgary, operated by James Condon, 1913, and located at 14th Street near 17th Ave., S.W. (Glenbow-Alberta Institute)

Childs Grocers Co. storefront, 144 Queen St. East, Toronto, 1916. (Multicultural History Society of Ontario)

The International Barber Shop in Montreal, 1967, catering to the Greek trade. (National Film Board)

The Regent, Montreal, which offered cultural events in the Greek language to immigrants in 1967. (National Film Board)

*King George II of Greece inspecting a Guard of Honour,
the Black Watch of Canada, June 30, 1942, Montreal.
(Public Archives Canada)*

*King George II of Greece met at Windsor Station,
Montreal, June 28, 1942. (Public Archives Canada)*

Rev. John Karapanegiotis and family, Greece, 1940, in the George Karry (Karapanegiotis) family album, Windsor. (Multicultural History Society of Ontario)

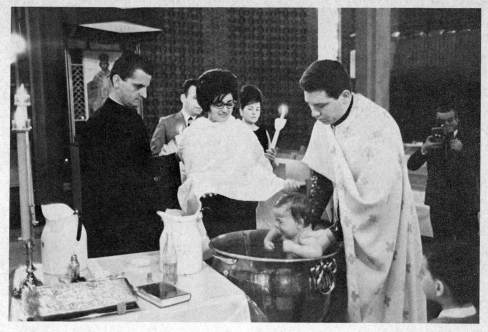

View of a Greek Orthodox baptism, Montreal, Quebec, 1967. (National Film Board)

Greek Orthodox priests conducting the Passover celebrations, Montreal, 1967. (National Film Board)

Independence Day Celebration, March 25, 1933. (Multicultural History Society of Ontario)

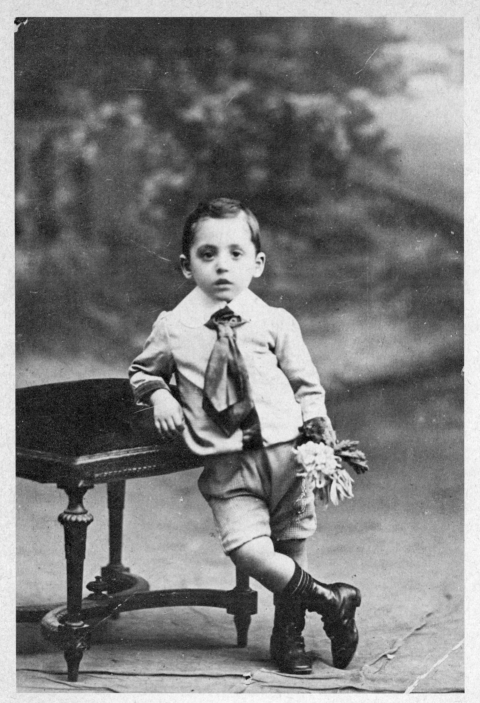

Portrait from the album of Mrs. Mary Marmon (nee Kartali) c. 1912.
(Multicultural History Society of Ontario)

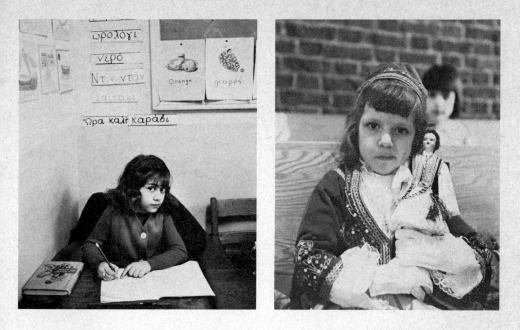

Various scenes from the Hellenic-Canadian School, and Montreal, 1967.
(National Film Board)

Native dancers celebrate the Greek Independence Day, Toronto, 1959. (Public Archives Canada)

Singer Katy Stergiani and guitarist Minas Katzalis at a concert celebrating Greek Independence Day, Toronto, 1959 (above); and Greek Orthodox Youth of America Dance group, Winnipeg, 1960 (below). (Public Archives Canada)

A Greek wedding reception in 1920. (Multicultural History Society of Ontario)

First gathering of all Greeks in Calgary, 1926. (Glenbow-Alberta Institute)

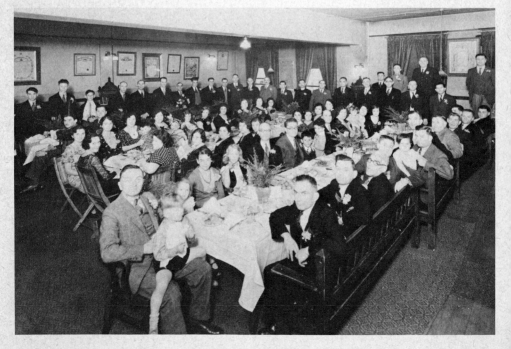

tionally gathered to eat, drink and talk.[38] These dances, like the *zembekiko*, require enthusiastic expression and systematic complex steps on the part of the dancers.

In the Greek communities of Montreal, Toronto, and Vancouver there are several organized Greek dance groups. The dancers are first or second generation Greek-Canadian youth of both sexes. The groups perform at ethnic festivals, Greek community functions and occasionally in ethnic television programmes. Traditional national and regional Greek costumes, often made by hand in Greek-Canadian homes, are worn by the dancers.

Greek Canadians are also fond of smaller gatherings such as namedays. According to Greek custom, a Greek Orthodox Christian celebrates the day of the patron saint after whom he was named. The most commonly given names are those of St. Constantine, St. Demetrios, St. George, St. Nicholas, St. John and St. Peter. Female patron saints are numerous and form an integral part of Greek Orthodoxy's deity structure, and the nameday celebrations of Greek women are as important as those of men.

Nameday celebrations consist of relatives and friends visiting the person being honoured to congratulate him or her with wishes of *chronia polla* ("many returns of years"). Congratulations are extended to the namesake's spouse, children and other close relatives. On such occasions the sentiments of family solidarity are strengthened and recreated.

Apart from these ethno-religious celebrations many Greeks entertain themselves in Greek nightclubs that are found in cities with large populations of Greek Canadians. In the nightclubs one may enjoy Greek food and Greek folk dances and folk music. The bands usually come from Greece and the *bouzouki* dominates the scene. When *bouzouki* music plays, the audience come to *Kefi* (musical euphoria) and some get up and dance the *zembekiko* (solo dance) with nostalgic vigour. This is the dance popularized in the Kazantzakis novel and movie *Zorba the Greek*, and it requires considerable energy and artistic and passionate expression.

Another social activity for some Greek Canadians is soccer. With the influx of many young Greeks after the 1950s, Greek soccer teams were founded in Canadian cities with large Greek-Canadian populations. They consisted mainly of young Greeks who had previously played soccer in Greece. The players are usually not professional athletes, but students or workers who join the team for sport or nationalistic purposes. Lambrou indicates, for example, that the Greek soccer team of Vancouver, the "Greek Olympics," is associated with Greek cultural identity. Accordingly, "to support the team is not only to be involved in an athletic institution but also to support the Greek culture, church and tradition."[39]

The only Greek soccer team in Canada that employs full-time professional players is the Panhellenic team in Toronto. Up to the late 1970s it was the only Greek-Canadian team that had participated in the National

Soccer League of Canada. Some of the players have been imported from Greece and others are part-time professionals.

Generally, the soccer teams are sponsored by sports-minded Greek-Canadian businessmen and other interested persons and the names given to the teams reflect Greek cultural tradition, including Apollo, Hellas, Hercules, Homer and Olympians. The games are usually held on Saturdays and Sundays and the matches involved two Greek soccer teams or a Greek and a non-Greek team. Other organized sport activities sponsored by the Greek-Canadian communities include basketball and hockey, as well as track and field.

Soccer is relatively new and steadily growing in Greek-Canadian communities. Whether it will continue to thrive depends on the number of young Greek immigrants entering Canada who either play or are interested in soccer, and the efforts of Greek communities to mobilize the interest of the second-generation Greek Canadians. It can be expected, however, that since soccer is becoming more popular in Canada more young Greek Canadians will become involved.

INTRAETHNIC CONFLICT

Of all the popular misconceptions about ethnic minorities in Canada, perhaps none exceeds the myth of ethnic solidarity. Greek Canadians, for example, have usually been perceived by outsiders as a cohesive, unified, co-operative group. However, internal conflict has existed within the Greek-Canadian community since its inception. Prior to World War II the Greek communities experienced only minor internal dissent and friction because they were still relatively small and traditionally oriented. Since 1950, however, when a new influx of Greek immigrants arrived in Canada, internal conflict has intensified. In the following pages an attempt will be made to examine the major factors which underlie most conflicts within the Greek-Canadian community. "Intraethnic conflict" refers to conscious dissociative forms of interaction within the ethnic community characterized by schisms, confrontations and hostilities. It involves a clash of interests, ideologies and values between or among groups of the ethnic community.

The Historical Role of the Church

Early sociologists of ethnic relations such as Thomas and Znaniecki looked up on the church in North America as the main unifying institution of the ethnic communities.[40] This observation, however, does not apply to the troubled Greek communities in Canada. Although the Greek Orthodox Church has shown strong devotion to traditional Greek culture and commitment to its ideals, many claim that the church's authoritarian structure and dominating influence have often exacerbated or even instigated conflict within the ethnic community. To understand the role of the church in ethnic life, and the ways in which the power of

the clergy has sometimes angered rather than unified the community, requires an historical perspective as well as contemporary sociological
analysis.

The political power of the Greek Orthodox Church leaders is deeply
rooted in the history of the Greek nation. During the period of Turkish
occupation (1453-1828) many Greek bishops were ethnarchs (governors).
They were not only spiritual but also political leaders of the enslaved
Greeks, this political mandate being assigned to them in 1454 by the
Sultan. The patriarch of the Ecumenical Patriarchate in Constantinople
became the head ethnarch (*millet-bashi* in Turkish) of the new politico-
religious domain. He acquired the *pronomia* (privileges) of administer-
ing, taxing and exercising justice over the Christians of the Turkish Empire. As Campbell and Sherrard indicate, the patriarch had far greater
power than he had possessed prior to the Turkish conquest, "a power extending not only over the Christians of his own Patriarchate but also
over those of other Orthodox Patriarchates and even over all non-
Orthodox Christians within the Ottoman Empire."[41]

Even after the independence of Greece in 1827, the Ecumenical
Patriarchate of Constantinople continued to serve as the head of the
Greek churches. But with the formation of the Kingdom of Greece in
1833 bishops of liberated Greece proclaimed the Greek church
autocephalus, breaking with its dependence on Constantinople. The new
Church of Greece acknowledged the King of Greece as supreme head in
governmental affairs but accepted the patriarch as a spiritual leader in
order to preserve its dogmatic unity with the Eastern Orthodox Church.[42]

The Greek churches in North America, however, continued to be
under the direct control of the Ecumenical Patriarchate until 1908.
Under a Patriarchal Decree, the Church of Greece was authorized to exercise jurisdiction over the Greek churches in North America, but it was
unable to provide the quality and organization needed at the time. In
1918 the Patriarch sent Archbishop Meletios of Athens to the United
States to establish a diocese as a central source of authority for the Greek
parishes. At first the efforts of Meletios yielded only frustrations as
Greek parishes were divided on political controversies going on in the
mother country.[43]

Not until 1921 did Meletios succeed in incorporating the Greek Orthodox Archdiocese of North and South America under the Religious
Corporation Law of New York State. When he became an Ecumenical
Patriarch in 1922 Meletios revoked the 1908 Patriarchal Decree and
restored the ecclesiastical authority and jurisdiction of the Patriarchate
over the Greek churches in North America. The same year (1922) the
Greek Archdiocese of North and South America was formally created
and its legal establishment ratified by the Patriarchate of Constantinople.[44] The archbishop acquired the highest ecclesiastical authority and
became responsible to the Patriarchate for the proper and effective administration and growth of the Archdiocesan institutions.[45] In the mean-

time the Church of Greece continued to provide Greek parishes in North and South America with priests, theologians and teachers.

Since the church was historically significant to Hellenism and its leaders had governmental experiences over Greek Christians it became the dominant force within the Greek communities in North America. Despite the challenges and criticisms by some parishioners, church leaders and their policies received much support from the conservative and traditionally oriented Greeks of the diaspora.

In understanding the administrative function of the church, it must be understood that the Greek Orthodox Church in Canada is not an independent ecclesiastical unit, but is a district of the Greek Archdiocese of North and South America with its headquarters in New York.[46] A report given in Ottawa in 1961 by Athenagoras, the acting Greek Orthodox bishop of Canada, clearly stated that Greek-Canadian parishes constitute a part of the Greek Archdiocese in New York and have to abide by the decisions of the clergy-laity conferences and contribute according to their membership to the financial support of the archdiocese as all other communities do in the United States.[47]

The administrative powers of the Greek clergy became stronger under the pastorship of Archbishop Iakovos. In 1964 the 17th Biennial Clergy-Laity Congress gave the Greek Orthodox clergy in North and South America unparalleled power over the administrative affairs of the ethno-religious community.[48] On March 31, 1971, in a speech to parishioners of the Holy Trinity Greek Orthodox Church in New York City, Archbishop Iakovos claimed that during his 12 years of pastorship he had raised the status of the priests by providing them with more administrative powers: "I provided the priests with more rights and responsibilities and appointed them to be the heads of the communities and not community clerks as were previously considered, and unfortunately still are, in some isolated cases."[49] The expansion of the administrative power of the clergy has been seen by many Greek Canadians as contributing to conflict within the Greek-Canadian communities.

The priest, by virtue of his ecclesiastical appointment, has been the head of the parish (*parikia*), a position which involves civic as well as spiritual leadership. According to the Uniform Parish Regulations of the Greek Orthodox Archdiocese:

> Each parish shall be administered by the priest and the parish council. The priest as a head of the parish, and by virtue of the ecclesiastical authority vested in him, shall guide and oversee the total parish program and is ultimately responsible for the whole life and activities of the parish.[50]

The regulations of the archdiocese also indicate that the parish council, which consists of elected church members, is responsible for conducting "all parish affairs in keeping with the aims and purposes of the Greek Orthodox Faith."[51] However, the clergy exercise great influence upon the parish council. For example, an election for parish council must be first verified in writing by the parish priest and then ratified by the Greek Orthodox Archdiocese in New York.[52]

The centralized authority of the priest has been resented by many Greek Canadians who see it as unnecessary intervention in the civic affairs of the Greek community. The clergy, however, argue that by virtue of their ecclesiastical authority they are expected to play important leadership roles and participate in decision and policy making. Thus, the ecclesiastical dominance on one hand and the demand for civic administration on the other have resulted in community conflict. For example, conflicts may arise over decisions regarding the hiring of a Greek school teacher, building a new church, approving candidates for council, or organizing school committees. These encounters usually divide the ethnic community into two conflicting groups, the priest and his "supporters" on one hand and some council members and other parishioners on the other. The supporters are usually traditionally-oriented members of the church, sympathetic to ecclesiastical authority. At times, however, the priest finds himself trying to please both his ecclesiastical superiors and those parishioners who form the opposition.

When the conflicting parties of the ethnic community are unable to resolve certain conflicts, such as whether to dismiss a priest or not, the matter is referred to an auxiliary bishop whose decision when confirmed by the archdiocese is deemed to be final.[53] The results of such referrals have not been always satisfactory to the parties concerned and the conflict may persist.

As noted earlier, conflicts within the Greek communities became more prevalent after World War II. This is mainly due to the fact that post-war Greek immigrants were generally better educated and more liberal ideologically and thus more prepared to challenge the traditional authority of the clergy. Since the early 1960s, leaders from the Greek communities of Montreal and Toronto have taken a strong position challenging the authority of the clergymen in community affairs.[54] The following statement made by the president of the Greek Community of Metropolitan Toronto Inc., Dr. L. Polymenakos, reflects the stance taken by many Greek Canadians toward clergy authority:

> The matter for us is very simple. We do not intervene in religious or ecclesiastical matters. We have never been entangled in dogmatic disputes with the clergy of our own church whom we respectfully recognized as spiritual leaders. Neither we intend to do so in the future. However, we are not disposed to accept open or covert intervention in the purely civic matters of our community.[55]

The objection to the administrative power of the Greek clergy by many Greek Canadians in Vancouver was published in an *Hellenic Echo* editorial. The following quotation describes the demand for change within the power structure of the Greek community in Vancouver:

Don't you think that the time has passed when priests and the Holy Archdiocese of North and South America involved themselves in affairs that were not in accordance to their religious duties? The only thing we want from you is advice and guidance and not orders.[56]

The leaders of the Greek church, on the other hand, continue to insist that the ethnic community is purely an ecclesiastical organization. For example, Bishop Sotirios of the Greek Orthodox Church in Canada stated of the Greek community in Toronto:

The Greek community is not a civic organization; it is purely an ecclesiastical organization which unreservedly and irrevocably is under the jurisdictions of the Greek Orthodox Church of North and South America. It is perfectly natural, therefore, for church leadership to demand from the Greek Community of Metropolitan Toronto Inc. to comply with church regulations. The problems of the Greek Community of Metropolitan Toronto Inc. will be solved only when the community itself consciously accepts the fact that it is an ecclesiastical organization.[57]

The remarks of Bishop Sotirios undoubtedly reflect the policies and objectives of the Greek Orthodox Archdiocese. The *Orthodox Observer* (an official newspaper of the Greek Orthodox Archdiocese) has explicitly stated that the function of the Greek Orthodox Church in North America cannot be confined to the religious sphere. In order to survive, the church must continue to play its traditional political function as well:

Those who demand that the church not concern herself with politics as neither more nor less than that the church in the New World limit herself to the functions of custodian of the temple, that she sway from leadership and become a tagger-along; that she cease providing direction to her congregation and devote herself to the issuance of baptismal and marriage certificates and to the oration of funeral eulogies. In reality, however, the church would deliver only the funeral eulogies of the omogenia, if she follow such advice. For it is impossible for her to survive anywhere, much more so it is impossible for the Greek Orthodox Church to survive in the Americas, if she is not a living institution, dynamic and inspired, leader and saviour. In other words, if she is not the Body of Christ.[58]

The various points of view mentioned above reflect the antagonism within the structure of the Greek-Canadian communities. There has been a slowly growing movement for one autonomous civic administration to deal with the complex problems of the modern ethnic communities. The leaders of the church, however, have resisted civic autonomy, fearing that the ethno-religious community will become more secularized and eventually lose its cultural identity. On the other hand, the Greek Orthodox archdiocese, according to the critics, is concerned about losing the economic and political advantages it has enjoyed since its establishment. Such critics note the control over the affairs of the ethnic community by the clergy and the fact that the archdiocese secures an annual contribution of seven per cent of the gross income of each Greek-Canadian parish.[59] The archdiocesan council also has the power to suspend or otherwise discipline a parish for its failure to meet its archdiocesan financial obligations.[60]

Critics also complain that the archbishop, as the head of the Greek Orthodox people in North America, holds strong political leverage within the American political system. His conservative political leadership has been welcomed by some Americans and supported by the conservative governments of Athens. That leaders of the Greek Orthodox Church in North America did not protest against the 1967-1974 right-wing dictatorship in Greece has been cited as indicative of such conservatism. One Greek-Canadian newspaper expressed the anger of many when it criticized the archbishop for paying a visit to Athens in 1968 to discuss with Junta leaders issues of concern to both parties.[61]

The traditional right of the Greek clergy to take political initiatives has been protested by many prominent leaders of the Greek ethnic group who believe that such powers are not functional in contemporary North American Greek communities. One ex-president of the Greek organization AHEPA has stated that since the Greeks are not enslaved they do not need an ethnarch, and that if the clergy want to be political leaders they must submit themselves to the ballot.[62]

The administrative power of the clergy has not been maintained in the home society. In contemporary Greece, the clergy are excluded from participating in civic matters. The role of the priest in contemporary Greece has been described by McNall:

> For one thing, under the Turks, the priest was the Greek village government, a role now, of course, assumed by the elected village councils. Then as schools were introduced, a second source of leadership came to the village. Once responsible for religion, government, and education, the church is now responsible only for religion. Under the Turks it was not infrequent for the priest to act as an arbitrator between the Greek community and the Turkish powers. The church also controlled some basic economic resources that could be distinguished, making the priest, for all practical purposes a patron. He is so no longer.[63]

It may also be argued that as a result of Turkish domination (including the political power of the ethnarchs) and the political instability of exploitative governments, the Greeks have become suspicious and mistrustful of politico-religious bureaucracies. Such political experiences have led the Greeks "to rely more closely on the family and kinship as one's relatives were often the only persons he could trust."[64] These characteristics of the Greek value system which emerged during a long

93

period of political suppression were carried to Canada and have hindered to some degree the solidarity of the Greek-Canadian community.

The conflicts between the clergy and some leaders of the Greek-Canadian community have been brought to the attention of the Greek government. For example, in 1964 Greek-Canadian leaders of Toronto made formal complaints to the government of Athens regarding the intervention of the clergy in the civic affairs of the community. The liberal government of George Papandreou endorsed the complaints and asked church officials to restrain the clergy. After the fall of Papandreou's government in July, 1965, direct government influence over the church seemed to wane. With the subsequent accession of the military dictatorship to power (1967-1974) co-operative relations between church leaders and the new regime were observed.[65]

The seriousness of conflicts based on the traditional power of the clergy varies from one community to another. The Greek communities of Montreal and Toronto have experienced the most crucial conflicts, resulting in court involvements, interpersonal violence between individuals and groups, and the establishment of administratively "independent" churches. The buildings of such churches are owned mainly by the parishioners either through the form of no-share capital corporation or through nominated (or elected) trustees. The priests for these churches are appointed by the bishop with the approval of the Greek Orthodox archdiocese in New York. The congregation pays the salary to the priest and in addition submits the annual contribution to the archdiocese. The administrative councils or boards of directors of these churches conform to the Uniform Parish Regulations and have no objection to being under the jurisdiction and authority of the archdiocese. These churches appeared mainly in Toronto, but are not under the administrative auspices of the Greek community of Metropolitan Toronto Inc. According to some Greek-Canadian church critics, the establishment of the "independent" churches was part of the archdiocese's "divide and rule" policy aimed at maintaining church power in the community.

According to some critics, conflicts between members of the ethnic community and the clergy have in part occurred because of the latter's lack of preparation for leadership. The clergymen who come from Greece to serve in Canada were brought up in Greece, educated in Greek theological schools, and had little knowledge of the English language or Canadian culture. Some of them had served for a short time in American parishes before they were assigned to Greek communities in Canada. Saloutos, in discussing the difficulties experienced by the Greek clergymen who came to Greek-American communities, writes:

> The clergymen, qualified or unqualified, had adjustment problems of their own. The transition from Greek rural to an American industrial environment comprised of people of many ethnic groups

and religious backgrounds, posed many difficulties. Greek Orthodoxy was a strange religion to the average American.[66]

Influenced then by their cultural background and traditional authority many of the Greek clergymen who came to Canada found it difficult to cope in their new environment. Their congregation consisted of urbanizing second-generation Greek Canadians who needed understanding and guidance in dealing with complex problems, post-World War II immigrants who were ideologically and academically prepared to challenge the authority of the church, "outsiders" who joined the ethno-religious community by marrying Greek Canadians, and university graduates who differed from the clergymen in their views about the social realities and problems of the Greek community. Neither were the clergymen adequately prepared to provide guidance or counselling to those confronted with marital and other familial problems. This situation created a communication gap and at times even resulted in hostilities between clergymen and parishioners.

On the other hand one should not conclude that priests were completely out of touch with the masses of Greek immigrants. Generally, the clergy shared the same socio-economic background as the majority of other immigrants and were not products of the elite. The clergy were also familiar with the political, social and economic problems experienced by post-World War II immigrants in the home society. Therefore, although in many ways Greek-Canadian clergy have been unprepared for their tasks, they have certain appropriate background experiences.

Much of the resentment has been directed towards the administrative power of the clergy and not at the Greek Orthodox religious institution as whole. Greeks proudly view Greek Orthodoxy as an integral part of their cultural inheritance. Faith and adherence to Greek Orthodoxy is considered an essential element of being Greek, or at least in identifying one's self with Greek culture and civilization. To illustrate this connection, authorities such as Irwin T. Sanders remind us that the coming of Greek Orthodoxy did not necessarily create a break with certain cultural and religious beliefs of ancient Greece. The deities of ancient Greece became the saints of Greek Orthodoxy.[67] It was ancient Greek philosophers such as Plato and Aristotle that provided the philosophical basis of the theology of Greek Orthodox theologians and other church fathers. Saint Basil, a theologian of Greek Orthodoxy, was influenced by the writings and ideas of Plato, Demosthenes and Xenophon.[68]

The conflict between clergymen and civic leaders may be a stimulus for important social changes. Without challenges to the ecclesiastical power and without pressures to examine the immigrants' problems more realistically, the Greek community might not adjust to the rapidly changing Canadian society.

The Greek Orthodox Church in Canada will probably continue to be an integral part of the Greek community's life through the performance of its religious functions and the propagation of traditions, values and ideals of Greek culture. On the other hand, the influence of the clergy on lay affairs may decline with the establishment of more non-sectarian associations and the entrance of influential young Greek Canadians into the community's administrative positions.

Change in Religious Doctrine

Since the Greek minority in Canada is an ethno-religious group, any change within the church inevitably affects the entire Greek community. For instance, in the 1960s Old Calendar churches appeared in the major Greek-Canadian communities.[69] In 1966 Father Akaikos and a group of parishioners split from the Greek Orthodox parish in Montreal and established an Old Calendar church. In 1969 a similar split occurred in Toronto when another Old Calendar church was established under the leadership of Father Karras. By 1976 there were five Old Calendar churches, three in Montreal and two in Toronto, and one missionary parish in London, Ontario, serving approximately 2,000 Greek-Canadian families. These churches were under the auspices of the Russian Orthodox Church outside of Russia[70] or the Church of the True Christians of Greece.

The transfer of allegiance of Greek clergy in Canada to the Old Calendar Church was in large part a response to the ideological and secular changes which were occurring within the Greek Orthodox Church at that time. For example, in 1965 Patriarch Athenagoras I in Constantinople (Istanbul) and Pope Paul VI in Rome simultaneously lifted the excommunication[71] which for an entire millennium had weighed heavily on Orthodox-Roman Catholic relations.[72] This change meant that the Greek Orthodox Church was becoming "ideologically tolerant" of Catholicism. On the other hand changes in the appearance of the priest (e.g., the casual suit and shaved beard) and the shortening of the liturgy indicated a trend toward secularization and more similarity with other non-Greek Orthodox churches in Canada. These changes, according to the Greek priests of the Old Calendar movement, presented a threat to the traditional Holy Orthodoxy. The main objective of the movement then was to preserve the traditional Holy Orthodoxy in a secular and rapidly changing Canadian society.

The followers of the movement were mainly Greek immigrants from various occupational backgrounds and geographical regions of Greece. Although some had been followers of the Old Calendar Church in Greece, others were ex-members of the new calendar churches (Greek Orthodox Churches) in Canada.[73]

Religious polarization had created some resentment and hostility between the two religious factions. For example, after the split the Greek Orthodox community of Toronto would not allow the children of Old Calendar parents to attend its Greek-language schools unless the children were baptized in the new calendar church. In certain instances kinship solidarity was affected when some families joined the Old Calendar Church and related families maintained their membership with the new calendar church. This caused some disruption in "get together" familial occasions such as celebrations of namedays and religious holidays.[74]

The Old Calendar parishes have been described by their spiritual leaders as relatively stable organizations, operating their own Greek-language schools and sponsoring various social activities. Their economic and social support has been based on "free will" offerings from the parishioners. Although the Old Calendar parishes do not, in the eyes of Canadians, represent the Greek communities of Montreal and Toronto, their members identify with Greek ethnicity and many belong to various nonsectarian associations.

Competition for Administrative Status

Some conflict within the Greek community emerges in electoral competition for administrative positions. The candidates try to gain electoral support from relatives, friends, business associates and compatriots who came from the same region in Greece, while at the same time trying to undermine their competitors. Greek TV and newspapers also play an important role in supporting candidates.

In the struggle for administrative power the "old timers" (pre-World War II immigrants) have frequently shown resentment towards the new immigrants. The newcomers, younger and better educated, are perceived as a threat to the established administrations. For example, in Montreal the administrative elite passed by-laws prohibiting newcomers from voting unless they had been members of the community for at least three consecutive years prior to the election.[75] However, the new immigrants eventually obtained the administrative posts. In 1976 the elected council members of the Greek communities in Montreal and Toronto were mainly post-World War II immigrants or second-generation Greek Canadians.

One might ask what leads certain Greek Canadians to compete for administrative positions. There is no doubt that while some of the candidates are prompted by patriotism or philanthropy, others compete for personal gain or interests. These reasons may include status as in the case of the successful but uneducated small businessman who craves social recognition and indirect promotion for his business (e.g. restaurant). Some professionals (lawyers, physicians) and large businessmen attempt to enter administrative positions in order to establish rapport with prospective clientele of the ethnic community.

Old Country Politics and Regionalism

The unity of Greek Canadians has always been affected by their political experiences and the internal political strife of the home society. When the Greeks came to Canada they brought their political beliefs and rivalries with them. In the new society where they found freedom to express political ideologies, the Greeks revived their old hostilities. At times, community meetings, ethnic celebrations and entertainments became battlegrounds for debating Old World political issues. A detail discussion of Old Country politics and their effects upon Greek-Canadian communities is found in Chapter Six.

Another source of political activity in Greek-Canadian communities stems from the regionalism of the homeland. A small percentage of immigrants who came to Canada did not identify themselves with Greek culture and the Greek community. These Macedonians, as they are called, were born in Greek Macedonia (northern Greece) but had no allegiance to Greece. They preferred to identify themselves with the Macedonian nation which unofficially consists of northern Greece, southwestern Bulgaria and southern Serbia.[76] Some of them who had served in the Greek armed forces during the 1950s came to Canada and identified themselves as Macedonians. They belong to Yugoslav organizations and attend the churches of the Autocephalus Church of Yugoslav Macedonia (Federative People's Democracy of Macedonia). The majority of the Greek Macedonians, that is, those who were born in Greece and consider themselves as Greeks, are reluctant to admit their regional origin for fear of being identified as Macedonian. The fact that some insist they are Macedonians while others from the same part of Greece refer to themselves as Greeks creates problems of terminology. For example, a Canadian ethnic directory[77] lists the Pan-Macedonian Association (a Greek association) under Macedonian Associations and Establishments in Canada. In recent years, however, an effort has been made by the Greek Community of Metropolitan Toronto Inc. to establish a terminology by adding the ethnic allegiance of the parties concerned: Greek Macedonian, Bulgarian Macedonian, or Yugoslav Macedonian.

Due to their historic adventures and hardships the Greek Macedonians have developed strong patriotic sentiments. While the ethnicity and state allegiance of other Greeks from the Peloponnesus and from mainland Greece was taken for granted, the Greek Macedonians during the last 80 years had to fight for their ethnicity against Bulgarian expansionism and in recent years against the political confusion created by the Skopje propaganda. In Canada they belong to their local associations such as the Pan-Macedonian Association, identify themselves with Hellenism and contribute to the social and economic welfare of the Greek community.

Another important aspect of the Macedonian dilemma involves the ethno-cultural claims by the pro-Bulgarian Macedonian immigrants. Historically, these immigrants were Slavs with Bulgarian allegiance who lived in areas liberated by Greece during the Balkan Wars (1912-1913) but who later emigrated to Bulgaria. It seems that these immigrants were not satisfied with the socio-economic conditions in Bulgaria and in the early 1920s began emigrating to Canada with settlements mainly concentrated in Ontario. They speak the Slavic Macedonian language which is a Bulgarian dialect with Greek and Slavic admixtures.

Although these immigrants came to Canada on Bulgarian passports, in their social and economic transactions with Canadians they identified themselves as Macedonians. This ethno-cultural claim has not been accepted by leaders of the Greek communities who believe that the ethnic group called Macedonians is an ethnological and linguistic hoax. They contend that the area from which the pro-Bulgarian Macedonians originated was never a Macedonian nation and that the population of the ancient kingdom of Macedonia was largely Greek speaking.[78] Organoff, from his analysis of the Soviet Encyclopedia dealing with the Macedonian question, concludes that "only in ancient Macedonia were there Macedonians in the ethnic and linguistic sense of the word."[79] He further argues that "no one and at no time ever proved the existence of a Macedonian nation or a Macedonian language."[80]

More importantly, however, Greek Canadians have been irritated by the expansionistic aims of the pro-Bulgarian Macedonians. During the last four decades the pro-Bulgarian Macedonians who came to North America, including southern Ontario, have initiated strong propaganda for the creation of an autonomous Macedonia comprising large portions of the areas belonging to Bulgaria, Greece and Yugoslavia, with the ultimate purpose of either becoming an independent state or being incorporated into Bulgaria. These ambitious plans have been viewed by Greece and the Greek communities in Canada as provocative.[81]

In conclusion, the Greek community in Canada has been organized around the church and various secular organizations. These organizations have had varying degrees of success in attempting to help Greek Canadians cope with the demands of modern Canadian society. The Greek community has experienced various conflicts based primarily on divergent political leanings, ethnic regionalism, opposing concepts of the role of the church, competition for power positions within the communities, and a rift between young, recent immigrants and their older predecessors. Nevertheless these problems are not beyond resolution and it is not unrealistic to expect a more tightly-knit Greek-Canadian national community in the future.

NOTES

1. In this analysis the term "parish" is used interchangeably with "community" (*kinotis*).
2. William I. Thomas and Florian Znaniecki, *The Polish Peasant in Europe and America*, Vol. V. (Boston: The Gorman Press, 1920), p. 41.

3. Theodore Saloutos, *The Greeks in the United States* (Cambridge Mass.: Harvard University Press, 1964), p. 122.

4. Scott G. McNall, *The Greek Peasant* (Washington, D.C.: A.S.A. Rose Monograph Series, 1976), p. v.

5. Saloutos, *op. cit.,* pp. 121-126.

6. The term "community" is used interchangeably with "parish." It constitutes an ethno-religious entity since Greek Orthodoxy plays an important role defining the Greek-Canadian minority in Canada.

7. The first Greek Orthodox Church of the Annunciation was opened in Montreal on December 16, 1910.

8. For more detailed information on the founding of Greek churches in Canada see Athenagoras of Elaia, *The Greek Church in Canada* (Toronto: Greek Orthodox Community, 1961).

9. Takis Petritis, "The Early Greek Immigrants in Canada," in *Afieroma* (Montreal: Cretan Association of Montreal, 1972-73), p. 11.

10. Active membership implies the annual payment of dues which entitles the member to certain rights and privileges such as attending regular and special community meetings, voting therein, and being elected a member or an office holder in the community council. Those who are not paid-up members identify themselves with Greek Orthodoxy and attend church services.

11. Any person of Greek origin, of paternal and/or maternal line who has attained his 18th birthday and who has been baptized according to the canons of the Eastern Orthodox Church is eligible for membership.

12. Approximately 95% of Greek Canadians are affiliated to some degree with the Greek Orthodox Church.

13. This refers to the highest governing authority of the Greek Orthodox Church in America deriving its authority from the ecumenical Patriarchate of Constantinopole. Certain Greek communities (e.g., Montreal and Toronto) have established themselves as corporations with constitutions which limit the power of the archdiocese over the administrative affairs of the community.

14. Campaign leaflets of St. George Greek Orthodox Cathedral, Montreal, 1976.

15. For more detailed information on the objectives of GOYA, see "Guidelines for Youth Adult Program" (New York: Greek Orthodox Archdiocese of North and South America, 1975).

16. The Pan-Hellenic Union was first organized in New York city in the autumn of 1907 by presidents of local Greek societies.

17. Saloutos, *op. cit.,* p. 248.

18. George A. Kourvetaris, "The Greek American Family," in *Ethnic Families in America*, eds., Charles H. Mindel and Robert W. Habenstein (New York: Elsevier, 1976), p. 172.

19. George Leber, *The History of the Order of AHEPA* (Washington, D.C.: The Order of AHEPA, 1972) pp. 147-149.

20. *Ibid.,* pp. 478-482.

21. George C. Vournas, "The Tragedy of Cyprus," *Journal of the Hellenic Diaspora*, Vol. 1 (November, 1974), p. 45.

22. See newsletter of the Hellenic Canadian Cultural Society, September 6, 1974, Toronto, Ontario.

23. Local organizations refers to those "societies," "associations" or "brotherhoods" consisting of members from a particular locality (e.g. village or town) in the home society.

24. Other nonsectarian organizations which had been established to deal with common problems of Greek immigrants were the Coordinating Committee of Social Services for the Greek Community of Montreal, Greek-Canadians National Neighborhood and the Federation des Societes Grecques Unie de Montreal.

25. For more detailed discussion of the latent functions of Greek formal organizations see Mary Treudley, "Formal Organizations and the Americanization Process," *American Sociological Review*, Vol. 14 (February, 1949), pp. 44-53.

26. Textbooks for the Greek schools in Canada have been made available free of charge by the Greek Ministry of Education.

27. K.G. O'Bryan *et. al., Non-Official Languages: A Study in Canadian Multiculturalism* (Ottawa: Thorn Press Ltd., 1976), p. 136.

28. Dr. A. Fousias, interview published in *Greek Canadian Weekly*, Toronto, 1976, p. 1 (translation).

29. The estimated number of children attending Greek schools in Canada is based on interviews with leaders of various Greek communities.

30. Saloutos, *op. cit.,* pp. 78-83.

31. *Ibid.,* p. 82.

32. See G. James Patterson, *The Greeks of Vancouver* (Ottawa: Canadian Centre for Folk Culture Studies, 1976), pp. 33-35.

33. Yianna Lambrou, *The Greek Community of Vancouver: Social Organization and Adaptation.* Unpublished M.A. Thesis, University of British Columbia, 1975, p. 71.

34. Patris, *Greek Canadian Weekly* (Vancouver), March 25, 1978, p. 2.

35. Ruth McKenzie, "The Study of the Greeks in Canada," *Citizen*, Vol. 9 (June, 1963), p. 12.

36. G. James Patterson, *The Greeks of Vancouver: A Study in the Preservation of Ethnicity* (Ottawa: National Museum of Man, Canadian Centre for Folk Culture Studies, 1976), p. 78.

37. *Ibid.,* p. 79.

38. *Ibid.,* p. 79.

39. Lambrou, *op. cit.*, p. 133.

40. Thomas and Znaniecki, *op. cit.,* p. 41.

41. John Campbell and Philip Sherrard, *Modern Greece* (London: Ernest Benn Limited, 1969), p. 189.

42. Saloutos, *op. cit.,* pp. 118-120. See also Edwin S. Gaustad, *Historical Atlas of Religion in America*, (New York: Harper and Row, 1976), p. 120.

43. Arthur C. Peipkorn, *Profiles in Belief: The Religious Bodies of the United States and Canada,* Vol. 1 (New York: Harper and Row, 1977), pp. 64-66.

44. Stephanos Zotos, *Hellenic Presence in America,* (Wheaton, Illinois: Pilgrimage, 1976), pp. 201-202.

45. See *Charter of the Greek Orthodox Archdiocese of North and South America* (Brookline Mass.: Holy Cross Orthodox Press, 1978) pp. 1-3.

46. In May, 1979, the auxiliary bishop of the Canadian district was elevated to a full bishop.

47. See *The Greek Orthodox Church in Canada,* Report of His Eminence Metropolitan Athenagoras of Elaia, Toronto, 1961, p. 38.

48. The 17th Biennial Clergy-Laity Congress also made the archbishop the final arbiter in almost all disputes (see Saloutos, *op. cit.,* p. 372).

49. *The Greek Orthodox Observer*, New York, May, 1971, p. 28. (translation).

50. *Uniform Parish Regulations of the Greek Orthodox Archdiocese of North and South America* (New York: 1973), p. 13.

51. *Ibid.,* p. 18.

52. *Ibid.;* p. 20.

53. *Ibid.,* p. 23.

54. The Greek communities of Montreal and Toronto became incorporated with their own by-laws which have restricted the power of the priest. According to the by-laws of the Greek Canadian Community of Montreal, for example, the priest is only a spiritual leader and not the head of and the director of the parish as indicated in the Uniform Regulations of the archdiocese.

55. Dr. L. Polymenakos interview published in *Greek Canadian Weekly,* Toronto, October 22, 1976, p. 10 (translation).

56. *Hellenic Echo,* Vancouver, October 1, 1973.

57. Bishop Sotirios' interview published in *Greek Canadian Action,* Montreal, October, 1976, p. 1 (translation).

58. See the editorial in *The Orthodox Observer,* New York, September 17, 1975.

59. It should be noted that the annual contribution to the archdiocese is used for organizational costs and maintenance of theological schools, religious publications and philanthropic institutions.

60. Uniform Parish Regulations, *op. cit.,* p. 25.

61. *Neos Kosmos,* Toronto, March 7, 1968, p. 8.

62. Peter L. Bell, "The Cyprus Battle," *Chicago Pnyx,* September 1, 1975, p. 7.

63. McNall, *op. cit.,* p. 66.

64. *Ibid.,* p. v.

65. Information is based on interviews with Greek-Canadian leaders from Toronto who at the time were directly involved in the issue.

66. Saloutos, *op. cit.,* p. 129.

67. Irwin T. Sanders, *Rainbow in the Rock: The People of Rural Greece* (Cambridge, Mass.: Harvard University Press, 1962), p. 259.

68. N.G. Wilson, *Saint Basil and the Value of Greek Literature* (London: Duckworth, 1975), p. 13.

69. The New Calendar (Gregorian Calendar) was legally introduced in Greece in 1923. This evoked strong opposition by traditionalist clergy who adhered to the Old Calendar (Julian Calendar). Thus, the Old Calendarists (*palaioimerologitai*) broke off communion with the official church and in consequence suffered persecution and discrimination by the Greek government. See Piepkorn, *op. cit.,* p. 66.

70. The Russian Orthodox Church Outside of Russia has refused to recognize the patriarchate of Moscow on the ground that the Soviet government completely controls the patriarchate. Bishop Petros of the Old Calendar Orthodox Church of Greece is in full communion with the Russian Orthodox Church episcopate in Santiago, California. See Piepkorn, *op. cit.,* p. 66.

71. In July, 1054, a mutual excommunication was exchanged by Michael Cecularius (Patriarch of Constantinople) and the Bishop of Rome, St. Leo IX. According to some historians this event occasioned the final break between the established church of the Byzantine Empire and the Western Roman Empire. The schism was mainly based on political events of the eleventh century such as the military aggression of the Normans, the commercial aggression of the Italian maritime cities, and the movements of the Crusades. See Steven Runciman, *The Eastern Schism* (Oxford: The Clarendon Press, 1963), pp. 28, 54, 159-170.

72. Theodore G. Stylianopoulos, "The Orthodox Church in America," *The Annuals of American Academy of Political and Social Science* (January, 1970), 387:47.

73. For more detailed information see *The Orthodox World* (Sacramento, California: Orthodox Christian Books and Icons, Vol. 4, No. 1, 1968), p. 29.

74. According to the Old Calendar Church, all religious holidays follow 13 days behind the new calendar.

75. Peter Stathopoulos, *The Greek Community of Montreal* (Athens: National Centre of Social Research, 1971), p. 30.

76. In 1944 Yugoslavia renamed one of its six republics, southern Serbia, as Federative People's Democracy of Macedonia with Scopje as capital. The objective of this Yugoslav plan was said to be to expand the new state by acquiring Greek Macedonia (northern Greece). However, the Yugoslav-backed Greek Communist revolutionaries (who theoretically had accepted the plan) were defeated in the 1946-1949 Civil War by the Greek pro-nationalists forces. See Th. Papacostantinou, "The Macedonian Myth," *Mesimvrini,* November 26, 1966.

77. See *Ethnic Directory of Canada,* compiled and edited by Professor Vladimir Markotic, University of Calgary, 1976.

78. *Encyclopedia Britannica,* 1970, Vol. 14, p. 510.
79. Christo Organoff, *Macedonska Tribuna,* January 15, 1976, p. 1.
80. *Ibid.,* p. 3.
81. Nicholas Andriotis, *The Federative Republic of Scopje and Its Language* (Athens, 1966), p. 55. According to Andriotis, "the Greeks have accepted the present ethnological reality in the Balkan peninsula and respect the new rights which history has created de facto in this part of the world. . . . They ask no more than their northern neighbours should themselves realize that the extent of provocation for which they have been responsible has reached the limit. There are limits which ought to be respected or else who could ever put an end to this vicious circle of mutual malice?"

FIVE

Family and Kinship

The need to examine some aspects of family life among Greek Canadians arises from the fact that in a multicultural society it is in the family that the distinctiveness of the ethnic group is or is not transmitted from one generation to the next. Family life in Greece, reflecting the Old World's values and institutions, shall be analyzed, and the demographic and social characteristics of the family in Canadian society shall be presented.

THE FAMILY IN GREECE

The family in contemporary Greece has been shaped by religious traditions, the rural nature of the country and the continuous political instability after the revolution of 1821. One of the greatest influence on the Greek family has been the Greek Orthodox Church. This is mainly due to the fact that Greece was occupied by Turkey from 1453 to 1821. During those four centuries of occupation the institution that managed not only to survive, but also to keep alive the Greek language and culture, was the church. The church remained strong, which explains why Greek Orthodoxy and Greek nationalism are almost inseparable.

The domination of contemporary Greece by a conservative and authoritarian church, especially in rural communities where the church has been a major source of social control, has contributed to the structure of the Greek family. For example, divorce and remarriage have been strongly discouraged by Greek Orthodoxy, and marriage is expected and even required by law to be a sacrament rather than simply a legal contract.

Historically, the strength of the Greek church has been its ability to reach the masses, especially the peasantry, and identify itself with them. The influence of the Greek church on family structure and relationships has been described by Campbell:

The family is also a religious community with its own "sacra" icons, and other objects. In the popular mind it is an earthly reflection of the Heavenly Family of God the Father, the Mother of God and Christ. Relations between members of a family ought to be modelled on the attitudes which, it is imagined, inspired the relations of the Heavenly archetype family and its members. A father ought to have wisdom and foresight, a mother compassion, a son courage and respect, a daughter virginity and so on.[1]

The agricultural economy of the country has also maintained certain characteristics of the extended family system. It was common, especially in the rural areas of Greece, to find extended families where aged parents were living with married children and their families. This family structure was suited to agricultural communities where the population consisted mainly of farmers or shepherds who needed the labour supplied by both children and grandparents. Although social change has affected family structure considerably, the care of the aged parents still remains a moral obligation for Greek children regardless of their socio-economic background and rural or urban residence. Children who have emigrated to Canada or other countries also provide financial support for their parents who were left behind.

One of the most important features of the Greek family has been its patriarchal and authoritarian nature. Generally, the women held a low status, marriages were arranged and the dowry system was dominant. The tradition of a male-dominated family structure is slowly disappearing among educated classes of Greek society, but still predominates among those with little formal education, and especially among the peasants.[2]

Another important aspect of the Greek family and kinship includes moral obligations based on family solidarity. Campbell, in his study of Greek family life in rural communities, found that "in the elementary family the principles of sibling solidarity and parental obligations are complementary and together guide its members in their duties and exclusive affections."[3] The solidarity within the kinship structure is reflected in the socio-psychological and economic support that kinsmen provided for each other when in need. Brothers are responsible for providing their sisters with dowry, aged parents are cared for by their adult children, and moral obligations are extended to relatives by marriage.

A prevalent value which influenced familial relationships in Greece was family honour. According to Campbell, "the intrinsic principles of honour refer to two sex-linked qualities that distinguish the ideal moral character of men and women: these are the manliness (*andrismos*) of men and the sexual shame (*entropi*) for women."[4] Members of the kinship structure were expected to show a strong commitment to family honour and defend it through physical violence if necessary. Campbell has observed:

Objectively . . . honour is an aspect of the integrity and social worth of the family as this is judged by the community; subjectively it represents the moral solidarity of the family, an ideal circle that must be defended against violation by outsiders.[5]

The above-mentioned family relationships and moral obligations were most pronounced and valued in Greek rural communities. However, the traditional features of the family are gradually decreasing under the influence of urbanization, technology and American and European contacts. The greatest changes have occurred in large urban communities such as Athens and Thessalonika.

Changes in the legal status of Greek women during the early 1950s have helped in the gradual modernization of the Greek family. In May, 1952, women were given full civil rights under the law and on April 1, 1953, Greece signed The International Convention on the Political Rights of Women of the United Nations. As a result of this and other social and political movements "the Greek woman is slowly but surely gaining her intellectual and spiritual freedom."[6] In 1975 the Greek Parliament adopted a constitution containing a clause that gave the two sexés equal rights and obligations. In 1976 a commission headed by Professor Andreas Gazis was appointed to draft new legislation which would eliminate sex discrimination and provide women with more equal status. According to proposed legislation:[7]

a) Men will be legally responsible for helping with house work and child care particularly if their wives are working.

b) Women will be responsible for contributing to the family's financial support.

c) Laws that discriminate on the question of work, pay and pensions will be eliminated.

d) There will be equal educational opportunities for both sexes at a higher level.

Equal opportunities for higher education in Greece have been improved in the 1970s. In 1976, for example, women accounted for about 50% of the students entering Greek universities, compared with about 25% in the early 1960s. Changes towards equal status for the sexes will, however, continue to be slow as long as Greece is dominated by conservative politico-economic institutions.

THE GREEK FAMILY IN CANADA

When the Greek immigrant came to Canada, he carried with him the customs and traditional beliefs of family life that he had learned in the home society. Upon his arrival he discovered that cherished ways of thought such as respect for elders, obedience to parents and teachers and male dominance were not observed by a great many Canadians, especially those from an Anglo-Saxon background. Greek Canadians have shown a relatively low degree of social integration into Canadian culture partly because their family life remains influenced by the home society's values and historical experiences. But as any immigrant participates in the socio-economic life of the host society his traditional ways of thinking cannot remain unaffected. Acculturation is a continuous social process and the immigrant slowly acquires the roles, values and lifestyles of his new society.

Size of Family

Immigrants who come from a traditional family system (characterized by an extended family structure with many children) often have large families. However, the size of the Greek family in Canada is smaller than the average in the general Canadian population. In 1971 only 18% of the Greek families in Canada consisted of five persons or more compared with 27% of families in the general Canadian population. (See Table 11)

The main reason for the differences in family size is that the Greek family had, on the average, fewer children than the family in the general Canadian population.[8] The smaller number of children may be due to the improvement of the Greek immigrants' economic status in Canada, since upwardly mobile couples tend to perceive children as economic liabilities. It could also be due to the fact that a large proportion of Greek-Canadian married couples are relatively young and thus their families are incomplete.

Family Dissolution

Leaders and clergymen of Greek-Canadian communities, especially smaller communities where most of the families are known to community leaders, report very few divorces and separations. According to Statistics Canada (see Table 12) the divorce rate amongst Greek Canadians is lower than that for the general population, though the difference is not statistically significant. (The lower percentage of widowed in 1971 is probably due to the relatively younger married Greek immigrant population.) No information is available on the rate of marital dissolution due to separations (non-legal and contractual) which have not culminated in formal divorce. We presume, however, that the strong familial ties and related traditional values serve to keep this rate low.

Divorce rates, of course, are not a precise index of serious marital conflict. Such conflict occurs in Greek marriages, but spouses who have been influenced by the Old Country's mores feel that divorce is a disgrace, and thus are more likely to put up with conflict rather than seek a divorce. Relatives at times may find it proper and necessary to intervene and advise in their children's, siblings' or even cousins' marital conflicts: intervention seems to be a moral imperative, and indicates, perhaps, the persistence of family obligations among Greek Canadians. It can

TABLE 11

**Families with Head of Greek Ethnic Origin
Compared to Families of the General Canadian Population,
By Size of Family 1971**

No. of Persons in Family	Greek Ethnic Group		General Canadian Population	
	Number	%	Number	%
2	6,985	23.2	1,591,600	31.4
3	7,840	26.0	1,046,375	20.6
4	9,815	32.6	1,056,925	20.8
5	4,135	13.5	662,855	13.1
6	995	3.3	358,645	7.1
7 or more	435	1.4	354,290	7.0
Total Families	30,135	100.0	5,070,685	100.0

Source: 1971 *Census of Canada,* Catalogue 93-714, Vol. II (Part II), June, 1973: Information for Greeks was specially processed for this study by Statistics Canada, August, 1974.

TABLE 12

**Percentages of Marital Dissolution of the Total Greek
and Canadian Married Population, 1971**

Marital Dissolution	Greek Ethnic Origin	General Canadian Population
Widowed	5.2	8.8
Divorced	1.3	1.7

Source: "Marital Status by Ethnic Group," 1971 *Census of Canada,* Catalogue 92-734, Vol. 1 (Part 4), February, 1974.

however, have negative consequences upon kinship relationships: intervention by relatives in marital conflicts can at times prevent reconciliation and lead to more serious family crises.

Kinship in the Host Society

In the home society the kindred[9] played an important role in the socio-economic survival of the Greek family. Kinsmen aided each other during family crises such as illness, loss of crops, or death, "matchmaking" negotiations, farm cultivation and the hostile environment of the Nazi occupation and the Civil War of 1946-49. In the new society the kindred are still considered important, as they provide each other with moral and socio-economic support in making adjustment to the new cultural setting. Established relatives who sponsored new immigrants in the 1950s and 1960s helped them to find homes and jobs, and reduced culture shock by providing a familial setting.

In business matters the immigrant has also looked to his relatives for economic assistance and co-operation. When the Greek immigrant needed a loan or a partner to open a restaurant he would turn to his relatives. Even the employees could be members of the immediate families or distant kinsmen. This interfamily co-operation accounts for the successful establishment of small businesses and spurs the upward social mobility of many Greek immigrants in Canada.

Economic support can also be extended to relatives in Greece. The Greek immigrants came to Canada not only to improve their own lives, but in many cases also to help relatives they left behind. Many immigrants, as soon as they acquire their first "fortune" in Canada, send clothing, food and financial aid to relatives back home. The money may be used to purchase a farm, start a business, remodel a house, or pay for the education of children.[10] Economic aid of this kind has always been welcomed, but was especially appreciated during the late 1940s and the 1950s when Greece was recovering from the economic catastrophes of World War II and the subsequent civil war. The economic support by Canadian and American Greek immigrants to their relatives at home, especially after World War II, has been an important factor in the improvement of the standard of living of many Greeks. Such improvement may have functioned as an insulator against potential political upheavals and Communist appeals. Similarly, the success of relatives in Canada and the vacation visits may encourage indigenous Greeks to model their political and economic structures on the democracies, as opposed to socialist and communist countries.

Solidarity among kinsmen can also be expressed at social events in which related families participate. The celebration of baptisms and namedays, for example, are occasions where exchange of personal wishes strengthen and renew kinship solidarity. To what extent social networks are extended to non-related families is not known, but immigrants who cannot speak the English language associate mainly with relatives, or at least with other Greeks. Earlier inquiries in Toronto[11] and in northern Ontario[12] have shown that friendship and leisure time activities of Greek families rarely extend to non-Greeks. A more recent survey has also shown a high rate of ethno-cultural homogeneity of friendship networks among Greeks, similar to those existing amongst Italian and Portuguese immigrants.[13]

Greek familism with its emphasis on solidarity, mutual support and moral obligations inevitably creates some conflict between kinsmen. Such conflicts, usually centred on family matters and business transactions, rarely result in permanent estrangements. According to the Greek custom, blood relationships are mutual and, at least symbolically, never broken. The idea that your kinsmen respond to your needs even after bitter conflicts is expressed in the proverb, "the blood never becomes water, and even if it will, it won't become muddied."

Spiritual relationships are also an important aspect of the Greek family's social network. They refer to those reciprocal relationships between individuals or families based on important religious sacraments such as baptisms and weddings. In a wedding two previously unrelated persons (the bridegroom and the wedding sponsor) are drawn into a spiritual relationship in which "their mutual esteem and respect are profoundly committed."[14] A relationship of this kind involves moral obligations and responsibilities between the concerned persons and thus enhances family solidarity. In other words, it is an institutionalized relationship and does not end with the wedding ceremony. According to Greek custom, the wedding sponsor usually becomes the godfather (*nounos*) of the first child. For the other children godparents are chosen by the parents from family friends, co-workers and other non-related persons of the Greek Orthodox faith.[15] Symbolically speaking, then, the godfather (or godmother) becomes the spiritual parent of the child. The godchild addresses his spiritual father as godfather (*nouno*) while the natural father and the spiritual father address one another as *koumbaro* or, in more formal terms, as *synteknos* (co-parent).[16]

An essential characteristic of the spiritual kinship system is that it provides spiritual kinsmen with socio-economic support and co-operation when the need arises. During the earlier periods of immigration many Greeks who came to Canada were sponsored by spiritual kinsmen who had already established themselves in Canada. When these immigrants first arrived in Canada, the spiritual relatives would help them to find a job and an apartment or a house to rent. Like the kindred, spiritual relatives are also involved in business transactions. When kindred are unavailable the Greek who needs a business partner may turn to his spiritual kinsmen. This is why Greeks may often attempt to find spiritual relatives (*kourmbari*) whose monetary resources and social position will aid them economically.

Selecting a Mate

The Greeks of Canada are predominantly endogamous. According to a recent inquiry by Paul Larocque, the Greeks, like the Portuguese, are concerned that spouses be similar on the three factors of birthplace, mother tongue and religion.[17] Other inquiries in Toronto[18] and in Thunder Bay, Ontario,[19] also indicated strong preference for endogamous marriages among Greek Canadians. In Thunder Bay, when Greek parents were asked if they would favour their children's marriage with someone outside their nationality, 73% were definitely opposed to such a marriage. This compared with 52% of the Slovaks and 11% of the Dutch immigrants in the sample. More extensive inquiries are needed, however, in order to make meaningful comparisons of interethnic marriages of first and second generation Greeks and determine how interethnic marriages are related to such variables as sex, age at immigration, and educational achievement.

Greek-Canadian immigrants seem to be more concerned about the ethnic than the religious background of their children's prospective spouses. In the study carried out in Thunder Bay, the respondents were asked if they would approve of their children's marriage with someone who was outside their ethnic group but of the same religion. It was found that Greek immigrants in the sample were less likely than Dutch and Slovak immigrants to accept religious endogamy without ethnic endogamy. The most common reasons Greek immigrants in Thunder Bay gave for objecting to interethnic marriages were the desire to maintain Greek culture and religion, belief that marriages can be happier if spouses have the same values, and belief that people from their nationality make better husbands and wives.[20] The same reasons for objecting to interethnic marriages were also given during informal discussions with many Greek parents in the cities of Calgary, Montreal and Toronto. These attitudes are similar to those observed among Greeks in the United States. Greek-American parents have emphasized the advantages of having a spouse of the same faith, and warned their children of mixed marriages and the loss of Greek identity.[21]

The strong resistance to interethnic marriages creates anxiety among Greek immigrant parents. In Greek families, when children reach the dating age the parents become disturbed lest their children date or marry non-Greeks.[22] Many parents realize that for the most part the tradition that calls for parents to choose their children's mates is inappropriate in Canada, yet the parents often do not approve of Canadian courtship patterns or of exogamous marriages. A long period of disappointment and grief is commonly observed among parents whose children defy their wishes and marry outsiders (*xeno*). These parents see this son or daughter as one who is "lost" (*hathike*). The term "lost" in the Greek context means that the person who practises exogamy will inevitably maintain social distance from his family and ethnic community and his children will not learn the Greek language and ways of life. In many instances the parents are eventually reconciled with the child who has married out, and the spouse is accepted into the family and the ethnic community.

Parental pressures on Greek children to marry within the ethnic group will continue to be strong and may slow down the assimilation process. Even in the mid-1970s arranged endogamous marriages can be observed. The "go-betweens" in the marriage arrangement are usually relatives or friends who may talk over the marriage prospect with the parents, and if they agree then the boy and the girl are encouraged to meet and perhaps cautiously date each other. If they are mutually interested, the courtship continues and the engagement follows. On the other hand, pressures for ethnic endogamy are expected to be less strong among second and third generation Greek-Canadian families whose values and social patterns are more similar to those of the host society.[23] However, ethnic exogamy among second-generation Greeks may be less than among certain other second-generation immigrants in Canadian society.

Husbands and Wives

As indicated earlier, the majority of Greek immigrants came from agricultural and traditional communities of Greece in which the husband was the head of the household and the family's representative in the community. His authority over the wife was absolute, and the wife was expected to be modest and submissive.[24] This type of relationship between the sexes was carried over from Greece to Canada by many immigrants. However, Canadian values and institutions have modified such familial structures, and wives are beginning to enjoy higher status and greater intellectual freedom. Along with these changes the Greek-Canadian wife is also enjoying more economic independence and technological conveniences.

Greek wives in Canada now play an important role in the discipline and socialization of children, and assist their husbands in business, domestic decisions and the family's economic welfare. The argument presented by Kourvetaris regarding husband-wife roles among Greek immigrants in the United States can also be applied in Canada:

> To an immigrant husband who left his parents at a young age, his wife was more than the sociological sex-role partner. She was the wife, the adviser, the partner, companion and homemaker. She also assisted her husband in his business and the family decision making. Wives/mothers usually exercised their influence in the family decision making indirectly through the process of socialization of the children because the Greek father had to work incredibly long hours away from home.[25]

Although *andrismos* (manliness) and the demand for paternal leadership are still persistent social attributes among Greek male immigrants, systematic studies of sex-role differentiation would probably indicate that more equalitarian relations between spouses are becoming prevalent. It can also be argued that the power relationship in marriage varies with the spouses' academic achievement, length of residence in Canada, and age at the time of immigration. In interethnic marriages, where the husband is a Greek immigrant and the wife a Canadian-born non-Greek reared in a more equalitarian family structure, traditional marital relationships may be also expected to be met with disapproval from the wife.

Power relationships in Greek immigrant families have been slowly shifting from traditional male dominance to companionship and cooperation between husbands and wives. What effect such changes have upon the "traditionally-directed" Greek husbands is not known. Nor do we know under what conditions or circumstances Greek husbands may take the authority back and prevent their spouses from doing what they want.

Parents and Children

The manner of rearing children is usually identified by Greek parents as one of the chief differences between Greek and Anglo-Saxon family life. The Greeks maintain that the majority of Canadian children enjoy unnecessary freedom and do not have sufficient respect for their parents, elders, teachers and other officials. There is a conflict between the Old World's traditional values and those of the new society, especially individualism and personal freedom.

Parental demands and familial control over children seem to be important factors accounting for the relatively low incidence of juvenile delinquency in various Greek communities throughout Canada.[26] The ethnic group's controls, which include gossip about deviant children and which encourages children to actively participate in the ethnic community's life, are also effective methods for preventing delinquency in small Greek communities. The fact that the immigrant anxiously strives for respectability and acceptance within the ethnic community and within Canadian society in general seems to account for this concern over children's behaviour. However, familial and other group controls seem less effective in large cities like Montreal and Toronto than in smaller centres. More deviant subcultures are found in a metropolis, and the ethnic group's "conformity pressure" over its members is decreased where intraethnic relationships are more impersonal.

Some observers (notably teachers and social workers) of Greek communities have described parent-child relationships as problematic, and the Greek family milieu as unfavourable to the child's social and academic development.[27] Such generalizations should be considered with caution as they are based on a few individual cases and not supported by systematic inquiries. It may be argued that an attachment to Greek values and institutions provides the child with psychological security and social control and, therefore, he or she is less likely to become involved in deviant behaviour such as delinquency and drug use. It may also be argued that the Greek family's milieu emphasizes academic achievement and enhances the child's upward mobility.[28]

The intimate social and physical contacts of the child's early life are also an important aspect of socialization in the Greek family. Campbell observed that "Greek children from the day of their birth are the centre of attention and interest in the family. The needs of the infant take priority over all others."[29] This kind of family interaction is also commonly observed in Greek-Canadian families. The child's early life involves a high degree of interaction with parents, grandparents and relatives. It would appear that the average second generation Greek child by the age of six receives much hugging, kissing, touching and playing from his parents, siblings and relatives. Such emotional and physical contacts extend even into adult life, as it is not unusual for adult friends and relatives of the same sex to greet each other with hugs, kisses and tears.

Prospects for Future Research

Extensive studies are needed in order to show more precisely the changes occurring within the Greek family and its adjustment to Canadian culture. The longer an immigrant has been in Canada the more likely he is to accept the familial roles of his new society. However, the age at which the immigrant arrives in Canada is more important than the length of his or her residence here. The younger the age at which an immigrant enters Canada, the more likely he or she is to internalize Canadian values and thus to accept the familial roles of Canadian society.

Further research may be enhanced by the inclusion of more sophisticated criteria to measure power in the family and by the comparison of the Greek family with other ethnic family systems in Canadian communities. The family power structure may be measured in terms of decisions such as who buys a house or business, disciplines children, buys home furniture and handles bank accounts, and of the dating patterns of adolescent children. Especially valuable would be a comparative analysis of family dissolution rates between marriages of pure ethnic descent (spouses both Greek) and mixed marriages (only one spouse Greek), while controlling the variables of educational achievement, religious background and parental approval.

The Greek family's involvement in external social relationships (formal and informal networks)[30] is also expected to vary with socio-economic status. We would expect that the higher the family's social class position, the more numerous are its members' connections to formal social networks within the Greek community and in the outside Canadian social structure. On the other hand, in an ethnic group such as the Greeks, where there is a strong sense of familism and ethnic identity, we might not be able to find a significant relationship between class position and informal social networks, – especially with related families. Familial obligations and socio-economic co-operation for survival in a foreign land increase the Greek family's contacts with relatives and families from their own background.

The Greek family in Canada, then, can be viewed as a relatively stable unit which provides its members with security, identity and community. Familial solidarity and socio-economic co-operation is extended to kindred and spiritual relatives from the Greek ethno-religious background, including those still residing in Greece. As a primary group, the Greek family plays an important role in maintaining the vitality of the Greek language and culture in the new land, through the socialization of the young and ethnic endogamy. As a social control agency it seems to be effective in directing children to conform to the accepted standards of

Canadian society while maintaining an equilibrium between the Canadian and Greek cultures. Although the Greek family still possesses many of its traditional attributes, it is in transition from a traditionally-oriented unit to one in which the size, roles and relationships resemble those of the English-Canadian and French-Canadian family systems.

NOTES

1. J.K. Campbell, *Honour, Family and Patronage* (Oxford: Clarendon Press, 1964), p. 37.
2. Constantina Safilios-Rothschild, "A Comparison of Power Structure and Marital Satisfaction in Urban Greek and French Families," *The Journal of Marriage and the Family,* 29, (May, 1967), p. 349.
3. J.K. Campbell, *op. cit.,* p. 54.
4. *Ibid.,* p. 269.
5. *Ibid.,* p. 193.
6. Athina Tatsoulis, "Greek Women Poets of Today," *Hellenia* 23 (July-September, 1953), p. 11. For a more detailed analysis of family change in contemporary Greece, see Panos D. Bardis, "The Changing Family in Modern Greece," *Sociology and Social Research*, 40 (September, 1955), p. 19-23.
7. See the *Globe and Mail,* November 4, 1976, p. F2.
8. According to 1971 Census data 18.6% of the Greek families had three or more children. This compares with 27.7% of the families in the general Canadian population.
9. Kindred refers to cognate relatives whose blood ties can be linked through the father's or mother's side as far as the degree of second or even third cousins.
10. It should be noted that other important contributions to the Greek economy by Greek immigrants include vacation visits and investments of Canadian dollars in small businesses.
11. Judith A. Nagata, "Adaptation and Integration of Greek Working Class Immigrants in the City of Toronto, Canada: A Situational Approach," *International Migration Review,* Vol. IV (Fall, 1969), pp. 44-67.
12. Peter D. Chimbos, "A Comparison of the Social Adaptation of Dutch, Greek and Slovak Immigrants in a Canadian Community," *International Migration Review*, Vol. 6 (Fall, 1972), pp. 230-244.
13. Paul Larocque *et al.,* "Operationalization of Social Indicators of Multiculturalism." Paper presented to the Fourth Departmental Seminar on Social Indicators: Department of the Secretary of State (November, 1974), p. 55.
14. J.K. Campbell, *op. cit.,* p. 222.
15. Occasionally godparents may be chosen from relatives such as cousins, aunts and uncles.

16. For a detailed analysis of wedding sponsor or godparent relationships, see Stanley E. Aschenbrenner, "A Study of Sponsorship in a Greek Village," Ph.D. dissertation (Minneapolis: University of Minnesota, 1971.

17. Paul Larocque, *op. cit.,* p. 54.

18. C.A. Price, "Report on the Greek Community in Toronto," M.A. Thesis (Toronto: York University, 1958).

19. Peter D. Chimbos, "Immigrants' Attitudes Towards Their Children's Interethnic Marriages in a Canadian Community," *International Migration Review,* Vol. 5 (Spring, 1971), pp. 5-16.

20. *Ibid.,* p. 9.

21. Theodore Saloutos, *The Greeks in the United States* (Cambridge, Mass.: Harvard University Press, 1964), pp. 313-314.

22. Greek parents do not object to the ethnicity of their children's friends in childhood or pre-adolescence. The nationality of the Greek child's friends becomes of greater parental concern when the son or daughter is approaching the age for dating or marriage. See Louesa Economopoulou, "Assimilation and Sources of Culture Tension of Second Generation Greek Pre-Adolescents in Toronto," M.A. Thesis (Toronto: Ontario Institute for Studies in Education, 1976.)

23. The study of Tavuchis indicates that in the second generation Greek-American family "there is a trend toward a less patriarchal structuring a high incidence of exogamy, and the development of patterns consistent with those exhibited by the dominant society." See Nicholas Tavuchis, *Family and Mobility Among Second Generation Greek Americans* (Athens: National Centre of Social Research, 1972), p. 33.

24. J.K. Campbell, *op. cit.,* pp. 150-154.

25. George A. Kourvetaris, "The Greek Family in America," in Charles H. Mindel and Robert W. Haberstein, eds., *Ethnic Families in America* (New York: Elsevier, 1976), p. 176.

26. This observation is based on interviews with leaders of the Greek community and probation officers in the large cities of Edmonton, Ottawa and Thunder Bay.

27. This refers, for example, to certain papers presented to the Greek Intercultural Seminar on March 29, 1974, at St. Barnabas Anglican Church in Toronto.

28. Earlier studies in the United States have shown how achievement motivation of second generation Greeks has its origin in early parent-child interactions which enhance the child's chance of upward mobility. Rosen, for example, found that Greek children had higher academic aspirations and thus were more upwardly mobile than children of other ethnic groups such as Italians and French Canadians. This, according to Rosen, is due to standards of excellence emphasized in the home by parents and the fact that academic achievement by children received the approbation of the entire Greek community. See Bernard C. Rosen, "Race Ethnicity and the Achievement Syndrome," *American Sociological Review,* 24

(February, 1959), p. 52. See also Peter D. Chimbos, "The Hellenes of Missoula, Montana: Social Adjustment," unpublished M.A. Thesis, Missoula, Montana: University of Montana, 1963, pp. 44-48.

29. J.K. Campbell, *op. cit.,* p. 154.

30. Formal networks refer to the family's social relationships with the school, church and other public institutions and voluntary associations. Informal networks are the patterns of social relationships with and among relatives, friends and neighbours. See Elizabeth Bott, *Family and Social Network* (London: Tavistock, 1957).

SIX

The Political Life of Greek Canadians

Living thousands of miles away from their homeland, Greek Canadians have always remained interested, and often even actively involved, in the political and social developments of Greece. They have financially assisted Greek political parties and have organized political associations. They have on several occasions held demonstrations dealing with political issues of the home society. On the other hand, their interest and involvement in Canadian political life has been limited.

This behaviour may seem unusual, since political developments and decisions in Canada directly affect their socio-economic life, while political developments in Greece affect them less. However, most Greeks have been in Canada only a short time, and Greek immigrants, like other immigrants, do not have the franchise prior to their naturalization as Canadian citizens. Furthermore, the vast majority of Greek immigrants had no knowledge of the two official languages and thus were unable to follow political developments in Canada before their arrival.

One can also argue that political beliefs and practices are inseparable from the previous cultural experiences of the new immigrants. They have learned and practised politics in their home society in different ways, and it is thus natural for them to be more interested in the politics with which they are familiar and to which they are sentimentally connected. Only gradually do they become familiar with the political scene of the host society, acquire voting rights, and become interested and involved. To what degree they become active in Canadian politics depends on such factors as socio-economic position, age at the time of immigration and self-interest.

THE PRE-WORLD WAR II YEARS

It was during the first years of this century that Greek communities were first organized in Canada. The Greek Canadians of that era came from a

*This chapter was written with the assistance of Bobis Giannakopoulos of Montreal.

119

north, the Metaxas regime was "accepted" by the liberals as the lesser of two evils.[3] The totalitarian rule of John Metaxas ended in 1941 with the occupation of Greece by the Nazi forces.

The evidence suggests that there was no extensive involvement by pre-World War II immigrants in Canadian politics, whether on a local, provincial or federal level. The reasons were, again, that most of them did not take out citizenship and their limited knowledge of English or French made it difficult for them to follow Canadian events and developments. Furthermore, the dominant political parties of Canada had little interest in involving Greeks, presumably because of the small size of the ethnic group at that time. Only the members of the small Greek-Canadian elite were somewhat involved in local politics. The vast majority of pre-World War II Greek Canadians were busily engaged in working hard under unfavourable economic conditions and dreaming of returning home or of becoming entrepreneurs.

THE POST-WORLD WAR II YEARS

The outbreak of World War II, the defence of Greece against Italian invaders (1941-1942), and later the revolutionary movement against German, Italian and Bulgarian occupation united all Greek Canadians in an effort to assist their homeland. Through the Greek Relief Fund, Greek Canadians collected and sent millions of dollars worth of assistance in the form of food, clothing and medical supplies to Greece through the Red Cross. The local Greek communities and Greek nonsectarian organizations such as the AHEPA lent their full support. For the first time Greek Canadians put their bitter political quarrels aside and united to help their homeland resist the aggression of the Bulgarian, German and Italian armies.

During the Civil War (1946-1949), the Greek Relief Fund continued soliciting funds, this time to assist the nationalist Greek government which was fighting against the communist revolutionary forces. Although there is no evidence of conflicting factions in Greek-Canadian communities at that time, it may be presumed that Greek Canadians did not want Greece to fall under communist domination. Such an event would have been incompatible with the ideologies and political policies of their new society. By this time, Greek Canadians had become concerned with the unemployment and poverty in post-war Greece and urged the Canadian government to allow more Greek immigrants to enter Canada. For example, on July 24, 1947, a resolution enacted by the Greek-Canadian AHEPA in Saskatoon, Saskatchewan, was sent to Prime Minister Mackenzie King requesting more liberal policies for Greeks wishing to enter Canada for the purpose of becoming permanent residents.[4]

With the defeat of the communist forces and the end of the Civil War in 1949, organized interest in Greek politics ceased. The old immigrants had been away from Greece for too many years and the political struggles with which they were familiar had been replaced by new struggles which they could not understand. Their children who had been brought up in Canada were naturally more interested in Canadian politics.

Active Greek-Canadian political movements reappeared in the mid-1960s. Growing democratic movements emerged in Greece against the right wing government and American influence in the country. In 1965, when King Constantine of Greece dismissed the elected Prime Minister George Papandreou, a large Greek-Canadian political rally was organized in Montreal. The people, who gathered in the Jewish Hall in the heart of the Greek "ghetto" on the corner of Mount Royal and Esplanade Streets, enthusiastically denounced the policies and actions of the throne and expressed their solidarity with the democratic movement in Greece. A similar political protest by Greek Canadians took place in Toronto.

The most dynamic political movements within the Greek-Canadian communities appeared after the right wing military takeover of Greece on April 21, 1967. Greek Canadians were among the first Greek emigrants to express their opposition to the *coup d'état*. For instance, the day after the *coup* several hundred Greek immigrants gathered in a hall on Park Avenue, Montreal, and denounced the military dictatorship. A few days later, a huge protest rally was organized in Toronto outside City Hall. In both cities anti-Junta organizations were immediately formed: the Panhellenic Democratic Association *Makrygiannis* in Montreal and the Anti-dictatorial Committee *Rigas Fereos* in Toronto.[5] Most of the organizers and followers of these organizations were ideologically liberal, although some of them had been previously involved in left-wing organizations in Greece, including the communist revolutionary movement of 1946-1949.

Organized protest against the new military regime grew in Montreal and Toronto, creating so much anxiety on the part of the Greek dictators that in August, 1967, they sent King Constantine to Toronto on a seven-day "goodwill visit." A reception for the king was organized by royalists and Junta sympathizers of the Greek community in Toronto. Greek-Canadian royalists from across the country came to Toronto to welcome the king and attend the royal dinner at the Park Plaza Hotel. Simultaneously, hundreds of anti-Junta Greek Canadians participated in a demonstration against King Constantine's visit, organized by a 25-man committee for the Restoration of Democracy in Greece. The protesters blamed the king for the rise of the dictators. According to them, the dictators were neo-fascists who had collaborated with the Nazi occupational forces in Greece from 1941-1944.

In 1968 the Panhellenic Liberation Movement was organized in Canada under the direction of Andreas Papandreou for the purpose of politically combatting the military Junta and restoring democracy in Greece. According to Papandreou:

123

The Panhellenic Liberation Movement . . . is unequivocally committed to the co-ordination of the activities of resistance efforts in
Greece, to the end that the Junta be overthrown and that a genuine
democratic process guaranteeing the full and unconditional
sovereignty of the Greek people be established in Greece on a solid
and permanent basis. It rejects beforehand any undemocratic solution or any establishment-inspired "guided democracy" type of
solution for Greece.[6]

Andreas Papandreou served as an economic advisor to the Bank of
Greece (1961-62), and as a minister to the government in 1964 and 1965.
On the day of the *coup* Papandreou was arrested by officers of the new
regime and sent to prison with other Greek politicians. In December,
1967, he received amnesty and in January, 1968, was allowed to leave the
country with his family. In Paris he denounced the Greek Junta, and a
month later organized the Panhellenic Liberation Movement (PAK) with
headquarters in Stockholm where he had been offered a university chair
in political science. In 1969 he moved to Canada and worked as a Professor of Economics at York University in Toronto.[7]

The followers of Papandreou's Panhellenic Liberation Movement included politically liberal or socialist Greek Canadians from all walks of
life. Greek-Canadian university students, particularly from York University, were also strong supporters of this organization. The Panhellenic
Liberation Movement, like other anti-Junta organizations in Canada, attempted to inform the Canadian public about the military government of
Greece through public lectures, the mass media, newsletters and formal
demonstrations.[8] For about six years (1968-1974) the Penhellenic Liberation Movement remained one of the most powerful organized political
forces against the Greek dictatorship.

The Greek-Canadian anti-Junta movements were supported by Canadian political organizations and other non-sectarian associations, the
New Democratic Party being the most supportive. Leaders of the NDP
not only spoke out against the government of Greece but also participated in demonstrations. In August, 1968, Ontario NDP president
James Renwick told 300 members of the Toronto Committee for
Restoration of Democracy in Greece that Canada should not only break
off diplomatic relations with Greece, but should also "convene a meeting
of NATO to consider Greece's expulsion from the organization."[9] Among
other prominent Canadians who voiced their disapproval of the Greek
dictatorship and urged the restoration of democracy in Greece were the
president of the Ontario Labour Congress, Mr. D. Archer; Rabbi
Fineberg from the Toronto Jewish Community; the Liberal MP, Mr.
Charles Caccia; Dr. John Morgan of the Unitarian Church; and the
president of the Voice of Women in Canada, Mrs. M. Sears.[10]

The Government of Canada recognized the military regime of Athens,
but later became an outspoken critic of Greek domestic policy:

In addressing the NATO Assembly in Ottawa, Canada's Foreign Minister was also highly critical and the NATO Assembly itself condemned any repression of democratic freedom in Greece as "dangerous to the internal cohesion of NATO" and called on the government in Athens to undertake immediately serious steps leading to the restoration of democratic freedoms.[11]

Additional support for the anti-Junta movements in Canada came from the liberal Greek-Canadian press. The newspapers *Ellenikos Tahydromos* (Hellenic Postman) in Montreal, edited by Christos Kolivas, and *Neos Kosmos* (New World) in Toronto, edited by Paul Astritis, had fiercely attacked the Greek dictators during their seven years of military rule. Both of these newspapers frequently published long articles denouncing the military regime of Athens and urged all Greek Canadians to join the struggle for the restoration of democracy in Greece. Events such as anti-Junta protests in Canada and the oppression of civil rights and physical torture of political prisoners in Greece were discussed extensively in these two newspapers. On the other hand neutral or pro-Junta newspapers carried articles on the effectiveness of the dictatorship in combatting political corruption, public anarchy and economic recession.

As anti-Junta movements became stronger and more influential in Canada, the regime in Athens began to take a defensive stance. Through "goodwill" visits of Greek officials to Canada and the co-operation of certain Greek-Canadian newspapers and government publications, the Athens regime attempted to enlighten Greek Canadians about the socioeconomic progress of Greece and thus discourage opposition to the Junta. For example, in April 21, 1969, the second anniversary of the military *coup d'état*, an information officer from the Greek Embassy in Ottawa spoke to a Greek audience in Montreal stressing the legitimacy of the military regime of Athens and its support by the Greek people.[12]

While many Greek-Canadian individuals and associations had taken a stand against the dictatorship, others offered their support. The Greek church-community administration throughout Canada was sympathetic to the military government, since the main objectives of the *coup d'état* were ostensibly to prevent a communist takeover in Greece and build a new society based on Christian principles. In 1968 the dictator of Greece, George Papadopoulos, published a book entitled *Our Creed* in which he outlined his political philosophy and justifications for the nonviolent takeover. According to Papadopoulos, "new Greece is Greece of the Greek and Christian spirit. It is Greece of the Greek and Christian civilization."[13] These words undoubtedly appealed to the conservative-religious elements in Greece and abroad.

When in December, 1967, a palace engineered coup against George Papadopoulos failed and King Constantine was forced to flee Greece for Italy, many Greek-Canadian Royalists ceased to support the military Junta. Opposition grew stronger in September, 1968, when the military regime of Athens approved a new constitution for Greece in a national referendum. The constitution stripped the king of most of his powers and reduced the membership of Greek Parliament from 300 to 150 representatives.

The organizers of the anti-Junta movements blamed the Greek consulates, particularly in Montreal and Toronto, for organizing popular support for the regime of Athens and for intimidating its opponents in Canada. To what degree consulates affected the political life and orientation of Greek Canadians during the dictatorships is not clear. We cannot even assume that all staff of the Greek consulates willingly supported the Junta, since some of them had obtained their civil service positions prior to the *coup d'état* under the liberal government of George Papandreou. Bitter and mistrustful relationships among Greek Canadians formed during that time continued even after the downfall of the dictatorship in July, 1974.

A few Greek Canadians who had close ties with Junta representatives in Canada or Greece served as informants by collecting information on anti-Junta activities. Many Greek Canadians who openly opposed the military Junta were labelled "communists," "unpatriotic" and "undesirable" and were unable to visit Greece without facing prosecution. Some received threats against themselves or their families for their anti-Junta activities. According to one researcher,[14] the rumours of threats by the Greek military Junta and its sympathizers and of retaliation by opponents were so widespread in Montreal that Greek Canadians would not risk identifying themselves with any political stand. Similar reactions among Greek-Canadian interviewees were observed in northern Ontario (1968).[15]

Sirros writes of the political conflict among the Greeks of Montreal during the 1967-74 Greek dictatorship:

> To compound an already difficult situation there existed a definite lack of unity amongst even the immigrant population. In fact it may be said that there was a state of active disunity. Political events in Greece during 1967 served as a catalyst for such disunity. Many Greeks had left Greece for political reasons as well as economic ones. There were those who wanted to forget about any sort of politics, those who wanted to continue their fight against the Greek regime, those who supported the Greek regime and those who feared any sort of identification with any of these groups. Suddenly people who had previously been friends began to question each other on the issue of the *coup d'état*. Suspicion, long a trait of people who must fight for their survival, began to creep into almost all community affairs.[16]

Incidents of intimidation became so prevalent that victims of such acts appealed to the Canadian government to intervene. For example, in 1969 leaders of anti-Junta organizations wrote letters to the Minister of External Affairs, Mitchell Sharp. Many of the incidents were reported to the municipal police as well as to the RCMP.[17]

The majority of Greek Canadians did not become involved in any organized opposition to the regime and thousands of them visited Greece during the seven-year dictatorship. Many Greek Canadians took advantage of the regime's attractive "foreign investor's plan," whereby Greek Canadians who made money available for investment in Greece were eligible for a government loan at a very low interest rate. This not only encouraged investment of Canadian dollars in Greece but also served as good public relations for the dictators.

An uprising at the Athens Polytechnic School occurred in mid-November, 1973. The protesters were suppressed by army tanks, and hundreds of students and workers were killed or wounded. With this incident, opposition to the Greek Junta within Greek-Canadian communities reached its peak. More non-political organizations now openly declared their opposition to the dictators. Protests by anti-Junta organizations grew stronger and their influences extended outside of Canada. For example, the Chairman of the Panhellenic Liberation Movement, Andreas Papandreou, who at the time was still at York University, sent to the Ministers of External Affairs of the NATO countries the following message:

> The Greek people ask at this hour of your conference in Brussels if you will find the courage to acknowledge your moral and political responsibility for the slaughter of Greek youths in Athens on November 16. At least 400 are dead and the injured reaches 1,000. The massacre occurred at the hands of a military Junta imposed on Greece by the United States and supported by NATO. The weapons and bullets were yours. Your silence can only mean that you participated willingly.[18]

In July, 1974, when an Athens-directed military *coup d'état* took place in Cyprus, most Greek-Canadian associations participated in demonstrations that denounced this act and the overthrow of President Makarios. The replacement of Makarios as president by Nikos Sampson, a declared partisan of the union of Cyprus with Greece, was to give Turkey the pretext for which it had waited, direct intervention in the island.[19]

The Turkish military invasion of Cyprus a few days later united Greek Canadians of all political convictions in massive anti-Turkish demonstrations and in the creation of "Solidarity for Cyprus" committees. The deep-rooted political divisions within the Greek community resulted, however, in a shaky and tenuous alliance. Despite that, the Greeks of Canada worked hard and contributed significantly to the cause of the Greek Cypriots.

The collapse of the Greek dictatorship and its replacement by the government of Constantine Karamanlis inevitably influenced Greek-Canadian political movements. Greek communities were no longer dichotomized into pro-Junta and anti-Junta sides and the anti-dictatorial organizations disbanded. The political parties of the opposition that became legal in Greece continued to have their affiliated organizations or support groups in Canada.

Factions based on political ideologies still existed within the Greek-Canadian communities in 1979. As noted earlier, the young and liberal Greek Canadians have been perceived as threats by the older conservative elements who avoid any interruption of the status quo within the ethno-religious community. For example, when in 1977 a group of young Greek Canadians in an Ontario city attempted to form a Greek cultural society, the new organization was labelled radical and received little support from the Greek community.

PARTICIPATION IN CANADIAN POLITICS

As we indicated earlier, Greek Canadians have shown little interest in Canadian political life, especially prior to the 1960s. However, in the early 1960s there were organized efforts by Greek Canadians in Montreal to participate in Canadian politics. While the Quiet Revolution was taking place in Quebec, the Greek Association of the Liberal Party appeared in Montreal, its members being mainly Greek businessmen and second generation professionals. The association was active during the election campaigns, as most of its members were involved for reasons of political patronage. The second-generation professionals were seeking to advance their careers, while the small business owners such as restaurateurs were mainly seeking favours, such as liquor licences, from the politicians. The proportion of Greek immigrants who had voting rights, however, was small and did not constitute a significant political force.

In 1965, John Kambites, a corner store owner and broadcaster from Montreal, presented himself as a New Democratic Party candidate in the federal elections. This was the first time that a Greek-Canadian candidate had sought election on an ethnic platform in an area where the Greeks of Montreal were concentrated. He was quickly surrounded by a group of post-war working-class socialist Greek immigrants. The campaign they carried on was lively and passionate, much like the campaigns organized by Greeks in their home towns. Despite this enthusiasm, the small number of Greeks with voting rights and socialist convictions could not affect the result of the election. Later an attempt to form a Greek association of the New Democratic Party also failed, but many of those who had worked in the elections retained their party memberships.

Most of the Greek Canadians who participated in the New Democratic campaign in Montreal had been involved previously in socialist movements and campaigns in Greece. The immigrants' involvement in the NDP campaign enhanced their political solidarity and later facilitated their active involvement in the political issues of the home society. For example, in 1965 they organized the mass rally in Montreal against King Constantine's dismissal of George Papandreou. Later on they became the organizers of the anti-Junta movements in Montreal.

In the fall of 1976, Greek Canadians made their voices heard during the Quebec provincial election campaigns. This was an example of possibly the most active political participation in the history of Greek Canadians. The interest and involvement of Greek Canadians was largely a result of Bill 22 and the controversial language test which was forcing Greek children into the French school system. Greeks who traditionally had voted Liberal felt betrayed by the Quebec Liberal Party and on October 27, 1976, hundreds of Greek voters confronted Premier Bourassa in a Park Extension hall. The Greek voters "bitterly attacked the premier for treating them like second-class citizens and demanded an end to the language test if he wants their support in the November 15 provincial election."[20] Although Greek Canadians would accept French as Quebec's official language, for socio-economic reasons they also wanted their children to be fluent in English. Their views are reflected in the following comments by a Greek parent in Montreal:

> When I came to Canada 15 years ago, the Greeks were forced into the English community because French schools wouldn't accept their children. Now we're being told we have to send our kids to French school. All my relatives and friends speak English. If my son goes to French school, he won't be able to communicate with them. Besides, for us, mobility is important. What if I want to move to Ontario or to the States? My kids will have to speak English.[21]

Three Greek Canadians became political candidates in the 1976 elections in the Laurier riding which was 30% Greek: Christos Syros (Democratic Alliance), George Savoidakis (Union Nationale) and John Kambites (Parti Québécois). Political rallies were organized and public debates among the three candidates were heard by thousands of Greek Canadians on local Greek radio programmes. The candidates also advertised their political objectives and policies in Greek-Canadian newspapers.

Although the Quebec Liberal Party was not successful in recruiting a Greek-Canadian candidate, it received campaign support and votes from Greek Canadians who had remained devoted to its ideals. On the other hand, the Greek political faction called *Belogiannis* gave its fullest support to the Communist Party of Quebec. Its members participated in political meetings, door to door campaigning and advertising for the Communist candidates in the Laurier, Outremont and Mercier ridings. All Communist candidates were Italian or French Canadian. A small group of Greek Canadians in Montreal also helped NDP candidates with their political campaigns.

The results of the November elections showed, however, that the attempts of the Greek-Canadian candidates to achieve political power had failed. Even in the predominantly Greek Laurier riding, no Greek-Canadian candidate was able to claim victory, presumably because of the division of the Greek vote and the traditional preference for the Liberal Party by many Greek Canadians. It was commonly believed in the Greek community of Montreal that a high proportion of Greek Canadians voted for the Liberal candidate André Marchand. This suggests that Greek Canadians are likely to vote for the political party of their choice rather than for the ethnic background of the political candidate.

There is no doubt that the victory of the Parti Québecois was enthusiastically welcomed by some Montreal Greek Canadians, especially those with socialist convictions. The editor of the Greek-Canadian newspaper *Hellenic Postman* (the most popular Greek-Canadian socialist newspaper in Canada) expressed his views about the victory of the Parti Québécois as follows:

> The electoral victory of the Parti Québécois opens new horizons in the life of our province. It brings a new message of progress, justice, happiness and security for all people of this beautiful and wealthy province. . . . With faith, trust and devotion to the new leaders of our province let's all virtually contribute to the creation of a NEW QUEBEC which will provide equality, justice and affection for all.[22]

But Greek Canadians were disappointed when early in 1977 the new PQ government proposed a more restrictive language law which prescribed that the instruction given in the kindergarten classes and the elementary and secondary schools of Quebec must be in French. This, the Greek Canadians claimed, did not concur with the PQ's election campaign promises that immigrants already established in Quebec would have freedom of choice in the language of their children's education. The reaction of many Greek Canadians to the proposed law may be characterized as one of anxiety, frustration and insecurity. In June, 1977, the Greek community of Montreal submitted a brief to the Quebec Parliamentary Committee indicating their dissatisfaction. According to the brief, Bill 101 impeded bilingualism, which is indispensable for both individual and collective development within the Greek-Canadian minority. The demands of the Greek Canadians of Montreal were summarized as follows:

> We wish first of all to state that French must be established as the main official language in all facets of public life in our province. However, we also support the position that knowledge of the English language is indispensable for success in any career in Quebec, in other parts of Canada and in the North American context. This knowledge is also indispensable for the proper optimization of the human resources of our community, within the framework of the desired development and progress of the Quebec society.[23]

Despite the formal protests by Greek Canadians and other ethnic minorities of Quebec, Bill 101 became law prior to September, 1977. As a result, Greek community leaders argued, many Greek-Canadian families moved from Montreal to other provinces or returned to Greece. And for the majority of Greek Canadians who decided to stay in Quebec, the language issue is expected to reinforce their political consciousness in future political campaigns.

Concerning the extent to which Greek immigrants participate in the political life of the host society through voting, earlier studies with small samples in different Greek-Canadian communities have presented contradictory results. In her 1968 study of 100 working class Greeks in Toronto, Nagata describes new Greek immigrants as being reluctant either to take out citizenship or to be active politically:

> Many of the respondents of my sample, of course, were not qualified to make applications, either for limitations of language or length of residence. In addition most of them felt that the problems involved in becoming a citizen must be enormous. In the majority of cases, no thought had been given to the question, and it was apparent that life in Canada was considered quite tolerable and acceptable without citizenship, particularly in view of the general political apathy in matters concerning this country.[24]

A survey[25] in the Greek community of Thunder Bay, Ontario, dealing with voting patterns indicated, however, that Greek immigrants had been active voters in both federal and provincial elections. For example, 86 of the 90 eligible voters in the sample voted in the 1965 federal elections, while voter participation of all eligible voters from Thunder Bay in the 1965 federal elections was reported at 84%.[26] In the 1968 federal elections, 91% of the 105 eligible Greek voters participated in voting. This compared with 78% voter participation of all eligible voters in the city of Thunder Bay.[27] Even in the 1967 Ontario provincial elections, 90% of Greek immigrant eligible voters participated in voting, as against 71% of all eligible Thunder Bay voters.[28]

There are two possible explanations why the Thunder Bay respondents showed more interest in Canadian politics than Nagata's respondents in Toronto: the Thunder Bay Greek immigrants had been in Canada for a longer period than Nagata's respondents and thus were better acquainted with the socio-political issues of the host society, and the Thunder Bay Greek immigrants had higher occupational status at the time of the survey. For example, 37 (52%) of the 71 family heads included in the sample were proprietors of small stores and restaurants. Nine (13%) were classified in skilled or semiskilled occupations. On the other hand, the Toronto respondents were mainly labourers and thus had fewer vested interests in Canadian politics than the business proprietors of Thunder Bay.

One may now ask which Canadian political party Greek immigrants generally vote for. Empirical research on the topic is limited, but the common belief within the Greek communities is that in federal elections the immigrants who came to Canada after the 1950s tend to vote for the Liberal Party, as was borne out in the 1968 Thunder Bay survey.[29] In the 1968 federal elections, 87 of the 105 eligible voters in the sample claim to have voted for the Liberal Party, whereas the Conservative and New Democratic parties received only eight votes each. The two remaining respondents refused to specify their political preference. The predominant reason for the strong support given to the Liberal Party by the Thunder Bay Greeks was that this party "provides more and better opportunities" for the immigrants and the workers in general.

To what extent the 1968 Thunder Bay findings can be applied to other and larger Greek-Canadian communities of the 1970s will have to be demonstrated by future inquiries. Although Greek immigrants tend to vote for the Liberal Party in federal elections, in provincial elections their political preferences are more varied. This is understandable since provincial as well as municipal political representatives (especially those from the party in power) have more influence on the ethnic community's socio-cultural life. For example, an ethnic community may be confronted with a need for provincial grants to establish an ethnic school and for this reason immigrants may vote for the party which they expect will provide such financial support. In ethnic celebrations such as Greek Independence Day the Canadian guests of honour are usually members of the political party in power.

Finally it should be re-emphasized that Greek Canadians as "ethnic voters" have not in the past (especially in the 1950s and 1960s) constituted a significant pressure group in Canadian politics. Even in the cities of Montreal and Toronto where we find large Greek populations the Greek Canadian "ethnic vote" had been relatively weak. This can be attributed to the continual preoccupation of Greek Canadians with Greek political events, especially during the 1960s, the lack of unity within the Greek community, the general reluctance of the charter groups to recruit Greek-Canadian political candidates, and feelings of powerlessness among working-class Greek Canadians. Gavaki's study in Montreal has shown that 75.2% of the 242 Greek immigrant respondents in the sample agreed that they felt "powerlessness when in conflict with stronger pressure groups." At least 58% agreed they had "no influence upon happenings in Canadian society." The level of powerlessness was higher among the blue-collar immigrants with relatively low academic achievement.[30]

With the passage of time and the stabilization of their residency, more Greek immigrants are becoming interested in Canada's political life, as was demonstrated in the 1976 Quebec provincial elections. More Greek immigrants are becoming aware of the need to obtain Canadian citizenship and use their voting power.

NOTES

1.   Public Archives, National Library, Ottawa, R.G. 13A2 Vol. 208 File 32.
2.   *The Loyal*, New York, Vol. 1, No. 1, April 5, 1919, p. 1.
3.   See Theodore Saloutos, *The Greeks in the United States* (Cambridge, Mass.: 1964), pp. 332-343.
4.   A letter sent to Prime Minister Mackenzie King by the Supreme Governor of AHEPA in Canada on August 6, 1947, Order of AHEPA (Canadian Jurisdiction), Brandon, Manitoba.
5.   The name "Makrigiannis" stands for the popular Greek military hero John Makrigiannis who fought against the Turks from 1821-1829. Makrigiannis was an anti-imperialist and anti-monarchist who in 1843 took an active role in the insurrection against King Othon of Greece. The name "Rigas Fereos" stands for the scholar who actively promoted the Greek revolution against the Turkish conquerors. In 1798 he was killed by the Turks.
6.   Andreas Papandreou, *Democracy at Gunpoint: The Greek Front* (New York: Doubleday, 1970), pp. 353-354.
7.   Immediately after the fall of the Greek dictatorship in 1974, Andreas Papandreou returned to Greece where he became the founder and leader of the Panhellenic Socialist Party of Greece. His party platform included abolition of the monarchy and a nonaligned policy for Greece including political independence from USA and the withdrawal of Greece from NATO. In the Greek federal elections of December, 1977, the Panhellenic Socialist Party became the official opposition party of Greece, and has been seen as a major political threat to the conservative government of Constantine Karamanlis. *Britannica Book of the Year* (Toronto, 1979, pp. 378-9.)
8.   On April 20, 1969, Andreas Papandreou spoke in Toronto to thousands of Greek Canadians and representatives of the various Canadian political parties and labour associations. In his speech Papandreou stressed his optimism for the restoration of democracy in Greece. See *Neos Kosmos*, Toronto, April 24, 1969, p. 3.
9.   *Neos Kosmos*, Toronto, October 3, 1968, p. 6.
10. *Ibid.,* p. 8.
11. Philipe Deane, *op. cit.,* p. 157.
12. See a film entitled "The 80 Go to Sparta," National Film Board of Canada, 1969.
13. George Papadopoulos, *Our Creed,* Vol. "B" (Athens' Management of General Press, 1968), p. 194. (Published in Greek.)
14. Efrosini Gavaki, *The Integration of Greeks in Canada* (San Francisco: R and E Research Associates, 1977), p. 51.
15. Peter D. Chimbos, "A Comparison of the Social Adaptation of Dutch, Greek and Slovak Immigrants in a Canadian Community," *International Migration Review,* Vol. 6 (Fall, 1972).
16. Christos Sirros, *The Mile End West Project: A Study of Community*

Development in an Immigrant Community (Montreal: Greek Community of Montreal, September, 1973), p. 6.

17. For detailed information on intimidation of Greek Canadians by pro-Junta agents and supporters in Canada see *Neos Kosmos*, June 19, 1969, p. 1.

18. Telegram by Andreas Papandreou on behalf of the Panhellenic Liberation Movement, Toronto, November, 1973.

19. Philip Deane, *op. cit.,* p. 135.

20. Sheila Arnopoulos, "Greeks Attack Bourassa on Bill 22," *The Montreal Star,* Montreal, October 28, 1976, p. A2.

21. *The Montreal Star*, October 27, 1976, pp. 1-2.

22. *Hellenic Postman,* Montreal, November 18, 1976, p. 1.

23. Brief prepared and submitted by the Greek Community-at-Large to Quebec Parliamentary Committee on Bill I, Greek Community of Montreal, June, 1977.

24. Judith Nagata, "Adaptation and Integration of Greek Working Class Immigrants in the City of Toronto: A Situational Approach," *International Migration Review,* Vol. 4, p. 59.

25. The survey was conducted by Peter D. Chimbos in the Fall of 1968. The sample consisted of 105 Greek immigrants. Of these (70%) were Canadian citizens and thus eligible voters at the time of the survey. In 1968 the Greek community of Thunder Bay consisted of approximately 125 families. The results of the survey have not been published elsewhere.

26. Statistics of the City Clerk's Office, Thunder Bay, Ontario.

27. *Ibid.*

28. *Ibid.*

29. Chimbos' Thunder Bay survey, *op. cit.*

30. Gavaki, *op. cit.,* p. 50.

SEVEN

Social Integration and Retention of Ethnic Identity

An important aspect of cultural pluralism in contemporary societies is the social integration of immigrants in the host society. The process of social integration refers to the gradual entrance into and involvement of the ethnocultural group in the socio-cultural matrix of the host society. Social integration does not necessarily mean assimilation, the loss of the individual's ethnic identity or his language and culture. It simply refers to a large degree of social and structural interaction between the ethnic minority and the rest of the society.[1] In Canada the process of integration is expected to be "equally beneficial to the receiving society and to the individual joining it. The individual must have complete freedom of choice in his integration; the receiving society must, through its institutions, assure him equal opportunities for personal fulfilment."[2]

Let us consider the extent to which Greek Canadians integrate in to Canadian society, and the factors which impede or facilitate this process. Social integration as a dynamic process of adjustment to the receiving society may be divided into two main subdivisions. The first, which we call cultural integration or acculturation, refers to the participation in the host society's cultural matrix through learning and adopting its values, language, norms and other elements.[3] On the other hand, in considering structural integration, we emphasize the social participation in the host society's life through social networks and institutional arrangements.[4]

CULTURAL INTEGRATION

Satisfaction with Canadian Life

The immigrant's satisfaction with life in the host society is an important step in cultural integration. Being satisfied with life in the new land not only alleviates the immigrant's insecurities but also provides a stable foundation for adjustment to the new culture. The survey by Larocque and his collaborators indicates that Greek Canadians were among the ethnocultural groups receiving the highest scores of "being generally satisfied with their life in Canada.[5] A more recent study by Gavaki in Montreal has shown that 188 (78%) of the 242 Greek immigrants in the sample were generally satisfied with their life in Canada and satisfaction had increased from the time of arrival to the time of the study for about 20%.[6]

The relatively high level of satisfaction found among Greek immigrants seems surprising when one observes that they dislike what they perceive as individualism and permissiveness in Canadian society and that they are strongly committed to the maintenance of their cultural heritage. There are two possible explanations for this. First, satisfaction is understood in terms of economic improvement; that is, a higher standard of living in the new country than in the homeland. This argument has been supported by Gavaki's Montreal study indicating that upwardly mobile Greek immigrants showed higher levels of satisfaction with life in Canada, while professionals who had experienced downward mobility scored lower on the same scale.[7]

Second, the presence of ethnic institutions, such as church, schools, associations, mass media, food markets, and entertainment, and of relatives in the host society, provide the new immigrants with a comfortable environment and make them feel at home. In Toronto and Montreal, where such institutions and services are readily available, new Greek immigrants experience little estrangement from their native culture. Nagata and her collaborators write of Greek institutions and services in Toronto:

> Greek language movies provide recreation and entertainment. For other essential activities such as dealing with banks and post offices and attending PTA meetings, linguistically more competent friends and family or other kin provide necessary interpretation services. For special advice and translation, as in the case of union contracts and tax forms, local Greek travel agents have extended their more traditional activities. Further, in some of the schools with the highest enrolment, attempts are made to accommodate Greek-speaking parents by printing Home and School notices in Greek and inviting Greek speakers to address PTA meetings. . . . The professional services of lawyers, doctors, real estate dealers, driving school instructors, accountants and dentists are all to be had "in Greek."[8]

However, satisfaction with life in the host society does not necessarily lead to a high level of social integration. Greek immigrants, although they expressed a high level of satisfaction about their daily life in Canada, as did Italians and Portuguese, were least acculturated in terms of having knowledge of Canadian ways of life and integration skills.[9]

Despite their satisfaction with life in Canada, many Greek Canadians show sentimental attachment to the motherland. The attachment is so strong that some new Greek immigrants live simultaneously in two different worlds. According to Gavaki's findings in Montreal, at least 208 (86%) of the 242 Greek immigrants in the sample said they were "homesick for Greece."[10] Thousands of Greek Canadians visit Greece every year to see their loved ones and to refresh themselves in the friendly, hospitable and warm motherland. Greek immigrants often speak of the importance of taking a trip to Greece in order to break the routine of their life in North American society. Some hope and plan to return to the homeland permanently. But as the years pass by and they establish themselves with their families in Canada, it becomes more and more difficult for them to repatriate to Greece. A popular Greek song which depicts the feelings of many new immigrants was commonly echoed in Greek-Canadian homes, nightclubs and restaurants during the 1950s and 1960s. The song is about a young Greek immigrant man sending a message to his mother in Greece that he is destined to remain in a foreign land:

> Mother stop weeping for me since it was my destiny in a foreign land to live and be. I came so young in this foreign land and now like a tree my roots are grown so deep, as I have a wife and children and my "branches" spread free.

Learning the Host Society's Language

Learning the language of the receiving society is perhaps the most important factor in the acculturation process.[11] Although Greek immigrants admit the need to increase their knowledge of the host society's language they, like the Italians and Portuguese, have ranked low on the English fluency scale.[12] The tardiness of many Greek immigrants in learning English or French may be due to the low level of their schooling in the home society and the continuous association with Greeks at work and other places of social interaction. As Nagata writes concerning the Greek immigrants who came to Toronto in the mid-1960s:

> Employment of newcomers is frequently obtained in a non-English-speaking environment: either employer and co-workers are also Greek, or they may be speakers of Italian or some other tongue. . . . Sponsored immigrants likewise are often placed by their sponsors in job situations where no English is spoken. It is apparent, therefore, that even where the newcomers are willing to learn English, conditions over which they have little control frequently prevent them from doing so. Even where English classes are available at night school or the international institute, shift work, overtime and general fatigue are usually sufficient to prohibit consistent attendance and study.[13]

On the other hand Greek respondents are among those ethnocultural groups which reported high desire for retention of their own language. Specifically, 55% of the first generation Greek respondents were "strongly in favour" of retaining the mother tongue. This compares with

43% of the Italians, 38.9% of the Chinese, and at the other end of the scale, 6.8% of the Dutch and 18.3% of the Hungarians. An additional 27% of the Greeks felt that retention of the Greek language was "somewhat desirable."[14]

Since their early years of settlement in Canada, Greek Canadians have shown a strong desire to preserve the culture of the Greek nation, acknowledged by historians to be the cradle of Western civilization. The transmission of this cultural heritage depends largely on the retention of the Greek language within the Greek-Canadian ethnic group. As leaders and professionals of the Greek community believe, "It is with this language as a means of communication that Greek Canadians retain their relationship with the Greek tradition. The Greek language is the carrier of Greek values, the composition of which constitute the cultural heritage."[15] The language can be preserved through Greek schools and by the use of Greek at home.

The Greek immigrants' concern for retaining their language has been expressed in their strong desire to speak Greek at home and to encourage their children's participation in Greek-run churches, schools and cultural organizations, and in that way learn the ancestral language. According to O'Bryan and his collaborators, 73% of the Greek respondents stated that they were "strongly in favour" of Greek-language retention by their own children, and an additional 18% were "somewhat in favour."[16] In Nagata's study in Toronto only one of the 76 Greek parents who were questioned on linguistic training expressed the desire for the offspring to be unilingually English. The remainder were in favour of having their children speak their mother tongue as well as English.[17]

In O'Bryan's survey the frequency of ethnic language use has been the highest among the Greeks. In Montreal 97% of the Greek respondents stated they used the Greek language "every day." This compares with 88% of the Greek respondents in Toronto.[18] The use of the Greek language has been mostly concentrated in the home and with close friends. At least 93.5% of the Greek respondents speak the Greek language within the family, with parents, spouses and children, and 81% speak it with close friends.[19]

Caution is required when using language as a measure of integration. The Greeks are relatively recent immigrants: in the sample used by O'Bryan, 24.2% had been in Canada less than five years, an additional 28.4% less than 10 years and a further 20.4% less than 15 years. Hence they have not had as much time to learn English or French as the more established ethnic groups. Nevertheless, as O'Bryan has stated, differences among groups in recency of immigration accounts for some, but not all, of the group differences in support for language retention.[20]

Identification with Canada

Anyone who chooses Canada as an adopted country is not only expected to adopt certain styles of life and behaviour patterns but also to feel that

The economic factor exercises an important influence and the English language, with its unquestionable dominance in North America, tips the scale strongly in its favour. Since economic, social and linguistic factors all play a part, the Francophone community, being economically weaker than the Anglophone, cannot easily attract immigrants. This is evident in Montreal and elsewhere in Canada.[25]

A small proportion of Greek Canadians in Quebec have identified themselves with the Francophone society. Some of these individuals have been educated in French-speaking institutions and hold professional positions in Quebec. Others having socialist convictions and, being fluent in French, have shown strong support for the separatist policies and objectives of the Parti Québécois. These are individuals who view the separation of Quebec as an essential step in bringing equality and justice to all ethnic minorities. In the November, 1976, provincial elections, many of these persons campaigned for the Greek candidate who ran for the Parti Québécois in the Laurier riding of Montreal.

STRUCTURAL INTEGRATION

Friendship Networks

Participation in friendship networks with members outside the ethnic group can be considered an important indicator of integration. By associating with non-Greeks, the new immigrant learns the skills needed for his social and occupational advancement in the new society. But according to the available studies, Greek immigrants tend to develop friendships networks within their own ethnic group. Larocque and his collaborators have shown that Greeks, like the Italians and Portuguese, indicate a high rate of ethnic group homogeneity. According to these investigators such networks can form the bases for or against the person's socio-economic integration to the host society.[26] Nagata, in her study of Greek working-class immigrants in Toronto, observed that acquaintances, visits and friendship relations rarely cross ethnic lines.[27] Lambrou in her study of the Greek community in Vancouver observed that social networks among Greek immigrants are mainly confined to the ethnic group.[28]

A study by the writer in Thunder Bay, Ontario, provides additional information on the Greek immigrant's integration through friendship networks. As an index of integration, the immigrant's amount of participation in leisure time activities such as parties and sports with Greeks and with Canadian-born people not of Greek background was adopted. Immigrants from three ethnic groups (Dutch, Greek, Slovak) were asked to indicate what parties or sport activities they took part in most often: those with Canadian friends or those with friends or their own ethnic group. The highest percentage of immigrants participating in parties or

he or she is a part of the country. The question then is
Greek immigrants identify themselves with Canada. The ?
mation suggests that the Greek immigrants' level of ider
Canada is generally low. According to Larocque and hi:
the Greeks were among the few ethnocultural groups ha\
identification as "hyphenated Canadians" (Canadians of
with their second identification in the "ethnic" (Gree
smallest representation was the "Canadian" identificatio
the heaviest representation in the Canadian identity cate
Dutch, Germans and Scandinavians.[21]

Gavaki's study in Montreal has provided additiona
about the identification of Greek immigrants with Can
Using indicators such as preference of neighbourhood,
Canadian sport teams, identification of nationality and fe
"Greekness" or "Canadianness," Gavaki was able to ;
overall rate of Greek identification with the host society i:
213 of the 242 respondents indicated a low level of iden1
Canada. The following question was used by Gavaki to
Greek immigrants' feelings of ethnic identification: "Wh
you what are you, what do you usually say"? Of the 242
225 (93%) identified themselves as Greeks. Respondents w
to indicate whether they felt more Canadian than Gr(
(21.1%) of the 242 respondents said they "feel more C
Greek."[22]

Gavaki has suggested that the Greek immigrants' ident
Canada is related to their low socio-economic status and re
exposure to the host society. She argues that given a
economic level and more years of exposure, more Greeks
themselves with Canada than Greece.[23] The low identificat
immigrants with Canadian society can also be partly exp.
academic training and experiences of Greek children in the I
From age six, Greek school children are exposed to an
system which emphasizes patriotism, religious ideals and
past of Greek civilization.[24] This education instils strong et
national pride and admiration for the homeland in individua
such persons resistant to integration into a society like Cana(
phasizes multiculturalism.

Greek Canadians, like the majority of the ethnocultur
Canada, identify themselves with the Anglophone rath
Francophone culture. When a Greek immigrant asserts "I
Canadian" or a "Canadian" he means an English-speakin
This is probably due to the fact that the Anglophone group is
ly associated with the mainstream of North American cult(
mises better socio-economic opportunities for the new imm
cording to the *Report of the Royal Commission on Bilin*
Biculturalism:

sport activities consisting of friends of their ethnic group came from the Greek sample (72%).[29] Reasons for their choices were given by the respondents, the most common among Greeks being that they felt comfortable with people of similar customs and traditions. Preference for the entertainment of the motherland was mentioned only by Greek respondents.

Another question regarding the immigrant's preference for friendship networks was, "Do you visit with Canadian friends or friends of your own ethnic group when you want to go out and spend the evening chatting with others?" Seventy-five per cent of Greek immigrants visited only friends of their own ethnic group, and three per cent visited Canadian friends only. The most common reasons given by the immigrants for their preference for friends of their own ethnic group involved having the same customs and traditions and speaking the same language.[30]

Formal Organizations

Membership in the formal organizations of the host society is another indicator of structural integration for ethnocultural minorities. Clubs and associations provide opportunities for learning skills and behaviour patterns useful in the immigrant's socio-economic mobility. The study of Larocque and his collaborators indicates that Greeks participate little in formal organizations. At least 88% of the Greek respondents had not participated in organized clubs or societies.[31] However, the Greeks indicated a "medium degree" of participation in business and political organizations. This can be related to the involvement of many Greek immigrants in small businesses and their historical experiences of political conflicts.

The low participation of Greek immigrants in formal organizations can be attributed to their low academic level in the homeland. The more educated a person is, the more likely he or she is to be affiliated with voluntary organizations.[32] This also explains why active participation in formal organizations varies directly with socio-economic status. Participation in formal organizations may be expected to be higher among upwardly mobile Greek Canadians.

The insignificant Greek-Canadian membership in social organizations is also a reflection of their rural background and the influence of dictatorial governments in the home society. Membership and participation in voluntary associations are more commonly found in societies characterized by democracy and urban-industrial ways of life. The anti-democratic regimes of contemporary Greece have discouraged and even prohibited participation in voluntary associations, except those provided by the government in power. On the other hand, societies like Canada and the United States are nations of joiners.[33]

Although we have no empirical evidence on Greek organizational membership, one may suppose that academically and economically mobile Greek Canadians are more likely to join ethnic associations like the AHEPA, Daughters of Penelope and even the youth organization GOYA. On the other hand, the working classes are least involved in Greek organizations and particularly church membership.

For those who join them, Greek organizations may serve to cushion any culture shock experienced by new immigrants and even facilitate assimilation. Vlachos writes of the functions of Greek-American organizations:

> Greek-American organizations play a decisive role in the assimilation process. On the one hand they help maintain and promulgate Greek culture and interaction between Greek members, and on the other hand by their functioning they accustom their members to basic requirements and working procedures of the culture of the larger American society. Depending on the kind of organization participation there exist possibilities of positive or negative influences on the process of assimilation.[34]

Employment

Sociological studies dealing with the integration of Greek immigrants in Canadian society through employment in non-Greek agencies or business are rare. It seems, however, that pre-World War II Greek immigrants were more likely to invest their saving in their own small businesses than work for Canadian employers. In cities such as Montreal a considerable proportion of new Greek immigrants have worked for Greek employers (especially in restaurants), lived in the Greek "ghetto" and carried on most of their social activities within the boundaries of the Greek group. Direct contact of these immigrants with the Anglo-Saxon and French communities has been minimal.[35] On the other hand, the masses of unskilled imigrants who came to Canada after the 1950s were more likely to obtain employment in factories and other Canadian-owned businesses. For them, it was in the sphere of employment where the greatest accommodation to Canadian norms had to be made.[36] However, for many the opportunities for linguistic improvement and economic integration at higher levels were limited. Working in a factory where co-workers speak Greek provides the newcomers with little opportunity to learn English or French. Most of Nagata's working class respondents in Toronto "felt the amount of English learned on the job was minimal. Often it is restricted to key jargon terms only, and rarely is much competence in English syntax achieved."[37] Many of the Greek immigrants who came to Canada after the 1950s indeed experienced employment situations where co-workers and even foremen were Greek speaking. Furthermore, low wages and long hours of hard work hardly provided the new immigrants with the money and leisure needed to become actively involved in the host society's cultural activities.

In the light of the above discussions it would appear that Greek Canadians have shown a low degree of integration to Canadian society. This is not surprising when one considers the socio-economic background and historical experiences of the Greeks and the nature of the socio-political policies of Canadian society. The fact that the overwhelming majority of Greek immigrants in Canada in the mid-1970s had arrived after World War II also partly explains their low degree of integration into the Canadian society.

The extent of integration also varies within the Greek minority's social structure. The professionals and the economically successful who have moved into affluent suburbs of Canadian cities include both Greek and non-Greek Canadians in their associations. Giannakopoulos, in his observations of integration patterns of Greek Canadians in Montreal, suggests that:

> The social relations of the middle class Greek immigrants are not limited only to other Greek families, but also include non-Greek neighbours, and business associates or colleagues. Furthermore, their children do not face problems of class discrimination and they tend to lose faster their mother tongue and culture. Clearly, therefore, the middle class families have followed on the steps of the pre-war Greek immigrants and tend to become integrated with the Anglophone middle class community in Montreal.[38]

On the other hand, the relatively low integration of the working-class Greek immigrants has been associated with their feelings of powerlessness. According to Gavaki's study in Montreal, the immigrants with low academic achievement and occupational status scored higher on the scale of powerlessness than the more successful. For example, the working-class respondents with little schooling were less likely than others to agree with items such as "can influence government decisions," "can change course of Canadian events," and more likely to agree with items like "feel helpless with Canada," and "feel powerless when in conflict with strong pressure groups."[39]

THE MAINTENANCE OF GREEK CULTURAL HERITAGE

The determination of Greek Canadians to preserve their culture and identity is reflected in the high retention of their native language and their industriousness in maintaining ethnic institutions and organizing ethnic communities. These institutions play specific roles in maintaining the ancestral language and culture in the host society.

The Greek School

As noted earlier the Greek school has played an important role in teaching children the Greek language and acquainting them with Greek culture and historical experiences. On Greek ethnic holidays (the 25th of March and the 28th of October) Greek school children throughout the

Greek-Canadian communities actively participate in the celebrations. They enthusiastically stand on the stage of the community hall and recite patriotic poems, sing Greek songs and folk dance. These are the occasions when children of Greek parentage collectively show understanding, reverence and pride for the Hellenic language and culture.

An important concern of Greek Canadians is the role that various educational agencies should play in retaining the Greek language in Canada. According to O'Bryan and his collaborators, over 62% of the Greek respondents felt it is primarily the responsibility of Canadian elementary and secondary schools to teach the Greek language. Only 15% of the respondents felt that the responsibility of teaching the Greek language and culture to Greek-Canadian children should lie in "ethnic schools" or "church schools."[40]

The Church

The Greek Orthodox Church is another institution which has contributed significantly to the preservation of Greek identity through the use of Greek language in religious services and its devotion to Greek ideals. Since affiliation between Greek Orthodoxy and contemporary Greek society is strong, the Greek minority in Canada can be considered as an ethno-religious group.[41] The church has conveyed to Greek Canadians the necessity for adjustment to Canadian culture and the spread of Hellenism and Christian Orthodoxy. Bishop Athenagoras of Elaia has described the mission of the Greek Orthodox Church in Canada as follows:

> It is not then right to think that we did come here to enjoy the beauty, the opportunities and the wealth that Canada offers to all. We did not come just to take but to offer as well. Yes, we did come to offer our loyalty, our love, our traditional patriotism, our work for the promotion of this country. In addition we came to offer something deeper than all these, and this is our rich Greek culture and the venerable tradition of Christian Orthodoxy.[42]

The Family

The Greek family more than any social agency plays an important role in teaching children Greek language and values, and providing them with some sense of identity with the Greek culture. Greek immigrant parents often speak the Greek language at home and send their children to afternoon Greek schools. In O'Bryan's study, Greek respondents showed stronger parental support for children taking non-official language courses than respondents from any of the other nine ethnic groups: at least 66% indicated that they would insist upon or encourage their children to take Greek courses, only 7.5% that they did not care and less than one per cent that they would discourage their children from taking such courses.[43] The reasons given by Greek parents for language

144

retention by their children were: "keeping up customs and traditions," 25%; "communication with parents," 22%; and "useful as a second language," 48%. Five per cent of the respondents gave "other reason" or "no reason."[44]

Although the Greek family and kinship system is historically related to those of other minority groups and to a certain degree to that of the dominant Anglo-Saxon and French cultures, it is exogamy that parents and church leaders are most concerned about. Church leaders and the majority of the parents believe that endogamy is essential for the preservation of Greek culture and identity, and they emphasize this to children. Schermerhorn's observation on Greek endogamy in the United States suggests some similarities with that of Greek Canadians:

> It has been the Greeks who have clung to endogamy with more tenacity than any European ethnic group in the United States and this is definitely an exclusionist policy that still sets the group apart. To a lesser degree, their participation in the Orthodox rather than the Roman Catholic Church creates another institutional enclosure that separates them from interaction with others even though these two religious institutions are variants on a common Christian theme.[45]

The avoidance of ethnic and religious exogamy by Greek Canadians plays a major role in the persistence of Greek identity and cultural survival in Canada. We expect, however, that attitudes toward ethnic exogamy will become more permissive with each new generation.

The Greek Mass Communications Media

Greek-language newspapers in Canada appeared as soon as Greek immigrants increased in number and developed a community. The first Greek newspaper, *Estia*, appeared in Montreal in 1924 under the editorship of Heraklis Papamanolis. With an increasing Greek immigrant population in Canada and the establishment of Greek communities, more Greek newspapers appeared in Montreal, Toronto and Vancouver. From 1925 to 1977 at least 31 different Greek-Canadian newspapers appeared in Canada (See Table 13). Some of these disappeared because of the precarious financial position they faced. During the 20-year period from 1957-1977, 70% of the Greek newspapers survived for three years or more, 60% for five or more years, and 42% for ten or more years. Of those in existence in 1977, four had been publishing for over a decade, including one in Toronto boasting a 21-year publication record. In 1977 there were at least 15 Greek-language newspapers in Canada, mostly published in Montreal and Toronto. Among the best-known weekly Greek-language newspapers in Canada are the *Hellenic Free Press, Hellenic Tribune, Hellenic Postman* and the *Greek Canadian Weekly*.

The modern Greek-Canadian newspapers are more professionally pro-

TABLE 13

**Greek-Language Newspapers
in Canadian Cities, 1925-1977**

City	Number	%
Montreal	14	45.1
Toronto	11	35.5
Vancouver	4	13.0
London	1	3.2
Ottawa	1	3.2
Total	31	100

Source: Data compiled by Mrs. Paraskevi Buckthought.

duced than the early efforts, which amounted to no more than a few pages, sometimes hand written and mimeographed. They are usually published by the offset process and supported by advertising, which amounts to about 40% of the total content of each issue. Advertising rates are comparable to those of the English-language dailies.

The Greek-language press in Canada has been an important aspect of the Greek community's life. It informs the new immigrants about political and social events in Canada and Greece and advertises Greek retail businesses and employment opportunities within the Greek community. The Greek-language press in Canada follows the same patterns of journalism as the Greek-language press in the United States, described by Saloutos:

> The Greek-language press . . . carried international news, especially stories about the affairs of Greece, including events in the villages and provinces, as well as about the Greek colonies in the United States. It kept the immigrant with little or no knowledge of English in contact with happenings in the homeland, perpetuated Old World feuds and gave rise to new ones.[46]

Among Greek Canadians there is a substantial Greek language readership, indicating that the Greek-language press constitutes a valuable resource for the retention of Greek language and culture. According to O'Bryan more than 56% of the Greek respondents claimed to have read Greek newspapers or bulletins at some time during the year preceding the data collection.[47] This figure may be considered high since the majority of Greek immigrants had had little schooling.

Greek Canadians are also avid listeners to Greek radio programmes. For example, 46% of the Greek respondents in O'Bryan's study were regular listeners to Greek programmes (among the group with some knowledge of the ethnic language), and at least 36% stated they listen to Greek programmes occasionally.[48] The Greek respondents were not only the most frequent listeners to ethnic radio and television programmes among those in the sample, but also showed the strongest support for more and better non-official language radio and television broadcasting. At least 56% of the Greek respondents felt that better non-official language radio and television programming was very important and 17% considered it as somewhat important.[49]

The frequency of listenership, however, depends upon the availability of Greek radio and television programmes. In Montreal and Toronto, where there are large Greek populations, Greek Canadians were able to enjoy Greek radio and television programmes and a variety of content. The radio programmes included Greek music of various kinds, news (local, national and international) and advertisements for Greek businesses and employment opportunities. The television programmes which operated on limited air time provided Greek audiences with national (including Greek community) and international news, advertising Greek businesses, Greek movies and Greek guest speakers discussing issues of interest to the Greek community.

Ethnocentrism

Ethnocentrism means judging other cultural groups solely in terms of one's own cultural standards. Since other cultural groups are different, ethnocentric persons view other customs, traditions and ways of life with suspicion and distrust.[50] The Greek immigrants' perception of some Canadian customs and values as threatening to social life and group survival has reinforced the persistence of Greek culture and identity, and yielding to or acquiring certain customs, many immigrants believe, is immoral or deviant. These attitudes have created feelings of xenophobia among many Greek immigrants. It is not uncommon for Greek immigrants to disapprove of or feel threatened by what they perceive as common practices in Canada such as early dating, disrespect for elders and parents, drug use, weak family bonds and overall permissiveness. At the same time, however, they may show appreciation of Canadian democracy, political freedom, *laissez-faire* and modern conveniences or efficient services in governmental agencies.[51]

Since the Greek Canadians have clung tenaciously to the home society's culture, certain customs observed in Greece 50 years ago and brought to Canada by pre-World War II immigrants have remained almost unchanged to the late 1970s in Canada. Meanwhile these customs have changed considerably in Greece. For example, the typical parents in Greek urban areas no longer discourage dating or arrange marriages for their children as many of the older Greek immigrant parents do in Canada. Self-consciousness and ethnocentrism in a strange land were reasons why the Greek immigrants guarded certain customs with zeal.

Social change was taken for granted by the people in Greece, but to Greek immigrants in Canada almost every change in their customs and traditions meant loss of ethnic identity.

Greek Canadians have preserved many aspects of the material culture, especially food. In the average Greek family, Greek cooking is common, meaning that aside from the purely Greek dishes more spices, seasoning, predominance of lamb, foods preserved in brine, olive oil, and a great number of flaky pastries are served.

Greek Canadians are less assimilated to North American cultural life than are the Greeks of the United States. This is due on the one hand to the relatively large number of new Greek immigrants who came to Canada after 1950 and thus developed greater institutional completeness[52] and cultural conservatism, and on the other hand to the policy of multiculturalism in Canada which has encouraged ethnocultural groups to preserve their cultural traditions and ethnic identity. Canadian policy contrasts with the pressure put on immigrants in the U.S. to "blend into the melting pot." As one Canadian study indicates, Greek Canadians are overwhelmingly in favour of Canada's "multiculturalism" policy.[53]

Greek Canadians will continue to show less assimilation than their Greek-American counterparts for many years to come. Patterson has predicted the comparative assimilation of Greeks in Canada and the United States as follows:

> If fifty to sixty years from now Canadian Greeks will be as assimilated as Greeks in the United States are at present, rates of assimilation in the two nations for Greeks could be said to be similar. We suggest, however, that there will be less assimilation in the future for Greek Canadians than there has been in the United States, simply because the United States until very recently has pursued a policy of encouraging its immigrants to join the melting pot and become Americans. That this policy has not worked completely, that many ethnic groups in the United States are now asserting their individuality, does not mean that considerable assimilation, even of Greeks, has not taken place. Canada on the other hand, has a continuing flow of new immigrants from Greece, it has a public policy of supporting ethnic multiplicity, and despite some of its citizens, is committed to ethnic diversity and cultural multiplicity.[54]

Although Greek Canadians are strongly determined to preserve Hellenism and Greek Orthodoxy, they also show concern for integrating into the economic structure of the host society. Larocque and his collaborators found that:

> Greeks are concerned about opportunities for integrating socio-economically and mixing socially so that while they wish to retain and develop their culture they wish to do so in a manner which will

not jeopardize their contribution to and enjoyment of the benefits of living in Canadian society. They also identify a concern over their group's becoming too isolated in terms of overall Canadian society.[55]

HELLENIZING THE SECOND GENERATION

Greek parents want their children to grow up as good Canadian citizens and succeed socio-economically. But would they also acquire and preserve the Greek language and culture? This question has been raised not only by parents but also by priests, leaders of the ethnic community and the Greek associations. Such anxieties have resulted in the formation of Greek schools and Greek youth organizations. Some parents have gone so far as moving back to Greece in order to provide their children with the opportunity of acquiring Greek culture and ideals and growing up in a society which is relatively free of drugs, lawlessness and unnecessary permissiveness. Thousands of Greek-Canadian parents send or accompany their children to Greece during the summer in order to visit relatives, familiarize themselves with Greece and learn the Greek language more fluently.

To what extent do second-generation Greek Canadians identify themselves with their parent's ethno-cultural background? Studies dealing with this question are sparse. According to Economopoulou's study in Toronto the second generation Greek pre-adolescents were significantly more assimilated than they perceived their parents to be in all levels tested (i.e., identification with the Canadian way of life, use of the English language and values). However, the Greek pre-adolescents did not have identical values to the Canadian (English speaking of Anglo-Saxon background born in Canada) pre-adolescents of Toronto. Economopoulou draws the following conclusion:

> In essence, what was found was that Greek pre-adolescents feel more "Canadian" than their parents in a number of their values but at the same time feel highly significantly more "Greek" than their Canadian peers. Upon examining Greek pre-adolescent, Greek parent and Canadian peer value means, it becomes evident that the Greek pre-adolescent is closer to those values held by his parents than those held by his peers.[56]

Within the Greek-Canadian community many of the Greek families have been able to socialize their children to conform to the expectations of the ethno-religious community and remain a part of it. These young people speak modern Greek fluently, serve on church committees and in ethnic youth organizations and comply with their parents' wishes of endogamous marriages. They are favourable to the Greek way of life and enjoy activities stemming from Greek culture. They take an active part in ethnic holiday parades, caravans, bazaars and money campaigns for the church. Those who have visited Greece are strongly infuenced by the Greek culture and display pride in their ancestry. Phrases such as "I am proud of being a Canadian of Greek descent" or "I am proud to come from a Greek background" are commonly heard from these youngsters. They form a group who, though born in Canada, are not entirely of Canada.

There is a group of second-generation Greek Canadians who since early childhood have been taught the Greek values but at the same time reverence for the host society's ideals. When they grow up, the bicultural way of life will seem natural. In this group there is a social balance between the two cultures despite some occasional parent-child friction during the process of learning the Greek language and values. As Economopoulou has reported, parent-child tension in the Greek family may result when parents order their children to go to Greek school and speak Greek at home.[57]

On the other hand there is a group of second-generation Greek Canadians who rarely identify with the Greek community and its system of values. Although they do not deny their ancestry, they have limited knowledge of the Greek language and participate very little in the ethnic community's organizations and social activities. A small number have lost contact entirely with the Greek community. They call themselves Canadians and usually show hostility towards the Greek minority and its way of life. Later in life they are able to escape from their ethnocultural background by "passing": they change their names,[58] associate with members of the dominant Anglo-Saxon group and marry outside the Greek group. The lack of interest in Greek culture and community life by some second-generation Greek Canadians is perhaps due to the home environment in which they were raised. For example, children who are not encouraged by parents to learn the Greek language and culture are less likely to identify themselves with the Greek community.

There may also be other factors or circumstances which discourage second-generation participation in the Greek community's institutions. Many of the people are alienated by the continuous conflict which exists among the various segments (religious, political, social class) of the ethnic community. As noted earlier, much of the energy of the Greek community's leaders and the active members in general is diverted to conflicting issues based on the home country's politics and internal power struggles rather than guiding the youth in participating in the local ethnic community.

Internal feuding may weaken the ethnic community and facilitate assimilation into the dominant culture. It has also been suggested that children of Greek immigrants find themselves in an ambivalent position towards both the Greek and the North American cultures. This situation usually results in cultural marginality. The individual may experience anxieties and conflicts as he has no clear-cut identification with either

Greek or the host society's culture.[59] Marginality has some positive consequences, as it lends flexibility, variety and colour to the individual's social life, especially in multicultural societies such as Canada. Humans can learn to adapt and enjoy multiple cultural experiences when a society values multiculturalism and provides equal economic opportunities and security for all.[60] Thus the personality problems that may be observed among certain second-generation Greek Canadians are more likely to result from family socialization, discrimination or other situational pressures.

Overall, it is evident that Greek immigrants have a relatively lower degree of integration into Canadian society than many other ethno-cultural groups. Factors responsible for this low level of integration include low socio-economic background, short length of residence in Canada and the unfavourable employment conditions for many new immigrants in earlier years. Moreover, Greek Canadians are strongly determined to preserve their culture and ethnic identity in the host society. The Greek Orthodox Church, Greek schools, the Greek mass media and the family have played important roles in the preservation of Greek culture and its transmission to the second and even third generation.

Fortunately, the achievement of a degree of cultural integration and upward mobility by Greek Canadians does not require assimilation. Upwardly mobile Greek Canadians are able to retain their ethnic identity and directly support the institutions of the ethnic community. Thus, Greek Canadians are able to prosper and integrate in Canadian society without sacrificing their traditional values, norms and institutions, or without turning their backs on their ethnic community.

NOTES

1. Efrosini Gavaki, *The Integration of Greeks in Canada* (San Francisco: R and E Research Associates, 1977), p. 8.
2. *Report of the Royal Commission on Bilingualism and Biculturalism* (Vol. 4, Ottawa, 1969), p. 5.
3. See Gavaki, *op. cit.,* pp. 15-16.
4. Cf. Milton Gordon, *Assimilation in American Life* (New York: Oxford University Press, 1964).
5. Paul Larocque *et al. Operationalization of Social Indicators of Multiculturalism.* Discussion paper for the Fourth Departmental Seminars on Social Indicators, Citizenship Branch, (Ottawa, November 26, 1974), pp. 62-3.
6. Gavaki, *op. cit.,* p. 37.
7. *Ibid.,* p. 38.
8. Judith A. Nagata *et al., English Language Classes for Immigrant Women with Pre-school Children* (Toronto: Institute For Behavioural Research, York University, 1970), p. 9.

9. Larocque, *et al., op. cit.,* p. 74.
10. Gavaki, *op. cit.,* p. 46.
11. Other relevant indicators of immigrants' acculturation may include knowledge of the Canadian way of life, willingness to participate in the host society's cultural events and adopt its food, drinking and clothing habits. Since information on these items is limited we are primarily concerned here with learning the host society's language and retaining that of the homeland (native language).
12. Larocque *et al., op. cit.,* p. 38.
13. Judy Nagata, "Adaptation and integration of Greek working Class Immigrants in Toronto, Canada: A Situational Approach," *International Migration Review,* Vol. IV (Fall, 1969), pp. 57-58.
14. K.G. O'Bryan *et al., Non-Official Languages: A Study in Canadian Multiculturalism* (Ottawa: Thorn Press Limited, 1976), pp. 94-97. O'Bryan's information was based on a sample of 171 Greek interviewees chosen from 84,877 Greek immigrants in the cities of Edmonton, Montreal, Toronto, Vancouver and Winnipeg.
15. See Anne Farmakides' Report on "Hellenism in Greek Communities Abroad," in Julius D. Metrakos *et al., Commission for Community Development: Interim Report,* Greek Community of Montreal, 1970, pp. 79-83.
16. O'Bryan *et al., op. cit.,* p. 120.
17. Nagata *op. cit.,* p. 56.
18. O'Bryan *et al., op. cit.,* p. 59.
19. *Ibid.,* p. 64.
20. *Ibid.,* p. 96.
21. Larocque *et al., op. cit.,* p. 61.
22. Gavaki, *op. cit.,* pp. 46, 87.
23. *Ibid.,* p. 100.
24. Scott G. McNall, *The Greek Peasant* (Washington, D.C.: Monograph Series of the American Sociological Association, 1974), pp. 38-39.
25. *Report of the Royal Commission on Bilingualism and Biculturalism,* Vol. 4, p. 5.
26. Larocque, *et al., op. cit.,* pp. 54-55.
27. Nagata, *op. cit.,* p. 54.
28. Yanna Lambrou, The Greek Community of Vancouver: Social Organization and Adaptation. Unpublished M.A. Thesis, University of British Columbia, 1975, p. 75.
29. Peter D. Chimbos, "A Comparison of the Social Adaptation of Dutch, Greek and Slovak Immigrants in a Canadian Community," *International Migration Review,* Vol. 6 (Fall, 1972), pp. 238-239.
30. *Ibid.,* pp. 241-242.
31. Larocque *et al., op. cit.,* pp. 49-50.
32. Murray Hausknecht, *The Joiners: A Study of Voluntary Associations in the United States* (Totowa, N.J.: Bedminster Press, 1962), p. 24.

33. James Curtis, "Canada as a Nation of Joiners: Evidence from National Surveys" in James E. Gallagher and Ronald D. Lambert (ed.) *Social Processes and Institutions: The Canadian Case* (Toronto: Holt, Rinehart and Winston, 1971), p. 160.

34. Evangelos Vlachos, *The Assimilation of Greeks in the United States* (Athens National Centre of Social Research, 1968), p. 90.

35. See Charalabos Giannakopoulos, *The Development of the Greek Ethnicity in Quebec,* Montreal: Concordia University, 1977, Chapter IV. (work in progress)

36. Nagata, *op. cit.,* p. 62.

37. *Ibid.,* p. 62.

38. Giannakopoulos, *op. cit.,* p. 138.

39. Gavaki, *op. cit.,* pp. 49-52.

40. O'Bryan *et al., op. cit.,* p. 127.

41. For an interesting hypothesis on the persistence of ethnic identity in multicultural societies see Alan Anderson, "Ethnic Groups; Implications of Criteria for the Examination of Survival," A Paradigm presented in the Workshop on Ethnicity and Ethnic Groups in Canada, at the Annual Meetings of the Canadian Sociology and Anthropology Association, University of Alberta, Edmonton, May 1975.

42. Athenagoras of Elaia, *The Greek Orthodox Church in Canada* (Toronto: Greek Orthodox Community, 1961), p. 3.

43. O'Bryan *et al., op. cit.,* p. 132.

44. *Ibid.,* p. 123.

45. R.A. Schermerhorn, *Comparative Ethnic Relations: A Framework for Theory and Research* (New York: Random House, 1970), p. 126.

46. Theodore Saloutos, *The Greeks in the United States* (Cambridge, Mass.: Harvard University Press, 1964), p. 88.

47. O'Bryan *et. al., op. cit.,* p. 66.

48. *Ibid.,* p. 72.

49. *Ibid.,* pp. 150-151.

50. For a more detailed definition of ethnocentrism see Georgia Theodorson and Achilles G. Theodorson, *Modern Dictionary of Sociology* (New York: Thomas Y. Crowell Company, 1969), p. 135.

51. See G. James Patterson, *The Greeks of Vancouver: A Study in the Presentation of Ethnicity* (Ottawa: National Museum of Man, Canadian Centre for Folk Culture Studies, 1976), pp. 37-44.

52. For a detailed discussion on institutional completeness and social integration see Raymond Breton, "Institutional Completeness of Ethnic Communities and the Personal Relations of Immigrants," *The American Journal of Sociology,* Vol. LXX (1964), 193-205.

53. O'Bryan *et al., op. cit.,* p. 155.

54. Patterson, *op. cit.,* p. 137.

55. Larocque *et al., op. cit.,* p. 71.

56. Louisa Economopoulou, Assimilation and Sources of Culture Tension

of Second Generation Greek Pre-Adolescents in Toronto. University of Toronto, Unpublished M.A. Thesis, 1976, p. 86.

57. *Ibid.*, pp. 73-77.

58. It should be noted, however, that "passing" is not always based on denying one's own ethnic group. Individuals may be motivated to change their names and identify with the dominant group simply to escape discrimination. For a discussion on "passing" see Paul B. Horton and Chester L. Hunt, *Sociology* (New York: McGraw Hill, 1972), p. 369.

59. Vlachos, *op. cit.*, p. 186. For discussion of cultural marginality as being a problematic situation see Everest V. Stonequist, *The Marginal Man: A Study of Personality and Culture Conflict* (New York: Russel and Russel Inc., 1961).

60. For critical analysis of the concept of "marginality" see David Reisman, "Some Observations Concerning Marginality," *Phylon,* 12 (Sec. Quarter, 1951), pp. 113-127.

Conclusion

In the preceding chapters we have examined the Greek ethnic group in Canada from an historical and sociological perspective. We have dealt with a group of people who for more than 100 years have been active participants in the socio-economic growth of Canadian society. Through printed historical and contemporary data, supplemented by personal interviews, the author has attempted to give a comprehensive account of Greek Canadians.

Greek Canadians started emigrating to Canada before the turn of this century, even though the vast majority came after 1950. Forced by poverty, wars and political upheavals in their homeland, they came to Canada to seek a better life for themselves and their children. Leaving their relatives, friends and hospitable villages behind, and with no knowledge of the host society's language and culture, these daring and aspiring Greeks took a gigantic step towards a new future.

From the beginning of their settlement in Canada, Greek immigrants have tended to concentrate and work in the large urban centres such as Montreal, Toronto and Vancouver. It was in the city where the new immigrants could find fellow Greeks, steady employment and the opportunity to gradually enter the complex and fast-paced Canadian society. In the city the new immigrant could participate in and remain close to ethnic institutions and thus feel more at home and less prone to culture shock. Hence Greek immigrants clustered in particular residential, commercial and entertainment areas.

Despite their willingness to work hard and their desire for socio-economic advancement, Greek immigrants, like those of other lands, experienced many hardships in their struggle for survival in Canadian society. Having received little academic training and few occupational skills in the homeland, the majority of Greek immigrants initially entered menial jobs. Many of these entailed long hours of hard work and low wages, sometimes under harsh conditions. The new immigrants found themselves at the bottom of the Canadian stratification ladder in the post-World War II period. Perhaps the earlier Greek pioneers had experienced even greater hardships as they struggled to survive in a period of industrial transition and social unrest in the newly-emerging Canadian society.

The masses of post-World War II Greek immigrants, however, found the socio-cultural setting of Canadian society more favourable than did the pioneers. Canada has become increasingly tolerant of ethnic differences and has provided newcomers with more opportunities to improve their socio-economic status while maintaining their cultural and ethnic identity. Most Greek immigrants have improved their standards of living and moved out of their entrance status, although few have reached high economic, political and managerial positions. Economic success has also tended to result in political conservatism among the wealthy Greek Canadians.[1]

The absence of Greek Canadians in high socio-political positions can be mainly explained in terms of their recency of arrival, their low academic achievement and perhaps the failure of the charter groups to recruit educated Greek Canadians to such power positions. Over time more Greek immigrants, and especially future generations of Greek descent, are expected to enter high positions in the occupational structure, as has happened in the USA.

Greek Canadians began organizing into ethnic communities in the early 1900s. Historically, the Greek community has been centred around the church and the various ethnic sectarian and non-sectarian associations. The larger Greek-Canadian communities have often experienced serious internal conflicts. The ethno-religious community first began to experience structural changes with the flow of new immigrants during the 1950s and 1960s. The post-World War II immigrants were younger and politically more liberal than their predecessors, and they demanded changes in the traditional structure of the ethnic institutions. Conflicts occurred between recent and established immigrants, between young and old, between political factions (concerning issues in Greece), between the clergy (who sought administrative power in the community) and those who opposed them, and among secular competitors for influential positions. Although a certain amount of intraethnic conflict is inevitable and even functional, in the mid-1970s the preoccupation of Greek Canadians with such internal conflicts has diverted their talent and energy from other important responsibilities which they have within the ethnic community and the larger society.

In their achievement aspirations and conformity to the basic requirements and expectations of the host society, Greek Canadians are no different from other citizens. But with respect to social integration, especially through primary group contacts, they exhibit a high degree of intraethnic interaction. Their social contacts are usually confined to their relatives and friends from Greek backgrounds, and they demand ethnic endogamy from their children. Contacts with non-Greeks are more likely to increase over time as the immigrant becomes fluent in the host society's language, and becomes upwardly mobile in the Canadian occupational structure. The social integration of Greek Canadians may be viewed as a slow but steady process leading to a satisfactory adjustment.

Greek Canadians are strong believers in multiculturalism and appreciate the opportunities offered by Canadian society to maintain their cultural heritage and ethnic identity. The ethnic institutions are doing their part in keeping Greek culture alive in Canada. Commitment to the preservation of Greek culture does not seem to be a barrier to the immigrants' upward social mobility. Although the socio-economically successful Greek Canadians are more integrated in Canadian society than the rest, they also provide leadership and direct support for the maintenance of ethnic institutions.

How much the culture of an ethnic minority is appreciated by the receiving society is an important question in considering the social adjustment of immigrants. The more appreciative the host society is of the immigrant's heritage, the easier is his cultural adjustment. The average non-Greek Canadian has some knowledge of the brilliant contributions made by Greek philosophers and scientists to the growth of Western civilization.[2] The classic works of Aristotle, Plato, Euripides, Sophocles and other eminent philosophers and writers are commonly taught in Canadian schools. On the other hand, Canadians who visit Greek community centres and exhibitions may be surprised to see no statues or portraits of philosophers and mythological characters, nor any displays based on works of classical intellectuals, architects and playwrights.

In multicultural societies relationships between dominant and subordinate ethnic groups can be viewed as a continuous process of cultural transactions. The ethnic subordinate group is in a better bargaining position in the transactional process if it represents cultural elements which the dominant society appreciates and even incorporates into its intellectual life and socio-political milieu. For example, it was the bravery of the Greek army against the fascist forces of Germany and Italy (1940-1943) which gave Greek Canadians respectability among their fellow Canadians. Never before had so much interest and praise been displayed in the Canadian press about contemporary Greeks.[3]

Under Canada's multicultural policy, Greek Canadians are encouraged to maintain their cultural heritage and identity. Although the majority of immigrants came to Canada with the intention of making their fortunes and returning to Greece, they have now realized that they are here to stay. The many socio-economic opportunities, the political freedom and the tolerance of ethnocultural groups found in Canada have created satisfaction and nurtured the aspirations of Greek Canadians. Canada will remain a favourite place for Greek immigrants, and current and future immigrants will continue their upward mobility and cultural integration. In a rapidly changing world where millions of displaced people are unable to settle anywhere, the Greeks of Canada may consider themselves fortunate to be wanted and feel part of two free, hospitable, and culturally wealthy nations – their native Hellas and their adopted country Canada.

NOTES

1. See Joseph Lopreato, *Italian Americans* (New York: Random House, 1970), p. 175. Lopreato argues that this is partly due to a sense of gratitude to the host society for having made possible the realization of hopes and aspirations brought over from the Old World.
2. Two of the best-known studies are C.M. Bowra, *The Greek Experience* (New York: The New American Library, 1957), and Edith Hamilton, *The Greek Way to Western Civilization* (New York: The New American Library, 1955).
3. For example, see Frank Daley, *Greece: Gallant-Glorious* (Haverhill, Mass.: Record Publishing Company, 1941).

Appendix

TABLE 14

Number of Greek Immigrants Entered Canada by Chronological Period (1931-1971)

Year	Number of Immigrants	Year	Number of Immigrants	Year	Number of Immigrants	Year	Number of Immigrants
1931		1941	6	1951	2,855	1961	3,858
1932		1942	—	1952	1,691	1962	3,741
1933		1943	1	1953	2,059	1963	4,759
1934		1944	1	1954	2,892	1964	4,391
1935	77	1945	6	1955	3,014	1965	5,642
1936	91	1946	61	1956	5,236	1966	7,174
1937	114	1947	659	1957	5,631	1967	10,650
1938	120	1948	712	1958	5,418	1968	7,739
1939	45	1949	719	1959	4,965	1969	6,937
1940		1950	865	1960	5,009	1970	6,327
						1971	4,769

Source: Canada Department of Citizenship and Immigration.

TABLE 15

Destination of Greek Immigrants to Canada by Province and Chronological Period (1956-1971)

	Nfld.	P.E.I.	N.S.	N.B.	Que.	Ont.	Man.	Sask.	Alta.	B.C.	N.W.T. Yukon	Not Stated	Canada
1956	6		98	11	2,217	2,458	130	63	89	163		1	5,236
1957	1	1	89	12	2,581	2,502	97	73	60	215			5,631
1958	2		103	14	2,800	2,185	74	55	55	129	1		5,418
1959	2		95	7	2,587	1,956	92	44	64	118			4,965
1960	1		132	9	2,449	2,064	100	53	84	117			5,009
1961	1		87	7	1,764	1,634	81	39	94	150	1		3,858
1962			131	8	1,793	1,471	77	58	113	88	2		3,741
1963			54	8	2,348	1,929	137	60	85	138			4,759
1964	2		62	3	1,972	2,036	72	38	44	162			4,391
1965	1	2	78	13	2,390	2,815	81	36	82	144			5,642
1966	1		101	30	2,708	3,724	152	75	109	273	1		7,174
1967	1		67	21	3,642	6,187	169	77	115	361	10		10,650
1968	2	1	47	4	2,463	4,361	156	68	136	300	1		7,539
1969	4		33	5	2,383	3,898	139	54	128	291	2		6,937
1970	3		33	10	1,952	3,709	156	44	151	263	6		6,327
1971	2		35	11	1,685	2,565	115	31	108	215	2		4,769

Source: Canada Department of Citizenship and Immigration.

TABLE 16

Greece as Last Permanent Residence and Mode of Arrival of Immigrants

	Total	Directly to Canada		Via and from the U.S.A.	
		By Ship	By Aircraft	By Ship	By Aircraft
1964	4,391	2,131	1,389	61	810
1965					
1966					
1967	10,650	2,534	5,502	36	2,578
1968	7,739	1,529	3,735	118	2,357
1969					
1970					
1971	4,769	131	4,423	48	167

Source: Canada Department of Citizenship and Immigration.

TABLE 17

Population of Greece Aged 10 Years and Over by Geographic Region and Education Level

(5% SAMPLE ELABORATION OF THE 1971 POPULATION CENSUS QUESTIONNAIRES)

Males

	Greater Athens	Rest of Central Greece & Euboea	Pelopon- nesos	Ionian Island	Epirus	Thessaly	Maced- onia	Thrace	Aegean Islands	Crete
TOTAL	1,024,520	401,520	403,980	73,040	119,460	261,440	768,400	130,480	166,720	181,600
Graduated higher education	84,440	8,680	10,820	1,480	2,880	6,360	25,220	3,320	4,860	4,360
Completed secondary education	225,300	28,180	31,300	3,940	6,600	16,460	76,540	6,100	11,480	13,800
Completed primary education	532,200	236,340	247,300	42,720	72,300	147,180	418,360	59,600	87,840	113,020
Have not finished primary school	167,380	119,960	106,360	23,540	34,760	85,360	237,460	57,500	57,740	47,640
Have not declared education level	15,200	8,360	8,200	1,360	2,920	6,080	10,820	3,960	4,800	2,780
Illiterate* (do not know reading or writing)	36,280	29,020	22,280	6,420	7,100	18,480	51,300	23,340	17,680	10,800

(Continued)

Females

TOTAL	1,139,260	412,620	412,500	83,540	133,820	283,420	790,340	135,520	184,780	195,600
Graduated higher education	29,620	3,080	4,420	760	1,180	2,420	11,660	1,340	1,780	1,840
Completed secondary education	234,900	15,460	19,400	2,780	4,640	11,280	59,740	3,620	8,580	10,100
Completed primary education	536,280	173,480	180,360	32,760	53,580	113,200	345,580	45,960	82,960	92,700
Have not finished primary school	299,760	190,480	175,680	43,500	59,620	133,020	346,760	77,060	83,260	84,320
Have not declared education level	38,700	30,120	32,640	3,740	14,800	23,500	26,600	7,540	8,200	6,640
Illiterate* (do not know reading or writing)	127,560	120,600	110,200	28,720	42,780	85,900	164,800	49,480	40,680	46,580

Source: Statistical Service of Greece.

*The category of illiterate population has resulted from a question irrespective of the one asked on the level of education; in the latter [illiterates] are included partly in the category [Have not finished primary schools] and partly in the category [Have not declared education level].

TABLE 18

Economically Non-Active Population of Greece, by Geographic Regions and Reason for Not Working

(5% SAMPLE ELABORATION OF THE 1971 POPULATION CENSUS QUESTIONNAIRES)

	Greece, total	Greater Athens	Rest of Central Greece & Euboea	Pelopon-nesos	Ionian Island	Epirus	Thessaly	Maced-onia	Thrace	Aegean Islands	Crete
MALES	1,029,260	339,620	106,680	107,760	22,660	38,820	70,760	215,260	31,120	49,840	46,740
Pupils or students	510,980	155,300	51,660	56,100	9,420	21,140	36,720	118,580	17,300	19,600	25,160
Housework	—	—	—	—	—	—	—	—	—	—	—
Invalids	123,460	31,580	14,620	15,780	3,940	4,420	8,260	23,080	3,060	10,340	8,380
Other Reasons	394,820	152,740	40,400	35,880	9,300	13,260	25,780	73,600	10,760	19,900	13,200
FEMALES	2,857,040	918,280	314,820	307,860	57,380	95,340	217,420	572,960	86,840	150,900	133,240
Pupils or students	423,140	137,480	40,500	50,320	7,040	17,280	29,640	90,660	13,240	14,480	22,500
Housework	1,969,700	646,120	222,340	203,540	38,040	61,680	154,480	385,440	57,880	111,060	87,120
Invalids	105,040	21,140	11,060	17,160	3,480	3,320	6,780	20,940	3,160	8,380	9,620
Other Reasons	359,160	113,540	40,920	36,840	8,820	13,060	26,520	75,920	12,560	16,980	14,000

Source: Statistical Service of Greece.

*On the basis of usual employment concept.

TABLE 19

**Marital Status of Greek Immigrants in Canada (Identified by Ethnic Group)
As Compared with the Canadian Average, 15 Years of Age and Over, 1971**

	Greeks		Canadians (non-Greeks)	
Marital Status	Freq.	Perc.	Freq.	Perc.
Single (15 years of age and over)	19,160	22.6	4,283,390	28.2
Married	61,520	72.4	9,759,295	64.2
Widowed	3,420	4.0	962,130	6.3
Divorced	880	1.0	184,690	1.3
Total	84,980	100.0	15,189,505	100.0

Source: 1971 *Census of Canada*, Catalogue 92-734 Vol. 1 (Part 4), February 1974.

TABLE 20

**Blishen Score Differences Between First Occupation and Occupation in Canada
(July 1969) of Greek and Slovak Immigrants in Thunder Bay, Ontario**

	Score differences Blishen points*	Greeks	%	Slovaks	%
	11 – and more	50.7		1.9	
U	6 – 10	5.7	74.6	5.9	30.2
P	1 – 2	14.2		13.6	
	no change		25.4		64.9
D	1 – 2	—		3.9	
O	3 – 5	—	0.0	1.0	4.9
W	6 – 10	—		—	
N	11 – and more			—	
Total		100		100	
		(71)		(105)	

Source: Peter D. Chimbos, "Ethnicity and Occupational Mobility: A Comparative Study of Greek and Slovak Immigrants in "Ontario City," *International Journal of Comparative Sociology,* 15 (1974) p. 65.

*Ignoring the second digit (decimal point) in Blishen scale.

Bibliography

Anderson, Allan. "Ethnic Groups: Implications of Criteria for the Examination of Survival." Paper presented in the Workshop of Ethnicity and Ethnic Groups in Canada, at the Annual Meetings of the Canadian Sociology and Anthropology Association, University of Alberta, Edmonton, May, 1975.

Andriotis, Nicholas. *The Federative Republic of Scopje and Its Language.* Athens, 1966.

Antoniou, Mary. *Welfare Activities Among the Greek People in Los Angeles.* San Francisco: R and S Associates, 1974.

Archives of the Greek Consulate, Toronto, 1951.

Arnopoulos, Sheila. "Waitresses Paid $25.00 for Sixty Hours." *The Montreal Star,* December 16, 1976.

Aschenbrenner, Stanley E. *A Study of Sponsorship in a Greek Village.* Unpublished Ph.D. Thesis, University of Minnesota, 1971.

Asimopoulos, Constantina. *The Rela-tionship Between Social Mobility and Integration of Immigrants in Montreal.* Unpublished Ph.D. Thesis, University of Montreal, 1975.

Athenagoras of Elaia. *The Greek Church in Canada.* Toronto: Greek Community, 1961 (pamphlet).

Avery, Donald H. *Canadian Immigration Policy and the Alien Question, 1896-1919: The Anglo-Canadian Perspective.* Unpublished Ph.D. Thesis, University of Western Ontario, 1973.

Bardis, Panos. "The Changing Family in Modern Greece," *Sociology and Social Research,* 40 (1955), 19-23.

Bott, Elizabeth. *Family and Social Network.* London: Tavistock, 1957.

Breton, Raymond, "Institutional Completeness of Ethnic Communities and the Personal Relations of Immigrants," *The American Journal of Sociology,* LXX (1964), 193-205.

Brief Prepared and Submitted by the Greek Community at Large to Quebec Parliamentary Committee on Bill I. Greek Community of Montreal, June, 1977.

Britannica Year Book. Toronto, 1969.

Campbell, John K. *Honour, Family and Patronage.* Oxford: Clarendon Press, 1968.

Campbell, John and Philip Sherrard. *Modern Greece.* London: Ernest Benn Limited, 1969.

Canada Department of Citizenship and Immigration, Statistics Section, 1950-1970.

Canada Immigration Statistics, Series 1946-1964, Department of Citizenship and Immigration (Immigration Branch) Ottawa.

Canada Year Book, Ethnic Groups, 1971 Census of Canada, Catalogue 92-723 Vol. 1.

Canadian Immigration and Population Study. Three Years in Canada, Ottawa: Information Canada, 1974.

Canadian Manpower Statistics. Ottawa, 1971.

Canoutas, Seraphim G. *Christopher Columbus: A Greek Nobleman.* New York, 1943.

The Charlottetown Patriot, March 28, 1941.

Charter of the Greek Orthodox Archdiocese of North and South America. Brookline, Mass.: Holy Cross Orthodox Press, 1978.

Chicago Pnyx, September 1, 1975.

Chimbos, Peter D. "A Comparison of the Social Adaptation of Dutch, Greek and Slovak Immigrants in a Canadian Community," *International Migration Review,* 6 (1972), 230-244.

——. "Ethnicity and Occupational Mobility: A Comparative Study of Greek and Slovak Immigrants in "Ontario City," *International Migration Review,* 15 (1974) pp. 57-67.

——. "Immigrants' Attitudes Towards Their Children's Interethnic Marriages in a Canadian Community," *International Migration Review,* 5 (1971), 5-16.

——. The Hellenes of Missoula, Montana. Unpublished M.A. Thesis. University of Montana, 1963.

Coats, R.H. *The Immigration Program of Canada.* Newton, Mass.: Pollak Foundation for Economic Research, 1926.

Curtis, James. "Canada as a Nation of Joiners: Evidence from National Surveys" in *Social Processes and Institutions: The Canadian Case,* eds. James E. Gallagher and Ronald D. Lambert, Toronto: Holt, Rinehart and Winston, 1971.

Deane, Philip. *I Should Have Died.* Toronto: Longman Canada Ltd., 1976.

Department of Canadian Citizenship and Immigration. Ottawa: Deputy Minister's Records, 1952-1957 – File No. 3-51.

Department of Labour. Ottawa: Deputy Minister's Records, 1951, File No. 3-51.

Economopoulou, Louesa. Assimilation and Sources of Culture Tension of

Second Generation Greek Pre-Adolescents in Toronto. Unpublished M.A. Thesis, University of Toronto, 1976.

Encyclopedia Britannica, Vol. 6 (1974) p. 156.

Ethnos (Greek newspaper), Athens, October 10, 1951.

Gaustad, Edwin S. *Historical Atlas of Religion in America,* New York: Harper and Row, 1976.

Gavaki, Efronsini. *The Integration of Greeks in Canada.* California: R and E Research Associates Inc., 1977.

Giannakopoulos, Charalabos D. *The Development of the Greek Ethnic Community in Quebec* (work in progress), Concordia University, 1977.

Gibbon, John M. *Canadian Mosaic.* Toronto: McClelland and Stewart, 1938.

Globe and Mail, Toronto, November 1976.

Good, William and Paul K. Hatt. *Methods of Social Research.* New York: McGraw Hill, 1952.

Gordon, Milton. *Assimilation in American Life.* New York: Oxford University Press, 1964.

Greece-Basic Statistics. Greek Office of Information. London, 1949.

The Greek Canadian Tribune (Greek Canadian newspaper), Montreal, November 11, 1976.

Greek Canadian Weekly (Greek Canadian newspaper), Toronto, 1976.

The Greek Orthodox Observer. New York, May, 1971.

The Greek Sun (Greek Canadian newspaper), Montreal, November 28, 1972.

Greek Year Book. Toronto: The Greek Orthodox Church of St. George, 1934.

Guidelines for Youth Adult Program, New York: Greek Orthodox Archdioses of North and South America, 1975.

Harney, Robert F., and Harold Troper. *Immigrants.* Toronto: Van Nostrand Reinhold Ltd., 1975.

Hausknecht, Murray. *The Joiners: A Study of Voluntary Associations in the United States.* Totowa: N.J.: Bedminster Press, 1962.

Hellenic Echo (Greek Canadian newspaper), Vancouver, 1973.

Hellenic Postman, (Greek Canadian newspaper), Montreal, November 11, 1976.

Hirshi, Travis. *Causes of Juvenile Delinquency.* Los Angeles: University of California Press, 1969.

Horton, Paul B. and Chester L. Hunt. *Sociology.* New York: McGraw-Hill, 1972.

Iliopoulos, Nicholas D., *Who is Who of Greek Origin in Institutions of Higher Learning in the United States and Canada.* New York: Greek Orthodox Archdiocese Office of Education, 1974.

I.L.O. Labour Problems in Greece, Geneva, 1949.

I.L.O. Yearbook of Labour Statistics, 1966.

Jecchinis, Chris. *Trade Unionism in Greece: A Study in Political Paternalism.* Chicago: Roosevelt University Press, 1967.

Kaltchas, N. *Introduction to the Constitutional History of Modern Greece.* New York: Columbia University Press, 1940.

Kealey, Gregory, and Peter Warrian (eds.), *Essays in Canadian Working Class History.* Toronto: McClelland and Stewart, 1976.

Kiattipis, Bambis. *The Organization of the Park Extension Citizens,* Montreal: Park Extension Community Corporation, 1973.

Kordatos, Yannis. *The Great History of Greece 1453-1821,* Vol. 9. Athens: 20th Century, 1947.

Kourvetaris, George A. "The Greek American Family" in *Ethnic Families in America,* eds., Charles H. Mindel and Robert W. Habenstein. New York: Elsevier, 1976.

Lambiri-Dimaki, Jane. "Dowry in Modern Greece in *Toward a Sociology of Women,* ed. Constantina Safilions-Rothschild. Toronto: Xerox College Publishing, 1972.

Lambrou, Yianna. The Greek Community of Vancouver Social Organization and Adaptation. Unpublished M.A. Thesis, University of British Columbia, 1975.

Larocque, Paul *et al.* "Operationalization of Social Indicators of Multiculturalism," Discussion Paper for Fourth Departmental Seminar of Social Indicators. Ottawa, Department of the Secretary of State, November 26, 1974.

Leber, George. *The History of the Order of AHEPA.* Washington, D.C.: The Order of AHEPA, 1972.

Lieberson, Stanley. "Suburbs and Ethnic Residential Patterns," *American Journal of Sociology,* 67 (1962), 673-681.

London Greek Community Telephone Directory, London, Ontario, Greek Community, 1976.

Lundberg, George *et al. Sociology.* New York: Harper and Row, 1968.

Macdonald, Florence. *For Greece A Tear: The Story of the Greek War Relief Fund of Canada.* Fredericton, New Brunswick: Brunswick Press, 1954.

Mackenzie, Ruth. "The Story of the Greeks in Canada." *Citizen* 9(3), 1963.

Malafouris, Bambis, *Hellenes tis Amerikis 1528-1948.* (Greeks in America), New York, 1948.

Marcotic, Vladimir. *Ethnic Directory of Canada,* University of Calgary, 1976.

McNall, Scott G. *The Greek Peasant.* Washington, D.C.: A.S.A. Rose Monograph Series, 1976.

Merton, Robert K. *Social Theory and Social Structure.* Glencoe, Illinois: The Free Press, 1957.

Metrakos, Julius *et al. Commission for Community Development for the Greek Orthodox Community in Montreal.* Interim *Report,* Montreal Greek Orthodox Community, July 31, 1970.

Ministry of Coordination, Regional Development Services, Athens, Greece, 1963.

The Montreal Star, December 16, 1976 and October 27, 1976.

Morrison, Jean. "Ethnicity and Violence: The Lakehead Freight Handlers Before World War I,"

169

in *Essays in Canadian Working Class History*, (eds.), Gregory S. Kealey and Peter Warrian. Toronto: McClelland and Stewart Limited, 1976.

Nagata, Judith. "Adaptation and Integration of Greek Working Class Immigrants in the City of Toronto, Canada: A Situational Approach," *International Migration Review.* 4 (1969), 44-70.

——. et al. *English Language Classes for Immigrant Women with Pre-School Children.* Toronto: York University, Ethnic Research Programme, 1970.

Neos Kosmos, (Greek Canadian Weekly newspaper), Toronto, 1967-1973.

Newman, William M. "Theoretical Perspectives for the Analysis of Social Pluralism" In *The Canadian Ethnic Mosaic: A Quest for Identity.* Toronto: McClelland and Stewart, 1978 pp. 40-51.

O'Bryan, K.G. *et al. Non-Official Languages: A Study in Canadian Multiculturalism.* Ottawa: Thorn Press Limited, 1976.

O.E.C.O. *Economic Survey,* Greece and Paris, 1966.

Organoff, Christo. "Macedonska Tribuna," Toronto, 1976.

The Orthodox Observer, September 9, 1975.

The Orthodox World, Sacramento, California: Orthodox Christian Books and Icons. Vol. V., 1968 (pamphlet).

Papadopoulos, George. *Our Creed,* Vol. "B". Athens: Management of General Press, 1968.

Papandreau, Andreas. *Democracy at Gunpoint: The Greek Front.* New York: Doubleday, 1970.

Patterson, James G. The Greeks of Vancouver: A Study in the *Preservation of Ethnicity.* Ottawa: National Museum of Man, Canadian Centre for Folk Culture Studies, 1976.

Petritis, Takis. "The Early Immigrants in Canada" in *Afieroma.* Montreal: Cretan Association of Montreal, 1972-1973.

Piepkorn, Arthur, C. *Profiles in Belief: The Religious Bodies of the United States and Canada.* New York: Harper and Row, 1977.

Porter, John. *The Vertical Mosaic.* Toronto: The University of Toronto Press, 1965.

Price, C.A. *Report on the Greek Community in Toronto.* Unpublished M.A. Thesis, York University, 1958.

Report of the Neighborhood Association to the Advisory Committee of the Canadian Red Cross Society on the Adjustment of Greek Immigrant Children from Iron Curtain Countries. Toronto: Canadian Red Cross, July 7, 1956.

Report of the Royal Commission on Bilingualism and Biculturalism: "The Cultural Contribution of the Other Ethnic Groups," Book IV. Ottawa: Queen's Printer, 1970.

Richmond, Anthony H. *Ethnic Residential Segregation in Metropolitan Toronto.* Toronto: York University Ethnic *Research Programme,* 1972.

——. *Post-War Immigrants in Canada.* Toronto: University of Toronto Press, 1967.

Riesman, David. "Some Observations Concerning Marginality," *Phylon* 12 (1951), 113-127.

Rosen, Bernard C. "Race, Ethnicity and The Achievement Syndrome," *American Sociological Review,* 24 (1959), 47-60.

Ross, Edward A. *The Old World in the New.* New York: The Century Company 1914.

Runciman, Steven. *The Eastern Schism.* Oxford: The Clarendon Press, 1963.

Safilios-Rothschild, Constantina. "A Comparison of Power Structure and Marital Satisfaction in Urban Greek and French Families," *The Journal of Marriage and the Family,* 29 (1967), 345-353.

Saloutos, Theodore. *The Greeks in America: A Student's Guide to Localized History.* New York: Teachers College Press, Columbia University, 1967.

——. *The Greeks in the United States.* Cambridge, Mass.: Harvard University Press, 1964.

Sanders, Irwin. *Rainbow in the Rock: The People of Rural Greece.* Cambridge, Mass.: Harvard University Press, 1962.

Schermerhorn, R.A. *Comparative Ethnic Relations: A Framework for Theory and Research.* New York: Random House, 1970.

Sicilianos, Demetrios, E. *Hellenic Katagogi tou Christoforou Kolombou* (The Greek Background of Christopher Columbus: Athens, 1950).

Sirros, Christos. *The Mile End West Project: A Study of Community Development in an Immigrant Community.* Montreal: Greek Community of Montreal, 1973.

Stathopoulos, Peter. *The Greek Community of Montreal.* Athens: National Centre for Researchers, 1971.

Statistics Canada, Greek Ethnic Group by Income, Education and Occupation, Catalogue No. 8917-13549A.

Statistics Service of Greece, Athens, 1963-73.

Stonequist, Everett H. *The Marginal Man.* New York: Scribners, 1937.

Stylianopoulos, Theodore C. "The Orthodox Church in America," *The Annals of American Academy of Political and Social Science,* 387 (1970), 41-48.

Sweet-Escott, Bickman. *Greece: A Political and Economic Survey 1939-53.*

Tatsoulis, Athnina. "Greek Women Poets of Today," *Hellenia,* 23 (1953), 10-13.

Tavuchis, Nicholas. *Family and Mobility Among Second Generation Americans.* Athens: National Centre for Social Research, 1972.

Theodorson, Georgia and Achilles G. Theodorson. *Modern Dictionary of Sociology.* New York: Thomas Y. Crowell Company, 1969.

Thomas, William I. and Florian Znaniecki. *The Polish Peasant in Europe and America.* Vol. V. Boston: The Gorman Press, 1920.

171

Treudley, Mary. "Formal Organizations and the Americanization Process," *American Sociological Review,* 14 (1949), 44-53.

Uniform Parish Regulations of the Greek Orthodox Archdiocese Of North and South America. New York: Greek Orthodox Archdiocese, 1973.

United Nations Statistical Yearbook. New York: United Nations, 1974.

Vlachos, Evangelos. *The Assimilation of Greeks in the United States.* Athens: National Centre for Researchers, 1968.

Vlassis, George. *The Greeks in Canada.* Ottawa: Leclerc Printers Ltd., 1953.

Vournas, George C. "The Tragedy of Cyprus," *Journal of the Hellenic Diaspora,* 1 (1974), 43-50.

Wilson, N.G. *Saint Basil and the Value of Greek Literature.* London: Duckworth, 1975.

Woodsworth, J.S. *Strangers Within Our Gates.* Toronto: University of Toronto Press, 1909.

Zotos, Stepharos, *Hellenic Presence in America.* Wheaton, Illinois: Pilgrimage, 1976.

Index